Knitting
Fresh Brioche

Creating Two-Color Twists & Turns
Nancy Marchant

sixth&springbooks | NEW YORK

sixth&springbooks | 104 W 27th St, 3rd Floor, New York, NY 10001   www.sixthandspring.com

Managing Editor
LAURA COOKE

Senior Editor
LISA SILVERMAN

Book Design
DIANE LAMPHRON

Page Layout and Production
ARETA BUK

Yarn Editor
VANESSA PUTT

Editorial Assistant
JOHANNA LEVY

Supervising Patterns Editor
LORI STEINBERG

Patterns Editors
ANNE COHEN
ALEXANDRA RICHARDS

Technical Illustrations
NANCY MARCHANT

Photography
ALEXANDRA FEO

Fashion Stylist,
Hair & Makeup
ALEXANDRA FEO

■ ■ ■ ■

Vice President
TRISHA MALCOLM

Publisher
CAROLINE KILMER

Production Manager
DAVID JOINNIDES

President
ART JOINNIDES

Chairman
JAY STEIN

Library of Congress Cataloging-in-Publication Data

Marchant, Nancy, 1949–
Knitting fresh brioche : creating two-color twists & turns :
75 stitches—12 stunning scarves & wraps.
     pages cm
Includes bibliographical references and index.
ISBN 978-1-936096-77-0
1. Knitting. 2. Knitting—Patterns. I. Title.
TT820.M184 2014
746.43'2—dc23
                                        2014017015

Manufactured in China

9 10

First Edition

■ ON THE COVER
Willow, knit in
Madelinetosh
Tosh Merino Light
(2 hanks each in
Betty Draper's blue
and citrus)

A NOTE FROM THE AUTHOR
I have developed the abbreviations and terminology used in this book, my patterns, my website, and my classes specifically for brioche knitting. I realize that if you want to design with stitches from those sources, the copyright question can be awkward.

I encourage you to use the stitch patterns and the terminology, so a standard can be created for brioche to lessen confusion. However, I would appreciate acknowledgment. As in all good pattern writing, mention the source of the stitch, terminology, or idea. This has been my life's work, so please respect that.

Contents

page 166

page 172

page 178

page 182

page 184

page 190

page 196

page 200

page 204

page 210

page 216

page 222

† brioche An obsolete, fancy knit fabric; used for sofa cushions and waistcoats.[1]

† Archival marking. Indicates the entry applies to a textile, fabric, process, or term that is no longer current. This does not mean that this term is never used, but rather that it is not in common usage.

[1] Tortora, Phyllis G., and Merkel, Robert S., *Fairchild's Dictionary of Textiles*, 7th Edition (New York: Fairchild Publications, 2009), p. 72.

Introduction

Exploring Brioche

While researching the brioche stitch,
I discovered something that surprised me.
All the Northern European countries have used
the stitch since the late 1800s, yet not one
country, to my knowledge, claims it as part of
their knitting culture. The brioche stitch has
no tradition anywhere. Only a few examples
can be found in museums, and they are
mainly machine-made. When I combed stitch
dictionaries, I again found a few examples, but
not many, and they were mostly one color.

This luscious, cushy stitch, which so many of
us want to wrap up in, has no significant history.
The dictionary entry at left is an indication
of how this wonderful stitch has come to be
viewed: obsolete.

I figured it was time to give the brioche stitch
some history, and I am inviting you to be part
of its creation. This stitchionary of two-color
patterns is a compilation of my designs, using
only increases and decreases on a two-color
brioche fabric. I hope you will use these stitches
in your knitting, creating scarves, shawls,
collars, sweaters—anything can be made using
two-color brioche.

Since these stitch patterns translate so easily
into scarves and shawls, I have chosen twelve of
my stitch patterns and created scarf and shawl
designs that use them to beautiful effect.

This book deals only with stitches worked in
two-color brioche knitting. However, in the
appendix, you will find explanations of how to
translate these patterns into one-color brioche,
as well as how to work the patterns in the round.

Let's explore two-color brioche together
and give this stunning style of knitting the
attention it deserves.

The Technique

General Brioche Knitting Tips

Brioche knitting creates a cushy, reversible ribbed fabric that comes about by working one stitch and slipping the next. In brioche knitting, instead of carrying the working yarn in front or in back of the slipped stitch, you bring the yarn *over* the stitch, giving the stitch a little shawl over its shoulders. In the following row, this shawled stitch will be either "barked" or "burped" (see "brk" and "brp" in the list of abbreviations).

In two-color brioche knitting, two rows are worked for each counted row that appears on the face of the fabric. For example, the light side of the fabric is first worked using the light color and then worked again using the dark color. Then the dark side is worked using the light color and then worked again using the dark color. You need to use circular or double-pointed needles, so that you can slide the stitches to the other end of the needle, where the yarn you are about to pick up is hanging. In brioche color knitting, the yarn over of the row just worked is the last color that you used. It takes 8 to 10 worked rows before the pattern can be recognized.

Brioche works best on loose-fitting garments that require ease. Because brioche stitches create a very lofty fabric, it is advisable to go down a needle size or two if you want to control its "give." Brioche knitting uses more yarn than, say, stockinette stitch—up to twice as much.

I generally work with yarns that have a "bite," such as 100% non-superwash wool. Slippery yarns like alpaca, silk, and superwash wool have a tendency to grow lengthwise in brioche knitting, because each worked stitch sits between two yarn overs. These yarn overs allow the stitch in between to elongate. That being said, I have made many successful triangular scarves and shawls with somewhat slippery yarns. A triangular shape pulls the stitches back into place, whereas in a rectangular scarf, the weight of the yarn can stretch it downward.

Counting Rows and Stitches

In brioche knitting, a shawled stitch is considered *one* stitch. This is very important: the yarn over is not counted separately. When you count 4 stitches, you will actually have 6 loops of yarn on the needle.

Two rows are worked for each counted row that appears on the face of the fabric. Half of the stitches are worked in one row and the other half (the stitches that were slipped in the former row) are worked in the following row. When you need to count rows, count only the stitches going up one knit column. When you are told to work 4 rows, count 4 knit column stitches, even though you will have worked back and forth 4 times (2 worked rows = 1 counted row).

Measuring Gauge

Measuring a brioche swatch for stitch gauge is tricky. The larger the swatch, of course, the more accurate your measurements will be. Whether you block your swatch or not depends on whether you plan on blocking the garment.

To measure gauge, lay the swatch on a flat surface and measure it with a flat ruler. Note that a normal brioche gauge will have few stitches and lots of rows. Where stockinette stitch will measure roughly 24 stitches and 32 rows for a 4-inch sample, brioche knitting will measure more like 16 stitches and 40 rows. Remember, the shawled stitch counts as one stitch: the yarn over itself is not counted as a separate stitch.

Casting On and Binding Off

Keep in mind that, given the elasticity of brioche, you should cast on and bind off very loosely. I have included instructions in the book for my preferred cast-on for brioche knitting, the Two-Color Italian Cast-On. My favorite bind-off is the matching Italian Bind-Off. Similar to Kitchener stitch, it matches the Italian Cast-On beautifully.

Correcting Mistakes

I have been "brioching" for years and still find the stitch difficult to read. If you make a mistake in the middle of a row, don't tear out the entire row at once; instead, undo one stitch at a time. There is an entire section of this book dedicated to helping you correct mistakes without too much headache. ◼

Ring of Fire page 166
◄———●

Terminology & Abbreviations

I have developed the following set of abbreviations and terminology specifically for brioche knitting. It includes the standard knitting terminology, along with some that is specific to brioche: most often, simply a "br" (for "brioche") placed in front of a traditional knitting abbreviation.

If a term and its abbreviation are pattern-specific, they will be explained in the Pattern Notes for the project, rather than in this list.

LS = light side of the work. The knit columns on this side of the work are in the light color.

DS = dark side of the work. The knit columns on this side of the work are in the dark color.

LC = light color. Use the light-colored yarn.

DC = dark color. Use the dark-colored yarn.

LS LC = the side of the work facing you has light-colored "knit" columns, and you will be working with the light-colored yarn in that row.

LH = left-hand.

RH = right-hand.

pm = place marker.

sm = slip marker.

k = knit.

p = purl.

sl = slip (purlwise, unless told otherwise).

[ ] = action that needs to be repeated.

brk (brioche knit—also known as a bark) = knit the stitch that was slipped in the previous row together with its yarn over. (See page 18.)

brp (brioche purl—also known as a burp) = purl the stitch that was slipped in the previous row together with its yarn over. (See page 20.)

sl1yo = the action that creates the shawled stitch. This action works differently for a bark row than for a burp row, but one aspect remains standard: *the working yarn must always be in front before slipping the stitch.* On a burp row the working yarn is in place before slipping the stitch, but in a bark row you need to first bring the yarn to the front, and then slip the stitch. This slipped stitch, with its yarn-over shawl, is considered one stitch.

sl1yo following a k or brk st = bring the working yarn under the needle to the front of the work, slip the next stitch purlwise, then bring the yarn over the needle (and over the slipped stitch) to the back, in position to work the following stitch.

sl1yo following a p or brp st = the working yarn is already in front. Slip the next stitch purlwise, then bring the yarn over the needle (and over the slipped stitch), and then to the front under the needle, into position to work the following stitch.

INCREASES

brkyobrk (2-stitch increase) = brk1, leaving the stitch on LH needle, yarn over (yarn forward under needle, then over needle to back), then brk1 into the same stitch—2 stitches increased. When a brkyobrk increase is used, 3 single stitches bloom out of the center of 1 stitch. These 3 stitches will be worked separately in the following row, since they are not yet shawled. (See page 28.)

brpyobrp (2-stitch increase) = into one stitch, brp1, yo, brp1. (See page 30.)

br4st inc (4-stitch increase) = into one stitch, [brk1, yo] twice, brk1. (See page 30.)

br8st inc (8-stitch increase) = into one stitch; [brk1, yo] 4 times, brk1.

DECREASES

brLsl dec (2-stitch decrease that slants to the left, involving 3 sts) = slip the first stitch knitwise, brk the following two stitches together, pass the slipped stitch over. (See page 32.)

brRsl dec (2-stitch decrease that slants to the right, involving 3 sts) = slip the first stitch knitwise, knit the next stitch, pass the slipped stitch over, place the stitch on LH needle and pass the following stitch over. Place the stitch on RH needle. (See page 34.)

br4st dec (4-stitch decrease, involving 5 stitches) = slip 2 stitches separately knitwise, place following stitch on cable needle to the front, knit the next stitch, pass the second slipped stitch over, place the stitch on LH needle and pass following stitch over, place stitch on RH needle and pass first slipped stitch over, move stitch from cable needle to LH needle, place stitch on LH needle and pass stitch from cable needle over, place finished decrease on RH needle. (See page 38.)

Brioche purl decreases involve 3 stitches. The first and third stitches are purl column stitches, and the middle stitch is a sl1yo. Before you work the decrease, the working yarn is lying in front, since you have just worked a sl1yo in a "purl" row.

brpLsl dec (2-stitch decrease) = slip the first stitch purlwise. You are now going to switch the position of the following 2 stitches on the LH needle. Do this by going behind and skipping the following stitch, put the next stitch on RH needle purlwise and at the same time hold the skipped stitch to front with fingers, place skipped stitch onto LH needle and purl it, then pass the slipped stitches over, first the one closest to the working stitch and then the very first slipped stitch. (See page 36.)

brpRsl dec (2-stitch decrease) = brp 2 stitches together, change the mount of the following stitch on LH needle so that the left leg of the stitch lies in front on the needle, place the working stitch on LH needle and pass the remounted stitch over. Place stitch on RH needle. (See page 37.) ■

Two-Color Italian Cast-On

This is my favorite cast-on for brioche knitting. It is relatively invisible, has the perfect amount of ease so it's never too tight, and uses two colors. It takes a bit of practice, but the results are worthwhile.

Begin by tying a strand of each color yarn together into a knot. Hold the knot on top of the needle in your right hand. Create a "V" by carrying the light color around your index finger and the dark color around the thumb of your left hand. Hold the yarns together with your left fingers. The tip of the needle is pointed upward between the two strands.

The needle movement of this cast-on is the important thing to think about. Carry the needle around one strand and in front of the second strand. Then lay the needle down on the second strand and bring up a stitch.

Whether you want to begin your first working row with a knit or purl stitch will determine which stitch you cast on first. The knit strand is held around the index finger and the purl strand is held around the thumb.

If you cast on too many stitches, don't worry. You can undo the excess stitches after you have worked the first set-up row.

For this example, we are going to cast on an uneven number of stitches, starting and ending with a light-color knit stitch. In the images, the curved arrows indicate the movement of the needle tip.

Edge showing Two-Color Italian Cast-On

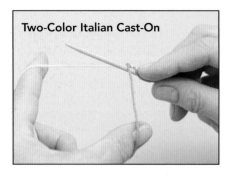

Begin by tying both strands into a knot. Hold yarns on needle as shown above, LC around index finger and DC around thumb.

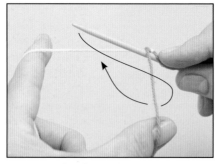

1 Knit LC st: Move needle counterclockwise over then under the thumb DC yarn . . .

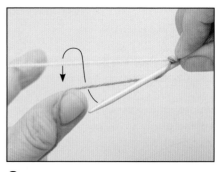

2 . . . then over and behind index finger LC strand to . . .

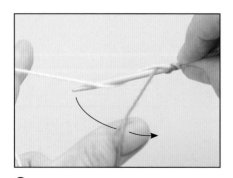

3 . . . catch LC strand on needle tip.

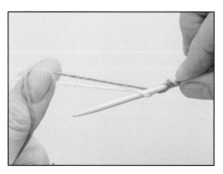

4 Bring needle back under thumb DC strand, returning to original position.

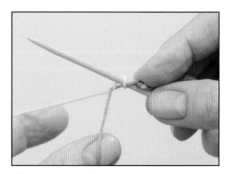

5 Pull both strands downward to complete your first stitch: a LC knit stitch.

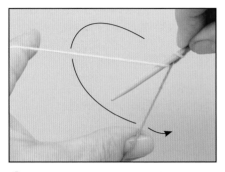

6 Purl DC st: Move needle counterclockwise over then under LC strand *and* under DC strand . . .

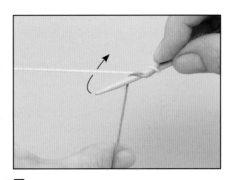

7 . . . then in *front* of DC yarn. Pick up DC yarn . . .

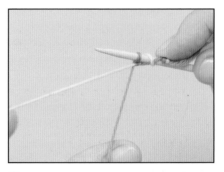

8 . . . and bring it back under LC strand and return to original position. This is your first DC purl stitch. Again, pull both strands downward to really form the stitch.

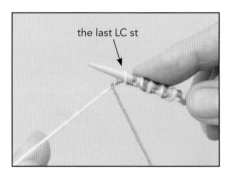

the last LC st

9 Repeat from step 1, creating knit and purl stitches. At end, cast on final LC knit stitch.

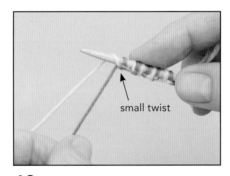

small twist

10 Hold last LC stitch in place with DC thread in back. Maintaining small twist between last two stitches, undo last LC stitch and . . .

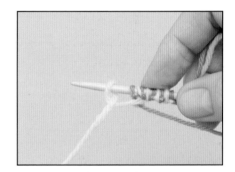

11 . . . work a half hitch with LC, as shown.

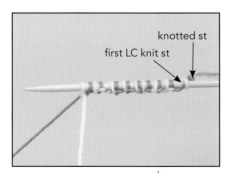

knotted st
first LC knit st

12 The beginning knotted "stitch" will be dropped after working the set-up row, so it does not count as a stitch. The sample above shows 17 cast-on stitches plus the knotted stitch. ∎

Two-Color Italian Cast-On with a Large Number of Stitches

Since the Italian Cast-On works so beautifully with brioche knitting, it is important to be able to cast on a large number of stitches. Since this cast-on is composed of twisted threads, it has a tendency to spiral around the needle, making the cast-on stitches difficult to control.

To aid in keeping track of a large amount of cast-on stitches, I run a third, contrasting strand as a lifeline along with the cast-

on. The lifeline weaves back and forth between the stitches and shows when the stitches are twisting around the needle.

I weave in the lifeline every 5 stitches, but you might prefer to weave in yours every 2 stitches.

After working a few rows, undo the knot and pull out the lifeline.

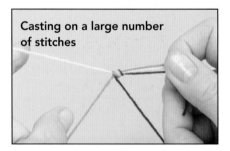

Casting on a large number of stitches

Begin by tying both strands into a knot, together with a third lifeline strand. I use a thin cotton yarn for my lifeline.

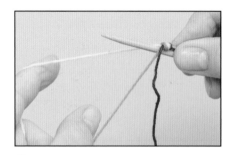

1 Letting lifeline hang, begin cast-on using LC and DC.

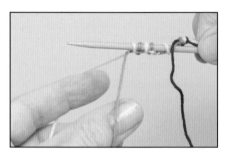

2 Cast on 5 sts. Example begins with LC knit st, so 5th st is also a LC knit.

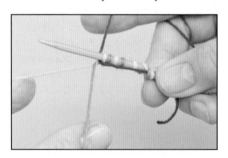

3 Weave lifeline from front to back.

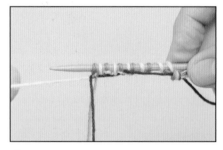

4 Cast on 5 more sts, beginning and ending with a DC purl st. Weave lifeline from back to front.

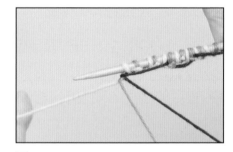

5 Continue casting on 5 sts at a time and weaving lifeline in between. Straighten cast-on sts before you begin to knit. ■

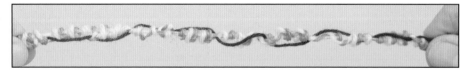

Notice how the cast-on stitches and lifeline want to twist around the needle.

Pull on the lifeline to remove the slack and to straighten out the stitches before you begin to knit. The lifeline also allows you to count your stitches more easily.

Tubular Treatment After the Italian Cast-On

If you want your cast-on edge to be firmer, you can tidy it up by working tubular rows after the cast-on, followed by set-up rows.

GLOSSARY
sl1 wyif = slip one stitch purlwise, carrying the working yarn in front.
sl1 wyib = slip one stitch purlwise, carrying the working yarn in back.

Using Two-Color Italian Cast-On, beg and end with LC knit st. Cast on a multiple of 2 sts + 1.

Tubular Row DS LC: p1, *sl1 wyib, p1; rep from * to end. Drop knotted st from Two-Color Italian Cast-On. Do *not* turn; slide.
Tubular Row DS DC: sl1, *k1, sl1 wyif; rep from * to last 2 sts, k1, drop DC to back, sl1. Turn.
You will now need to set up your brioche rows.

Set-Up Row 1 LS LC: k1, *sl1yo, k1; rep from * to end. Do *not* turn; slide.
Set-Up Row 1 LS DC: sl1, *brp1, sl1yo; rep from * to last 2 sts, brp1, drop DC to front, sl1. Turn.

Set-Up Row 2 DS LC: p1, *sl1yo, brp1; rep from * to last 2 sts, sl1yo, p1. Do *not* turn; slide.
Set-Up Row 2 DS DC: sl1, *brk1, sl1yo; rep from * to last 2 sts, brk 1, drop DC to back, sl1. Turn.

You are now ready to begin with Row 1 LS LC. ■

Using a Different Cast-On

If you would prefer to use a method other than the Two-Color Italian Cast-On, there are a few things you need to consider.

■ Make sure your cast-on is worked loosely. You can keep it loose by casting onto a larger needle than the size you'll be using.

■ If you use the Long-Tail Cast-On, you can work it in two colors. Instead of taking the tail of one ball of yarn, tie two colors together and carry one strand on your thumb and the other around your index finger.

■ If you'd rather use the Long-Tail Cast-On in only one color, cast on using the dark color. Turn the work, attach the light color, and work the first set-up row DS LC. ■

The Selvedge Edge

Because brioche is used so often for scarves and shawls, the edges are usually on display and need to look good. If the edges flutter, the project will sit in your closet, unworn.

The edges need to be consistent and to hold their shape. They should have the same amount of elasticity as the rest of the knitting.

For all the two-color brioche swatches in this book, I have worked a single-color selvedge edge. Some of the projects have a different edge treatment, but I tend to stick to the single-color selvedge. Many knitters comment that the edge is not a perfect chain up the side. It is more like a knobby edging, but it is very even and holds the edge beautifully.

This selvedge edge is created by working the edge stitches in one row and slipping them in the next. They are not slipped with a yarn over, they are simply slipped. You do not "brioche" these selvedge stitches, only the stitches in between. ■

The left side edge when viewed from the light-color side

The right side edge when viewed from the light-color side

sl1yo, brk1

This is the basis of all brioche knitting. Whether you hold the yarn in your right or left hand, when working the sl1yo, the working yarn must be in the front before slipping the following stitch. The next step is to "bark," or brk1. Again, note that you must be using circular or double-pointed needles.

Notice how the yarn over sits over its stitch on the needle after it is worked, beginning in the front.

English or American Method (right-hand carry)
I am an "English method" knitter: I carry the working yarn in my right hand, then "throw" it over the needle.

These images show how to work a sl1yo followed by a brk1, holding the yarn with your right hand.

1 After working a brk1 . . .

2 . . . bring the working yarn to the front by going under the RH needle.

3 Slip the following stitch purlwise.

4 Carry the working yarn over the slipped stitch, and at the same time begin working a brk1 . . .

5 . . . by knitting the following stitch together with its yarn over shawl. This is a finished sl1yo, brk1. ■

Continental or German Method (left-hand carry)

Left-hand yarn carriers have the advantage of working the sl1yo in one movement. Using the needle to bring the yarn forward, and then slipping the stitch at the same time, allows Continental knitters to brioche knit very quickly.

These images show how to work a sl1yo followed by a brk1, holding the yarn with your left hand.

1 After working a brk1, leaving the working yarn in the back, . . .

2 . . . take the RH needle behind the working yarn (this then brings the yarn to the front) and at the same time . . .

3 . . . sl1 purlwise. The yarn is carried over the stitch, creating its yarn over shawl.

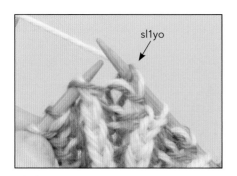

4 This is a finished sl1yo. The following stitch is a brk1 . . .

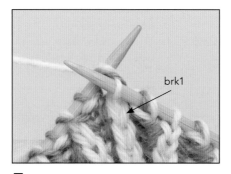

5 . . . worked by knitting the stitch and its yarn over shawl together.

6 This is a finished sl1yo, brk1. ■

sl1yo, brp1

When a brioche purl row is being worked, the working yarn is already in the front for the sl1yo.

English or American Method (right-hand carry)
These visuals show how to work a sl1yo followed by a brp1, holding the yarn with your right hand.

1 After you work a brp1, the working yarn is already in the front.

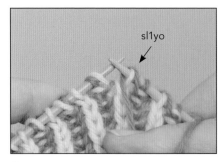

2 Slip the following stitch purlwise. Carry the working yarn over the slipped stitch and back to the front.

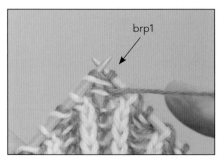

3 Brp the following stitch together with its yarn over shawl.

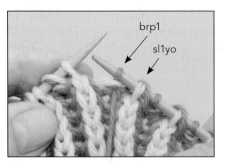

4 This is a finished sl1yo, brp1. ■

Continental or German Method (left-hand carry)
These visuals show how to work a sl1yo followed by a brp1, holding the yarn with your left hand. →

1 After you work a brp1, the working yarn is already in the front.

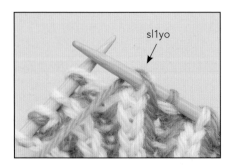

2 Slip the following stitch purlwise. Carry the working yarn over the slipped stitch and back to the front.

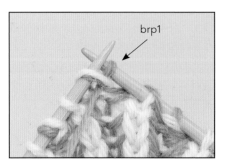

3 Brp the following stitch together with its yarn over shawl.

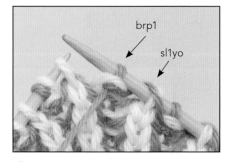

4 This is a finished sl1yo, brp1. ■

Cathedral *page 200*

Creating the Basic Fabric

We are creating a two-colored fabric with one-color selvedge stitch edges. When working a light color (LC) row, the selvedge stitches are simply knitted or purled. They are never worked in the brioche stitch.

When working a dark color (DC) row, the selvedge stitches are always slipped. You will begin working a DC row by slipping the first light-color selvedge stitch, then picking up the dark color to work. At the end of a DC row, it is important that you drop the DC before slipping the last light-color selvedge stitch. You will always be dropping the DC to the light side of the work. That way it is in the correct position when you pick it up to work it the next time it is used.

You will need to use circular or double-pointed needles. You will begin the basic fabric by working 2 set-up rows.

English or American Method (right-hand carry)

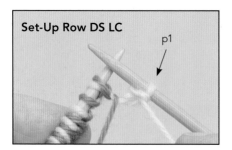

Set-Up Row DS LC

p1

1 Using light color (LC): p1 . . .

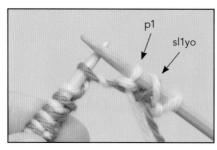

p1   sl1yo

2 . . . *sl1yo, p1; rep from * to end.

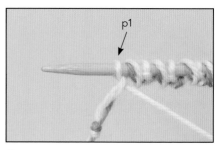

p1

3 At end of row, drop knotted st from Italian Cast-On. Do *not* turn; slide sts back to opposite end of needle to pick up the DC. ∎

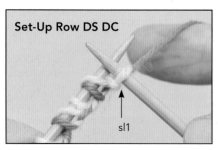

Set-Up Row DS DC

sl1

1 Using dark color (DC): sl1 . . .

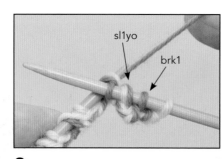

sl1yo   brk1

2 . . . *brk1, sl1yo; rep from * to last 2 sts . . .

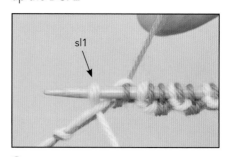

sl1

3 . . . brk1, drop DC to back, sl1. Turn. ∎

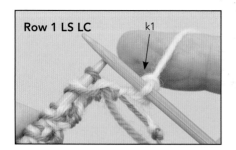

Row 1 LS LC   k1

1 Using LC: k1 . . .

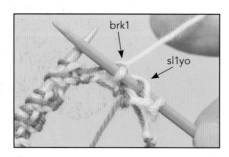

brk1   sl1yo

2 . . . *sl1yo, brk1; rep from * to last 2 sts . . .

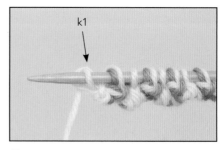

k1

3 . . . sl1yo, k1. Do *not* turn; slide. ∎

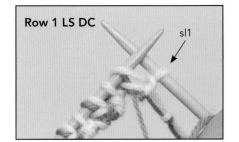

1 Using DC: sl1 . . .

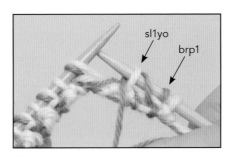

2 . . . *brp1, sl1yo; rep from * to last 2 sts . . .

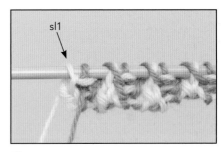

3 . . . brp1, drop DC to front, sl1. Turn. ■

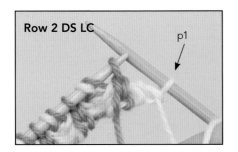

1 Using LC: p1 . . .

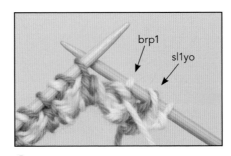

2 . . . *sl1yo, brp1; rep from * to last 2 sts . . .

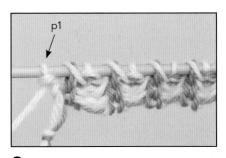

3 . . . sl1yo, p1. Do *not* turn; slide. ■

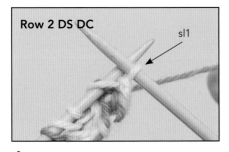

1 Using DC: sl1 . . .

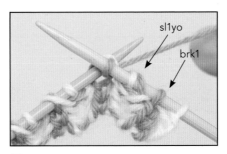

2 . . . *brk1, sl1yo; rep from * to last 2 sts . . .

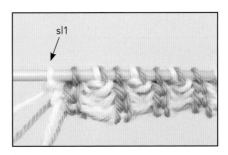

3 . . . brk 1, drop DC to back, sl1. Turn. Rep from Row 1 LS LC. ■

Continental or German Method (left-hand carry)

Set-Up Row DS LC

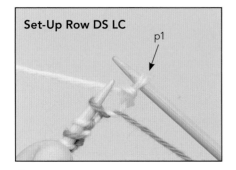

1 Using light color (LC): p1 . . .

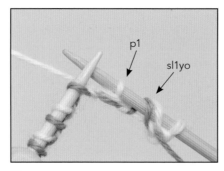

2 . . . *sl1yo, p1; rep from * to end.

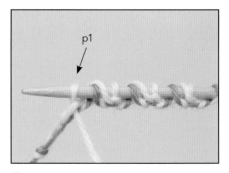

3 At end of row, drop knotted st from Italian Cast-On. Do *not* turn; slide sts back to opposite end of needle to pick up the DC. ■

Set-Up Row DS DC

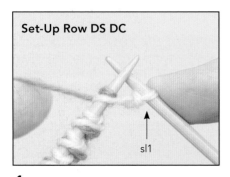

1 Using dark color (LC): sl1 . . .

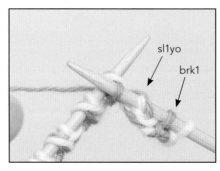

2 . . . *brk1, sl1yo; rep from * to last 2 sts . . .

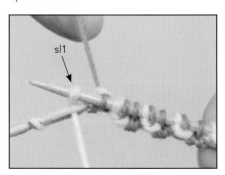

3 . . . brk1, drop DC to back, sl1. Turn. ■

Row 1 LS LC

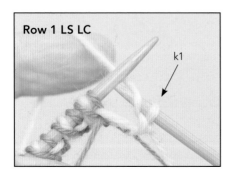

1 Using LC: k1 . . .

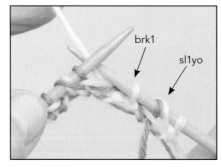

2 . . . *sl1yo, brk1; rep from * to last 2 sts . . .

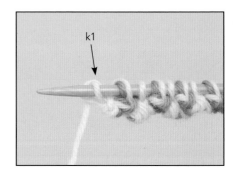

3 . . . sl1yo, k1. Do *not* turn; slide. ■

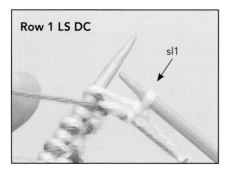

Row 1 LS DC

sl1

1 Using DC: sl1 . . .

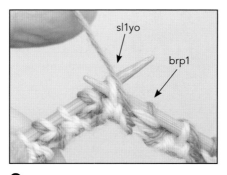

sl1yo

brp1

2 . . . *brp1, sl1yo; rep from * to last 2 sts . . .

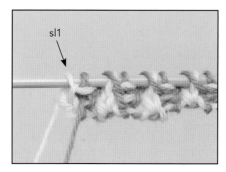

sl1

3 . . . brp1, drop DC to front, sl1. Turn. ■

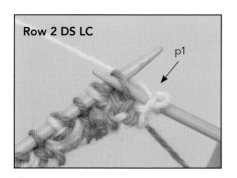

Row 2 DS LC

p1

1 Using LC: p1 . . .

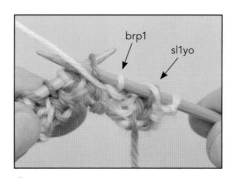

brp1

sl1yo

2 . . . *sl1yo, brp1; rep from * to last 2 sts . . .

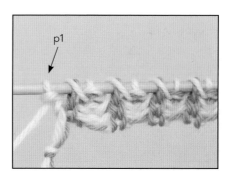

p1

3 . . . sl1yo, p1. Do *not* turn; slide. ■

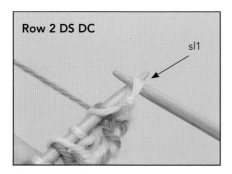

Row 2 DS DC

sl1

1 Using DC: sl1 . . .

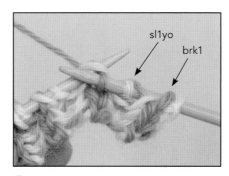

sl1yo

brk1

2 . . . *brk1, sl1yo; rep from * to last 2 sts . . .

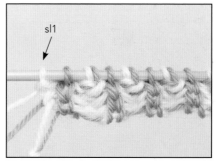

sl1

3 . . . brk 1, drop DC to back, sl1. Turn. Rep from Row 1 LS LC. ■

Italian Bind-Off

This is also known as the Kitchener Bind-Off. It matches the Italian Cast-On. The Italian Bind-Off uses only one of the two strands—I generally use the light color. In the sample shown, I used a third color so you can better see how to work this bind-off.

Cut the light-color yarn to 4 times the finished width you will be binding off. Cut the dark color and weave it in as shown, to avoid tangling. Thread the light color onto a blunt tapestry needle.

Edge showing Italian Bind-Off

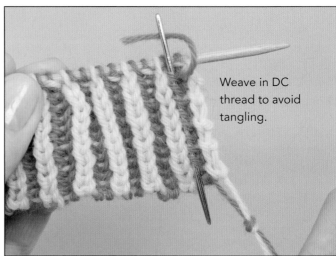

Weave in DC thread to avoid tangling.

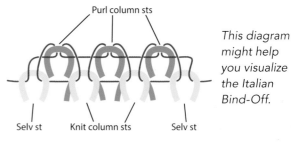

Purl column sts

Selv st   Knit column sts   Selv st

This diagram might help you visualize the Italian Bind-Off.

Sister Janie *page 196*

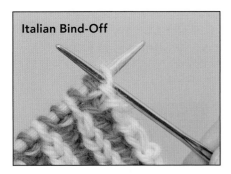

1 Insert tapesty needle (TN) purlwise into first (selvedge) st. Pull yarn through, leaving st on needle.

2 Going behind first st, insert TN knitwise into first purl column st.

3 Pull yarn through, leaving st on needle. This is difficult to see, but TN is in front of the right foot of the stitch.

4 Insert TN into the front of the first st and purlwise into next knit column st. (Note that TN catches the entire st with its yarn over.) Pull yarn through, dropping end (first) st from needle.

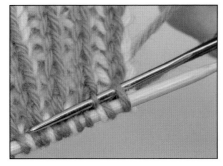

5 Insert TN purlwise into first purl column st again and knitwise into following purl column st. Pull yarn through, dropping end st from needle.

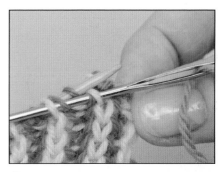

6 Rep from step 4 until 3 sts remain.

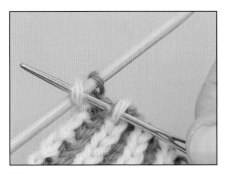

7 Insert TN into the front of the first st and purlwise into last knit column st. Pull yarn through, dropping end st from needle.

8 Insert TN purlwise into last 2 sts. Pull yarn through, dropping both sts from needle.

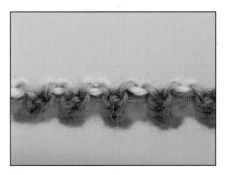

9 Finished Italian Bind-Off. ∎

Increases

To maintain the integrity of brioche stitch, increases should be worked in pairs.

When a brkyobrk increase is used, three single stitches bloom out of the center of one stitch. These three stitches will be worked separately in the following row, since they are not yet shawled with yarn overs.

brkyobrk
(2-st increase)
brk1, leaving stitch on LH needle, yarn over (yarn forward under needle, then over needle to back), then brk1 into the same stitch—2 stitches increased.

brkyobrk on LS   *brkyobrk on DS*

English or American Method (right-hand carry)

brkyobrk

brkyobrk will be made into this knit column stitch

1 In a LS LC row, work into a knit column stitch . . .

2 . . . brk1, leaving st on LH needle . . .

3 . . . yarn forward under RH needle, then over RH needle to back, creating yo . . .

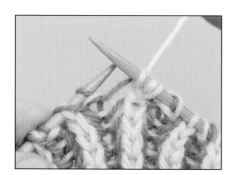

4 . . . brk1 into same stitch—2 sts inc.

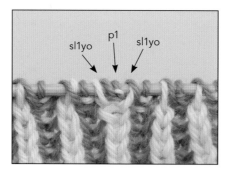

sl1yo   p1   sl1yo

5 In LS DC row following an inc row, work to inc, then work sl1yo, p1, sl1yo. Stitches are now back in brioche mode. ■

Continental or German Method (left-hand carry)

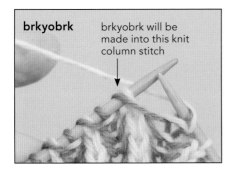

brkyobrk brkyobrk will be made into this knit column stitch

1 In a LS LC row, work into a knit column stitch . . .

2 . . . brk1, leaving st on LH needle . . .

3 . . . yarn forward under RH needle, then over RH needle to back, creating yo . . .

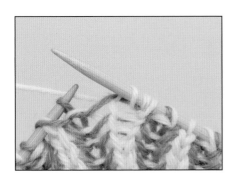

4 . . . brk1 into same stitch—2 sts inc.

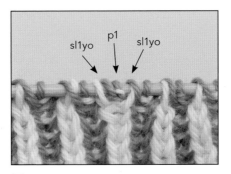

sl1yo   p1   sl1yo

5 In LS DC row following an inc row, work to inc, then work sl1yo, p1, sl1yo. Stitches are now back in brioche mode. ■

Multiple brkyobrks
(increasing by 4 or more stitches)

Follow the instructions for a brkyobrk increase, then keep going, adding another yo and another brk.

You can easily work a 6, 8, or even 10-stitch increase with this method. ∎

br4st inc
(4-st inc, 5 sts bloom out of 1 st)
Into 1 st, [brk1, yo] twice, brk1.

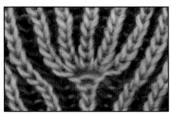

br8st inc
(8-st inc, 9 sts bloom out of 1 st)
Into 1 st, [brk1, yo] 4 times, brk1.

brpyobrp
(2-stitch increase)
brp1, leaving st on LH needle, yo (bring yarn over needle, then under needle to front), then brp1 into same stitch— 2 stitches increased.

brpyobrp on LS   *brpyobrp on DS*

In a LS DC row, work into 1 purl column stitch: brp1, yo, brp1.

After following DS LC row is worked, inc looks like this.

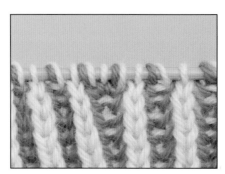

Inc looks like this on LS. ∎

Bart & Francis
page 222

Decreases

Decreases, like increases, need to be worked in pairs of stitches to maintain a brioche pattern.

Two-stitch decreases involve three stitches: a brk column stitch (A in photo), the following purl column stitch (B in photo), and the following brk column stitch (C in photo). The stacking order of these three stitches, when decreased, can be different, and the visual result varies as well.

A decrease that stacks stitches A (on top of stack), C, and B is called a brLsl dec. This places the middle "purl" stitch on the bottom and crosses the first knit column stitch over and on top of the third knit column stitch. A decrease that stacks C, A, and B is a brRsl dec.

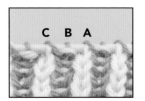

The stitch before the decrease is a sl1yo. The sl1yo is slipped as always, with the working yarn in front, but its yarn over will not be made until you begin to work the decrease.

When you are instructed to slip a shawled stitch, remember that this is considered one stitch and be sure to slip the stitch together with its yarn over.

brLsl dec
(2-stitch decrease that slants to the left, involving 3 sts)
Slip the first stitch (A) knitwise, brk the following two stitches (C and B) together, pass the slipped stitch (A) over.

brLsl dec on LS   *brLsl dec on DS*

English or American Method (right-hand carry)

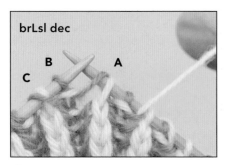

1 Sl A knitwise.

2 Brk C and B tog.

3 Pass A over.

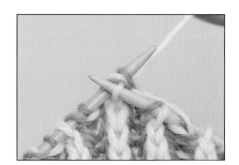

4 Finished brLsl dec. St A sits on top, slanting to left. ■

Continental or German Method (left-hand carry)

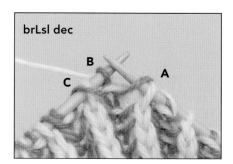

1 Sl A knitwise.

2 Brk C and B tog.

3 Pass A over.

4 Finished brLsl dec. St A sits on top, slanting to left. ■

brRsl dec

(2-stitch decrease that slants to the right, involving 3 sts)
Slip the first stitch (A) knitwise, knit the next stitch (B), pass the slipped stitch (A) over, place stitch on LH needle and pass the following stitch (C) over. Place stitch on RH needle.

brRsl dec on LS *brRsl dec on DS*

English or American Method (right-hand carry)

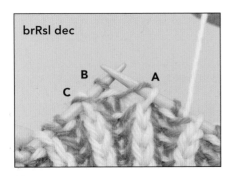

1 Sl A knitwise.

2 Knit B.

3 Pass A over.

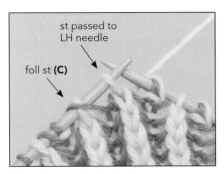

4 Place st on LH needle . . .

5 . . . and pass C over. Place st on RH needle—finished brRsl dec. St C sits on top, slanting to the right. ■

Continental or German Method (left-hand carry)

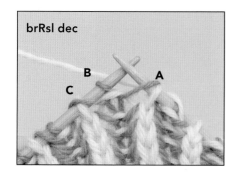

brRsl dec

B A

C

1 Sl A knitwise.

2 Knit B.

3 Pass A over.

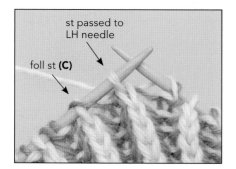

st passed to
LH needle

foll st (C)

4 Place st on LH needle . . .

5 . . . and pass C over. Place st on RH needle—finished brRsl dec. St C sits on top, slanting to the right. ■

Brioche Purl Decreases

These decreases involve three stitches. The first (A) and third (C) are purl column stitches, and the middle (B) stitch is a sl1yo. Before the decrease, the working yarn is lying in front, since you have just worked a sl1yo in a "purl" row.

Some manipulation is required when working brioche purl decreases. For a brpLsl dec, you will need to switch the position of stitches on the needle. For a brpRsl dec, you will need to change the mount of a stitch.

brpLsl dec
(2-stitch decrease)

Slip A purlwise, go behind B and put RH needle into C purlwise. Hold B to front with fingers as you slip C to RH needle. Place B on LH needle and purl it, then pass C over, then pass A over. A lies on top of the decrease and slants to the right when you look at it from the opposite side of the work. It slants to the left if viewed from the side where it was worked.

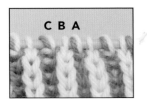

brpLsl dec on LS   *brpLsl dec on DS*

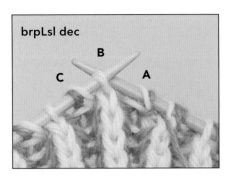

1 Sl A purlwise.

2 Go behind B and insert RH needle into C purlwise. Hold B to front with fingers . . .

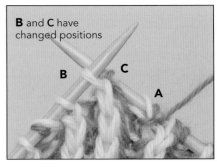

3 . . . as you slip C to RH needle. Place B onto LH needle . . .

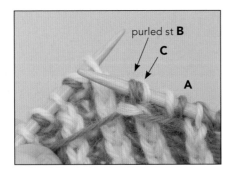

4 . . . and purl it.

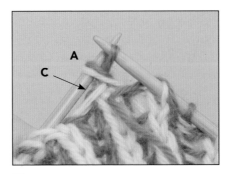

5 Pass C over, then pass A over.

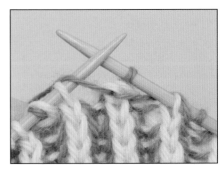

6 Finished brpLsl dec. St A lies on top of the decrease and slants to the right when viewed from the opposite side of the work. ■

brpRsl dec

(2-stitch decrease)

Brp A and B together, change the mount of C on LH needle, place the worked-together stitch on LH needle and pass C over. Place stitch on RH needle. C lies on top of the decrease and slants to the left when viewed from the opposite side of the work. It slants to the right if you could view it from the side where it was worked.

brpRsl dec on LS   *brpRsl dec on DS*

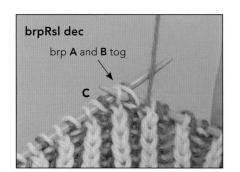

brpRsl dec

brp **A** and **B** tog

C

1 Brp A and B together.

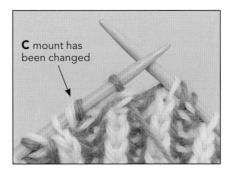

C mount has been changed

2 Change mount of C on LH needle so left leg of stitch is in front, place worked st on LH needle . . .

3 . . . and pass C over.

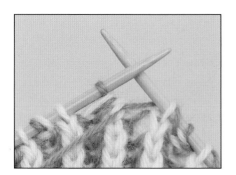

4 Finished brpRsl dec.

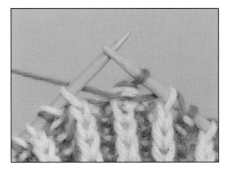

5 Place st on RH needle. C lies on top of dec and slants to left when viewed from opposite side of work. ■

Decreasing by 4 Stitches

The br4st dec is used to eliminate 4 stitches at once, placing the center stitch on top. This decrease really pulls in and can be very decorative. A wonderful little leaf can be created by working a br4st inc and then, a few rows later, a br4st dec right above it. The stitch before the decrease is a sl1yo. The sl1yo is slipped as always, with the working yarn in front, but its yarn over will not be made until you begin to work the decrease.

When you are instructed to slip a shawled stitch, remember that this is considered one stitch and be sure to slip the stitch together with its yarn over.

This decrease involves 5 stitches. The first (A), third (C), and fifth (E) are knit column stitches, and the second (B) and fourth (D) are purl column stitches.

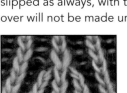
br4st dec on LS

br4st dec on DS

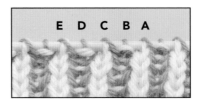

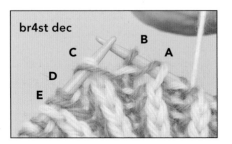

1 Slip A and B separately knitwise.

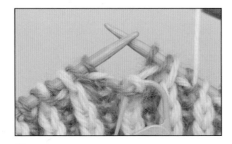

2 Place C on cable needle or stitch marker and hold to front.

3 Knit D.

4 Pass B over.

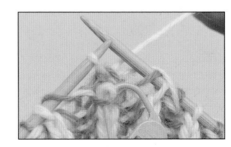

5 Place st on LH needle.

6 Pass E over.

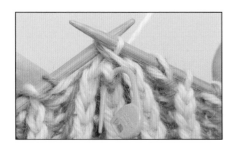

7 Place st on RH needle, pass A over.

8 Place C from cn on LH needle, place st on LH needle.

9 Pass C over, place finished dec st on RH needle. ■

Weaving in Ends

The brioche stitch creates nice little pockets in which to hide yarn ends. Thread the end onto a tapestry needle, then weave it between the yarn overs as shown. Try to catch a bit of the yarn over thread with your tapestry needle to help keep the end from slipping out.

Two ends that need to be woven in

1 Thread yarn end onto tapestry needle and sew across a yo strand.

2 Carry needle down between yo's of knit column. Make sure needle does not show on reverse side.

3 Pull yarn through and off needle. Clip end.

4 Carry 2nd yarn end between yo's up other side of knit column.

5 Pull yarn through and off needle. Clip end.

6 The end result. ■

Blocking

If you want your project to be stretchy and elastic (which also depends upon the material), then don't block it. I did not block any of my stitch swatches.

If you want the piece slightly relaxed, then steam block it lightly.

If you want all of the stitches fully displayed, you will need to wet block your item.

I generally block individual finished pieces before they are sewn together.

Steam Blocking
Spread a thin, damp cloth over the wrong side of the knitted piece and very gently touch the iron to the damp cloth, creating lots of steam. This will relax the yarn and ease the piece into shape. Don't press down and flatten the knitting. I steam blocked several of the projects in this book.

Wet Blocking
Immerse the piece in water, squeeze it out by rolling it in a thick towel, stretch it and pin it out to the exact measurements on a flat board, or you can pin the piece first and then wet it down with a water-filled spray bottle. Allow the piece to dry completely. I wet blocked the lacy scarves shown in the projects section of this book. ■

Repairing Mistakes

Repairing mistakes made in brioche knitting is indeed a challenge. The stitches are difficult to read. The problem is that brioche stitches are not just one knitted loop; they are a stitch with a yarn over, and when you rip out the work it's easy to confuse the stitch with its yarn over. Luckily, with two-color brioche this becomes somewhat easier.

If you make a mistake in the middle of a row, don't pull out the needle and tear out the entire row at once. Instead, rip back one stitch at a time onto a much smaller needle. This will make the stitches and yarn overs easier to pick up, and you can work off this smaller needle onto your original needle for the next row.

If you notice a mistake at the end of the evening, put your work down and address it later, when you are well rested. Trust me: no good comes from hasty brioche repairs.

Picking Up Stitches

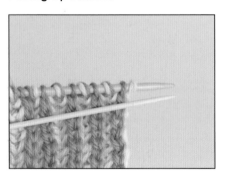

Use a smaller needle when you need to pick up stitches.

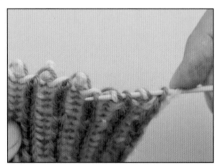

If your stitches fall off the needle, pick them up as carefully as possible with a smaller needle. Notice that one color column of stitches falls to the front, and the other color falls to the back. Remember that every other stitch has a yarn over. If some of the stitches have unraveled farther down the piece, place those onto a stitch holder. You can weave them up after you have picked up all the other stitches onto a needle.

Most often, after picking up all the dropped stitches, you will need to reorganize the stitches in the row once again. The stitch mounts may be incorrect, and some stitches have probably lost their yarn over shawls. You can also chain up any unraveled stitches at this time. ■

Ripping Back Several Rows at Once

If a mistake lies several rows down and you can't go down a column to repair it, you may need to rip out several rows at once.

It's best not to remove the needle and rip out all the rows at once. But if you do prefer this method, rip back only until one row above the mistake row. Then carefully rip back and pick up one stitch at a time, using a smaller needle.

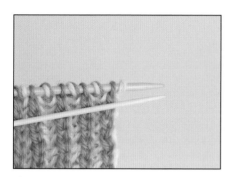

1 Use a smaller needle to pick up stitches.

2 Count down number of rows to unravel. Insert smaller needle into selvedge stitch of lowest row.

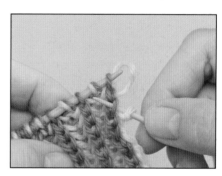

3 Drop stitch from needle and unravel.

4 Continue picking into stitches and unraveling until end of row. ■

Unraveling One Column of Stitches

The most common mistake in brioche knitting is a dropped yarn over. This creates a annoying little bar of color that just glares at you, crying out to be repaired.

The best way to repair this dropped yarn over is to unravel the column, fix your mistake, and then chain the stitches back up the column. Do this very carefully, trying to keep the stitches in front and their corresponding yarn overs hanging to the back.

Shown below is a tried-and-true method for repairing a dropped yarn over. Again, don't do this at the end of the evening. Wait until you can make the repair calmly and patiently!

A dropped yarn over that needs to be repaired.

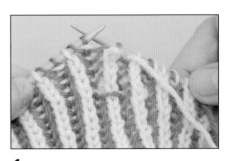

1 Pop the stitch off the needle.

2 Unravel and place st only, leaving yo behind, on curved cable needle or large safety-pin st marker.

3 Continue popping off sts, unraveling and placing onto cable needle. Single sts are hanging on cable needle and yo's are resting behind cable needle in place.

4 When you reach the dropped yo, place it together with its stitch onto a crochet hook.

5 Chain up single sts from cable needle. Don't remove from cable needle until all sts have been chained.

6 All sts have been chained and final st (with its yo) has been placed on needle. Now remove cable needle.

7 The end result. ■

Reading Two-Color Brioche Charts

Working two-color brioche stitch from written instructions is doable, but working from a chart makes a lot more sense. Written instructions have to be followed word for word, while charts are a visual interpretation of the stitch pattern.

Each stitch is represented by a symbol. The symbol's meaning is shown in the key or legend. Learning to read and interpret a brioche chart and to compare your knitting with its chart will make brioche that much easier.

Two-Color Brioche Charts

In two-color brioche knitting, all rows are worked twice. For that reason, there are two chart rows representing each light side, LS LC Row and LS DC Row, and two for each dark side, DS LC Row and DS DC Row.

In one chart row—for example, a LS LC row—half the stitches are slipped and the other half are worked in the light color (LC). Then, in the following charted row, a LS DC row, the worked stitches are slipped and the stitches that were slipped in the previous row are now worked using the dark color (DC). Both light side (LS) rows, which are odd-numbered rows, are read from right to left on the chart. Both dark side (DS), even-numbered rows are read from left to right.

Read the chart as if the light side (LS) were the right side (RS/public side) of the work and the dark side (DS) were the wrong side (WS).

A light color (LC) row is indicated on the chart with a white background. A dark color (DC) row is indicated on the chart with a gray background.

The red boundary box indicates the stitch repeat. The stitches outside the red boundary box are selvedge stitches and are not part of the repeat.

The blue boundary box is the repeat within the set-up rows, which are worked only at the beginning of a stitch pattern.

Symbols in the legend are given with both LS and DS instructions. Be sure to execute the symbol action that corresponds to the side of fabric and the yarn color you are working with. For example, the ⌂ symbol means brk1 on LS rows and brp1 on DS rows.

Most of the time, manipulations such as increases and decreases are worked on a LS LC row.

"No stitch" is indicated by a darker gray box, as in the Speed Knitter Chart on page 86.

When you have several repeats of a pattern, it is best to place a marker between each repeat and the selvedge stitches.

Each worked stitch is followed by a slipped one (sl1yo). After a while, you probably won't need to bother reading the sl1yo. Read only the stitches that are worked, such as brk1, brp1, brkyobrk, brRsl dec, and brLsl dec. These actions are always followed by sl1yo.

Take note: the symbols for decreases made in the DS DC rows are slanted in the opposite direction from how the decrease will appear on the DS. For example, the brLsl dec symbol ⬔ (worked as a left slant dec on the DS) slants to the right, which is the way it appears, when finished, on the LS of the work.

The general legend on the following page shows common brioche chart symbols. See pages 228–235 for guidance on translating two-color flat charts into two-color in the round, one-color flat, and one-color in the round stitch patterns. ■

Brioche Chart Symbols

Note: If a chart symbol is pattern-specific, it will be explained in the Pattern Notes of the project, rather than included in this general legend.

LEGEND FOR FLAT TWO-COLOR BRIOCHE KNITTING CHARTS

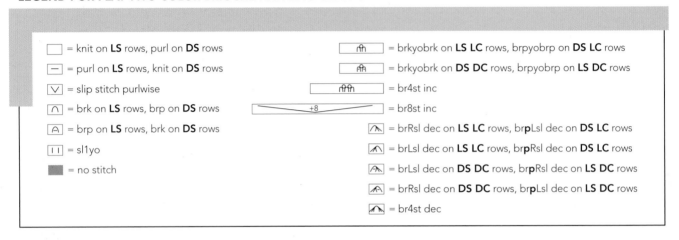

□ = knit on **LS** rows, purl on **DS** rows

— = purl on **LS** rows, knit on **DS** rows

V = slip stitch purlwise

∩ = brk on **LS** rows, brp on **DS** rows

A = brp on **LS** rows, brk on **DS** rows

| | = sl1yo

■ = no stitch

= brkyobrk on **LS LC** rows, brpyobrp on **DS LC** rows

= brkyobrk on **DS DC** rows, brpyobrp on **LS DC** rows

= br4st inc

+8 = br8st inc

= brRsl dec on **LS LC** rows, brpLsl dec on **DS LC** rows

= brLsl dec on **LS LC** rows, brpRsl dec on **DS LC** rows

= brLsl dec on **DS DC** rows, brpRsl dec on **LS DC** rows

= brRsl dec on **DS DC** rows, brpLsl dec on **LS DC** rows

= br4st dec

WHAT DOES THIS ALL MEAN?

Brioche chart symbols are meant to appear as if you are looking at the light side (LS) of the work.

Two-Color Brioche Chart

Note again that the symbols for decreases made in dark side (DS) rows are slanted in the *opposite* direction from the way the decrease will be made on the dark side. For example, the brLsl dec symbol, slants to the *right*, which is the way it appears, when finished, on the light side of the work. On the dark side, it is worked as a *left*-slant decrease. ■

This vertical column of stitches is a purl column on **LS** and a knit column on **DS**

This vertical column of stitches is a knit column on **LS** and a purl column on **DS**

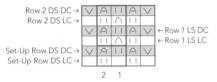

The gray background indicates a **DC** row.

The white background indicates a **LC** row.

The red boundary line represents repeats

The blue boundary line represents repeats in Set-Up Rows

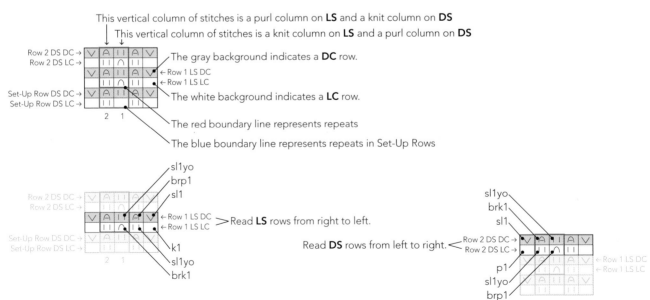

sl1yo
brp1
sl1
k1
sl1yo
brk1

> Read **LS** rows from right to left.

Read **DS** rows from left to right. <

sl1yo
brk1
sl1
p1
sl1yo
brp1

Light side (LS) of two-color brioche fabric

Dark side (DS) of two-color brioche fabric

The Basic Fabric

Two-Color Brioche Stitch with a Selvedge Edge
This is the plain two-color brioche stitch, with beautiful edges. I advise you to practice this stitch pattern before attempting to add increases and decreases.

Using the Two-Color Italian Cast-On (page 14), begin and end with LC knit st. Cast on a multiple of 2 sts + 1.

Set-Up Row DS LC: p1, *sl1yo, p1; rep from * to end. Drop knotted st from Two-Color Italian Cast-On. Do *not* turn; slide sts back to opposite end of needle.
Set-Up Row DS DC: sl1, *brk1, sl1yo; rep from * to last 2 sts, brk1, drop DC to back, sl 1. Turn.

Row 1 LS LC: k1, *sl1yo, brk1; rep from * to last 2 sts, sl1yo, k1. Do *not* turn; slide.
Row 1 LS DC: sl1, *brp1, sl1yo; rep from * to last 2 sts, brp1, drop DC to front, sl1. Turn.

Row 2 DS LC: p1, *sl1yo, brp1; rep from * to last 2 sts, sl1yo, p1. Do *not* turn; slide.
Row 2 DS DC: sl1, *brk1, sl1yo; rep from * to last 2 sts, brk1, drop DC to back, sl1. Turn.

Rep from Row 1 LS LC.

Bind off using the Italian Bind-Off (page 26). ■

S-Twist Brioche

This is the sample swatch for S-Twist Brioche Stitch. It requires a 6-stitch repeat worked over 4 LS and DS rows (the stitches within the red boundary box on the chart).

Note how the increase in Row 1 LS LC covers 3 grid spaces of the chart. That's because the increase makes 3 stitches bloom out of one stitch. The decrease to its left eliminates 2 stitches, so it covers 1 grid space. The stitch count and the grid both remain the same at the end of a pattern repeat.

This sample was worked over 27 stitches (a multiple of 6 stitches plus 3) and 28 rows. An increase and a decrease were worked in each Row 1 LS LC. ∎

This is the increase made in Row 1 LS LC (3rd pattern rep).

This is the corresponding decrease made in Row 1 LS LC (3rd pattern rep).

Note that increases and decreases can cause your knitted fabric to distort.

S-Twist Chart

	6	5	4	3	2	1	

Row 4 DS DC →
Row 4 DS LC →
← Row 3 LS DC
← Row 3 LS LC
Row 2 DS DC →
Row 2 DS LC →
← Row 1 LS DC
← Row 1 LS LC
Set-Up Row DS DC →
Set-Up Row DS LC →

Reading Mr. Flood's Chart

When you first see a brioche chart, it can look quite intimidating. That's because almost every square contains a symbol—and you probably don't recognize the symbols.

To learn to read a two-color brioche chart, start by isolating one row. I use removeable highlighting tape, but a sticky note, index card, or magnetic strip also works. You will only be paying attention to the row below the tape.

This is how I approach working Mr. Flood's Brioche Stitch (see page 109).

Cast on a multiple of 10 stitches plus 5, and work the set-up rows. Set-up rows are "plain" two-color brioche, meaning that there are no manipulations such as increases or decreases. →

Mr. Flood's Chart

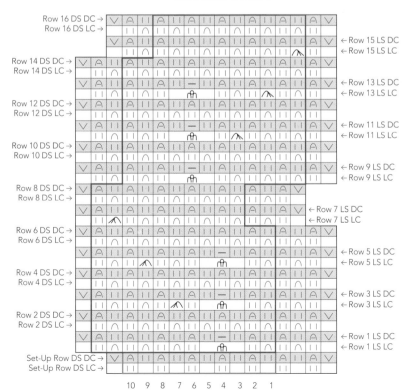

Reading Mr. Flood's Chart (cont.)

In the Set-Up Row DS DC on the chart, read p1, then work the actions given within the blue boundary box: sl1yo, p1, which are repeated up to the last 4 stitches. Finish the row with what is outside of the blue boundary box, which is [sl1yo, p1] twice.

From now on, as you read across the chart, ignore the sl1yo ⊡ symbols. This sl1yo action is part of the brioche sequence and will always occur after a brk1, brp1, an increase or a decrease, so it is a given. Take note of it only in the first set-up row.

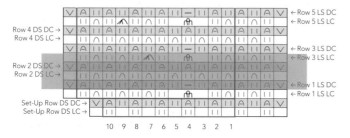

Cover the remaining rows on the chart, leaving the row you are about to work and the previously worked rows exposed.

To read Row 1 LS LC, begin with 4 selvedge stitches; a k1 ▢, then a sl1yo ⊡, then a brk1 ⋂, then another sl1yo ⊡. Read these as 1 knit and 1 bark stitch, working the sl1yos but not bothering to read them.

After the selvedge stitches, repeat one bark ⋂, an increase ⋔, and three barks ⋂ ⋂ ⋂. Notice again that I disregarded reading the sl1yos ⊡.

In other words, read the repeat part of the pattern as follows: 1 bark, 1 increase, 3 barks. The sl1yos are ignored because they always occur after the barks and increase. Notice that the chart is now 2 stitches wider because of the increase.

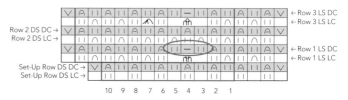

The following LS DC row is a plain brioche purl row, except for the 3 stitches above the increase in the previous row. Newly created stitches need to be brought into brioche mode with sl1yo, p1, sl1yo, since they do not yet have their yarn over shawls. This becomes logical after a few repeats.

All even-numbered DS rows are plain two-color brioche rows; the DS LC row is all brioche purls and the DS DC row is brioche knits. The increases and decreases happen on the LS LC rows. (This is true of most of the stitch patterns in this book.)

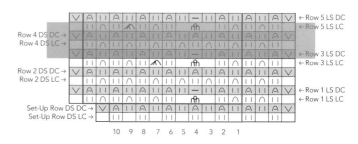

Row 3 LS LC: Work the selvedge stitches, then the repeat of 1 bark, 1 increase, 1 left-slant decrease ◪, 2 barks. The following LS DC row will be worked in plain brioche, bringing the new stitches from the increase into brioche mode.

Row 5 LS LC: Work the selvedge stitches, then the repeat of 1 bark, 1 increase, 1 bark, 1 left-slant decrease, 1 bark. The following LS DC row will be worked in plain brioche, except for the new stitches from the increase.

Row 7 LS LC: Work the selvedge stitches, then the repeat of 4 barks and 1 left-slant decrease. The chart has now decreased by 2 stitches. The following LS DC row will be worked in plain brioche, since there was no increase in the previous row.

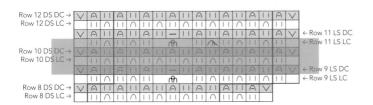

Row 9 LS LC: Notice that the position of our red boundary box has shifted. The selvedge edge pattern is now k1, sl1yo and the repeat within the red boundary box is 3 barks, 1 increase, and 1 bark. The following LS DC row will be worked in plain brioche, except for the new stitches from the increase; the chart is now 2 stitches wider.

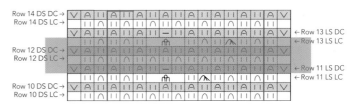

Row 11 LS LC: Work the selvedge stitches, then the repeat of 2 barks, 1 right-slant decrease, 1 increase, and 1 bark. The following LS DC row will be worked in plain brioche, except for the new stitches from the increase.

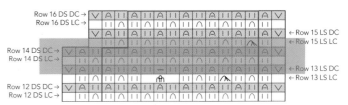

Row 13 LS LC: Work the selvedge stitches and the repeat of 1 bark, 1 right-slant decrease, 1 bark, 1 increase, and 1 bark. The following LS DC row will be worked in plain brioche, except for the new stitches from the increase.

Row 15 LS LC: Work the selvedge stitches, then the repeat of 1 right-slant decrease and 4 barks. The following LS DC row will be worked in plain brioche, since there was no increase in the previous row. The chart has now returned to its original 10 stitches. ∎

The Stitch Patterns

Two-Color Brioche Stitch Patterns

Like a lot of you, I have been knitting for most of my life. But I have yet to ever get bored with it—because I discovered the brioche stitch. I played with the stitch for many years before getting serious about it. Then, while I was writing my first book, *Knitting Brioche*, a world of possibilities opened up to me.

Even while working on that project, I desperately wanted to dive into developing new brioche stitch patterns. I have spent the past five years developing the stitches presented here, all of which were created using only increases and decreases worked on a basic two-color brioche knit fabric. There are no cables or crossed stitches, no textural variations, no play with variegated color or different yarn weights—only increases and decreases. And this is just a handful of brioche stitch pattern possibilities: there are still so many more to discover!

Right-Leaning Ladder

This little pattern uses a brkyobrk increase followed by a brRsl decrease in every LS LC row. Notice how the fabric biases to the right on the LS. If the pattern began with a brLsl decrease followed by an increase, the fabric would bias in the other direction, as with Left-Leaning Ladder.

Right-Leaning Ladder Brioche Stitch
Using Two-Color Italian Cast-On, begin and end with LC knit st. Cast on a multiple of 6 sts + 3. For the sample shown, I cast on 27 sts.

Set-Up Row DS LC: p1, *sl1yo, p1; rep from * to end.
Do *not* turn, slide.
Set-Up Row DS DC: sl1, *brk1, sl1yo; rep from * to last 2 sts, brk1, sl1. Turn.

Row 1 LS LC: k1, sl1yo, *brkyobrk, sl1yo, brRsl dec, sl1yo; rep from * to last st, k1. Do *not* turn, slide.
Row 1 LS DC: sl1, brp1, *sl1yo, p1, [sl1yo, brp1] twice; rep from * to last st, sl1. Turn.

Row 2 DS LC: p1, *sl1yo, brp1; rep from * to last 2 sts, sl1yo, p1.
Do *not* turn, slide.
Row 2 DS DC: sl1, *brk1, sl1yo; rep from * to last 2 sts, brk1, sl1. Turn.

Rep from Row 1 LS LC. ■

Right-Leaning Ladder Chart

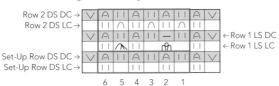

53

Left-Leaning Ladder

Left-Leaning Ladder Brioche Stitch
Using Two-Color Italian Cast-On, begin and end with LC knit st. Cast on a multiple of 6 sts + 3. For the sample shown, I cast on 27 sts.

Set-Up Row DS LC: p1, *sl1yo, p1; rep from * to end. Do *not* turn, slide.
Set-Up Row DS DC: sl1, *brk1, sl1yo; rep from * to last 2 sts, brk1, sl1. Turn.

Row 1 LS LC: k1, sl1yo, *brLsl dec, sl1yo, brkyobrk, sl1yo; rep from * to last st, k1. Do *not* turn, slide.

Row 1 LS DC: sl1, brp1, *sl1yo, brp1, sl1yo, p1, sl1yo, brp1; rep from * to last st, sl1. Turn.

Row 2 DS LC: p1, *sl1yo, brp1; rep from * to last 2 sts, sl1yo, p1. Do *not* turn, slide.
Row 2 DS DC: sl1, *brk1, sl1yo; rep from * to last 2 sts, brk1, sl1. Turn.

Rep from Row 1 LS LC. ■

Left-Leaning Ladder Chart

S-Twist

This fabric also biases to the right. It differs from Right-Leaning Ladder in that an extra set of LS and DS rows is worked, which elongates the pattern. And it uses a brLsl dec instead of a brRsl dec, which creates a curvy edge in the motif.

S-Twist Brioche Stitch
Using Two-Color Italian Cast-On, begin and end with LC knit st. Cast on a multiple of 6 sts + 3. For the sample shown, I cast on 27 sts.

Set-Up Row DS LC: p1, *sl1yo, p1; rep from * to end. Do *not* turn, slide.
Set-Up Row DS DC: sl1, *brk1, sl1yo; rep from * to last 2 sts, brk1, sl1. Turn.

Row 1 LS LC: k1, sl1yo, *brkyobrk, sl1yo, brLsl dec, sl1yo; rep from * to last st, k1. Do *not* turn, slide.
Row 1 LS DC: sl1, brp1, *sl1yo, p1, [sl1yo, brp1] twice; rep from * to last st, sl1. Turn.

Row 2 DS LC and all DS LC rows: p1, *sl1yo, brp1; rep from * to last 2 sts, sl1yo, p1. Do *not* turn, slide.
Row 2 DS DC and all DS DC rows: sl1, *brk1, sl1yo; rep from * to last 2 sts, brk1, sl1. Turn.

Row 3 LS LC: k1, sl1yo, *brk1, sl1yo; rep from * to last st, k1. Do *not* turn, slide.
Row 3 LS DC: sl1, brp1, *sl1yo, brp1; rep from * to last st, sl1. Turn.

After working last set of DS rows, rep from Row 1 LS LC. ■

S-Twist Chart

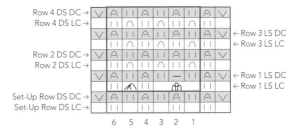

S- and Z-Twist

In this variation, the S-Twist pattern is mirrored. The biasing has been balanced out by using both right- and left-slanting decreases. Notice the beautiful fluted bottom edge, where the fabric is pulled up and down by the increases and decreases. This is reminiscent of zigzag or chevron knitting.

S- and Z-Twist Brioche Stitch
Using Two-Color Italian Cast-On, begin and end with LC knit st. Cast on a multiple of 12 sts + 3. For the sample shown, I cast on 39 sts.

Set-Up Row DS LC: p1, *sl1yo, p1; rep from * to end. Do *not* turn, slide.
Set-Up Row DS DC: sl1, *brk1, sl1yo; rep from * to last 2 sts, brk1, sl1. Turn.

Row 1 LS LC: k1, sl1yo, *brRsl dec, sl1yo, brkyobrk, sl1yo, brkyobrk, sl1yo, brLsl dec, sl1yo; rep from * to last st, k1. Do *not* turn, slide.
Row 1 LS DC: sl1, brp1, *[sl1yo, brp1, sl1yo, p1] twice, [sl1yo, brp1] twice; rep from * to last st, sl1. Turn.

Row 2 DS LC and all DS LC rows: p1, *sl1yo, brp1; rep from * to last 2 sts, sl1yo, p1. Do *not* turn, slide.
Row 2 DS DC and all DS DC rows: sl1, *brk1, sl1yo; rep from * to last 2 sts, brk1, sl1. Turn.

Row 3 LS LC: k1, sl1yo, *brk1, sl1yo; rep from * to last st, k1. Do *not* turn, slide.
Row 3 LS DC: sl1, brp1, *sl1yo, brp1; rep from * to last st, sl1. Turn.

After working last set of DS rows, rep from Row 1 LS LC. ■

S- and Z-Twist Chart

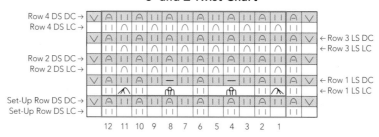

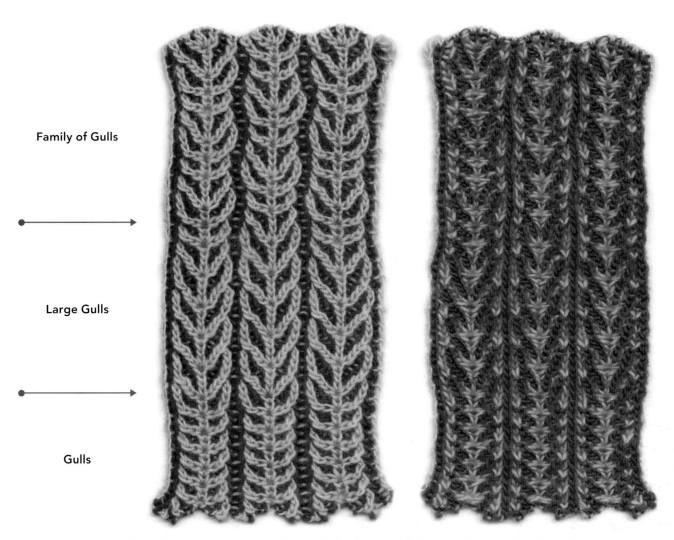

Family of Gulls

Large Gulls

Gulls

Gulls, Large Gulls, and Family of Gulls

With this sample, the increases have been meshed together. Instead of two, one slanting to the left and the other to the right, a centered increase of four stitches has been used. By playing with the placement of the decreases and using more or fewer rows between each manipulation row, different stitch patterns appear.

Gulls Brioche Stitch
Using Two-Color Italian Cast-On, begin and end with LC knit st. Cast on a multiple of 10 sts + 3. For the sample shown, I cast on 33 sts.

Set-Up Row DS LC: p1, *sl1yo, p1; rep from * to end. Do *not* turn, slide.
Set-Up Row DS DC: sl1, *brk1, sl1yo; rep from * to last 2 sts, brk1, sl1. Turn.

Row 1 LS LC: k1, sl1yo, *brRsl dec, sl1yo, br4st inc, sl1yo, brLsl dec, sl1yo; rep from * to last st, k1.
Do *not* turn, slide.
Row 1 LS DC: sl1, brp1, *sl1yo, brp1, [sl1yo, p1] twice, [sl1yo, brp1] twice; rep from * to last st, sl1. Turn.

Row 2 DS LC: p1, *sl1yo, brp1; rep from * to last 2 sts, sl1yo, p1. Do *not* turn, slide.
Row 2 DS DC: sl1, *brk1, sl1yo; rep from * to last 2 sts, brk1, sl1. Turn.

Rep from Row 1 LS LC. ■

Gulls Chart

Large Gulls

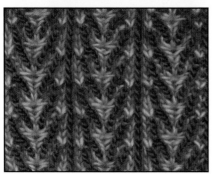

Large Gulls

By following the same pattern as in Gulls, but adding Rows 3 and 4, an elongated motif has been created.

Large Gulls Brioche Stitch

Using Two-Color Italian Cast-On, begin and end with LC knit st. Cast on a multiple of 10 sts + 3. For the sample shown, I cast on 33 sts.

Set-Up Row DS LC: p1, *sl1yo, p1; rep from * to end. Do *not* turn, slide.
Set-Up Row DS DC: sl1, *brk1, sl1yo; rep from * to last 2 sts, brk1, sl1. Turn.

Row 1 LS LC: k1, sl1yo, *brRsl dec, sl1yo, br4st inc, sl1yo, brLsl dec, sl1yo; rep from * to last st, k1. Do *not* turn, slide.
Row 1 LS DC: sl1, brp1, *sl1yo, brp1, [sl1yo, p1] twice, [sl1yo, brp1] twice; rep from * to last st, sl1. Turn.

Row 2 DS LC and all DS LC rows: p1, *sl1yo, brp1; rep from * to last 2 sts, sl1yo, p1. Do *not* turn, slide.
Row 2 DS DC and all DS DC rows: sl1, *brk1, sl1yo; rep from * to last 2 sts, brk1, sl1. Turn.

Row 3 LS LC: k1, sl1yo, *brk1, sl1yo; rep from * to last st, k1. Do *not* turn, slide.
Row 3 LS DC: sl1, brp1, *sl1yo, brp1; rep from * to last st, sl1. Turn.

After working last set of DS rows, rep from Row 1 LS LC. ■

Large Gulls Chart

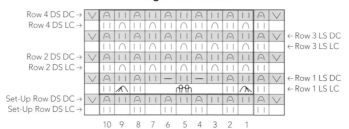

Family of Gulls

For this variation, the placement of the Gulls motif has been shifted and plain columns of two-color brioche stitch placed in between to create a new stitch pattern.

Family of Gulls Brioche Stitch

Using Two-Color Italian Cast-On, begin and end with LC knit st. Cast on a multiple of 20 sts + 13. For the sample shown, I cast on 33 sts.

Set-Up Row DS LC: p1, *sl1yo, p1; rep from * to end. Do *not* turn, slide.
Set-Up Row DS DC: sl1, *brk1, sl1yo; rep from * to last 2 sts, brk1, sl1. Turn.

Row 1 LS LC: k1, sl1yo, *brRsl dec, sl1yo, br4st inc, sl1yo, brLsl dec, sl1yo; rep from * to last st, k1. Do *not* turn, slide.
Row 1 LS DC: sl1, brp1, *sl1yo, brp1, [sl1yo, p1] twice, [sl1yo, brp1] twice; rep from * to last st, sl1. Turn.

Row 2 DS LC and all DS LC rows: p1, *sl1yo, brp1; rep from * to last 2 sts, sl1yo, p1. Do *not* turn, slide.

Row 2 DS DC and all DS DC rows: sl1, *brk1, sl1yo; rep from * to last 2 sts, brk1, sl1. Turn.

Row 3 LS LC: k1, sl1yo, *brRsl dec, sl1yo, br4st inc, sl1yo, brLsl dec, sl1yo, [brk1, sl1yo] 5 times; rep from * to last 11 sts, brRsl dec, sl1yo, br4st inc, sl1yo, brLsl dec, sl1yo, k1. Do *not* turn, slide.
Row 3 LS DC: sl1, brp1, *sl1yo, brp1, [sl1yo, p1] twice, [sl1yo, brp1] 7 times; rep from * to last 11 sts, sl1yo, brp1, [sl1yo, p1] twice, [sl1yo, brp1] twice, sl1. Turn.

Row 5 LS LC: as Row 1 LS LC.
Row 5 LS DC: as Row 1 LS DC.

Row 7 LS LC: k1, sl1yo, * [brk1, sl1yo] 5 times, brRsl dec, sl1yo, br4st inc, sl1yo, brLsl dec, sl1yo; rep from * to last 11 sts, [brk1, sl1yo] 5 times, k1. Do *not* turn, slide.
Row 7 LS DC: sl1, brp1, *[sl1yo, brp1] 6 times, [sl1yo, p1] twice, [sl1yo, brp1] twice; rep from * to last 11 sts, [sl1yo, brp1] 5 times, sl1. Turn.

After working last set of DS rows, rep from Row 1 LS LC. ■

Family of Gulls

Family of Gulls Chart

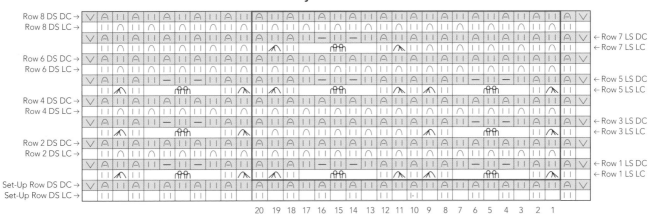

Small Bead

Seed Bead

Seed Bead and Small Bead

The subtle Seed Bead motif would work well in between other, larger brioche stitch motifs.

Seed Bead Brioche Stitch

Using Two-Color Italian Cast-On, begin and end with LC knit st. Cast on a multiple of 6 sts + 3. For the sample shown, I cast on 27 sts.

Set-Up Row DS LC: p1, *sl1yo, p1; rep from * to end. Do *not* turn, slide.
Set-Up Row DS DC: sl1, *brk1, sl1yo; rep from * to last 2 sts, brk1, sl1. Turn.

Row 1 LS LC: k1, sl1yo, *brLsl dec, sl1yo, brkyobrk, sl1yo; rep from * to last st, k1. Do *not* turn, slide.
Row 1 LS DC: sl1, brp1, *sl1yo, brp1, sl1yo, p1, sl1yo, brp1; rep from * to last st, sl1. Turn.

Row 2 DS LC and all DS LC rows: p1, *sl1yo, brp1; rep from * to last 2 sts, sl1yo, p1. Do *not* turn, slide.
Row 2 DS DC and all DS DC rows: sl1, *brk1, sl1yo; rep from * to last 2 sts, brk1, sl1. Turn.

Row 3 LS LC: k1, sl1yo, *brkyobrk, sl1yo, brRsl dec, sl1yo; rep from * to last st, k1. Do *not* turn, slide.
Row 3 LS DC: sl1, brp1, *sl1yo, p1, [sl1yo, brp1] twice; rep from * to last st, sl1. Turn.

After working last set of DS rows, rep from Row 1 LS LC. ∎

When extra rows are added between the manipulations worked for Seed Bead, the Small Bead motif becomes much more obvious.

Small Bead Brioche Stitch
Using Two-Color Italian Cast-On, begin and end with LC knit st. Cast on a multiple of 6 sts + 3. For the sample shown, I cast on 27 sts.

Set-Up Row DS LC: p1, *sl1yo, p1; rep from * to end. Do *not* turn, slide.
Set-Up Row DS DC: sl1, *brk1, sl1yo; rep from * to last 2 sts, brk1, sl1. Turn.

Row 1 LS LC: k1, sl1yo, *brLsl dec, sl1yo, brkyobrk, sl1yo; rep from * to last st, k1. Do *not* turn, slide.
Row 1 LS DC: sl1, brp1, *sl1yo, brp1, sl1yo, p1, sl1yo, brp1; rep from * to last st, sl1. Turn.

Row 2 DS LC and all DS LC rows: p1, *sl1yo, brp1; rep from * to last 2 sts, sl1yo, p1. Do *not* turn, slide.
Row 2 DS DC and all DS DC rows: sl1, *brk1, sl1yo; rep from * to last 2 sts, brk1, sl1. Turn.

Row 3 LS LC: k1, sl1yo, *brk1, sl1yo; rep from * to last st, k1. Do *not* turn, slide.
Row 3 LS DC: sl1, brp1, *sl1yo, brp1; rep from * to last st, sl1. Turn.

Row 5 LS LC: k1, sl1yo, *brkyobrk, sl1yo, brRsl dec, sl1yo; rep from * to last st, k1. Do *not* turn, slide.
Row 5 LS DC: sl1, brp1, *sl1yo, p1, [sl1yo, brp1] twice; rep from * to last st, sl1. Turn.

Row 7 LS LC: as Row 3 LS LC.
Row 7 LS DC: as Row 3 LS DC.

After working last set of DS rows, rep from Row 1 LS LC. ■

Seed Bead

Seed Bead Chart

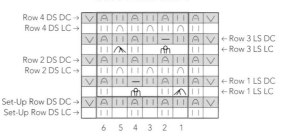

Small Bead

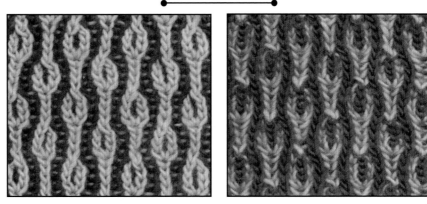

Small Bead Chart

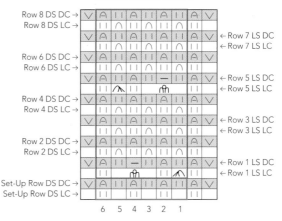

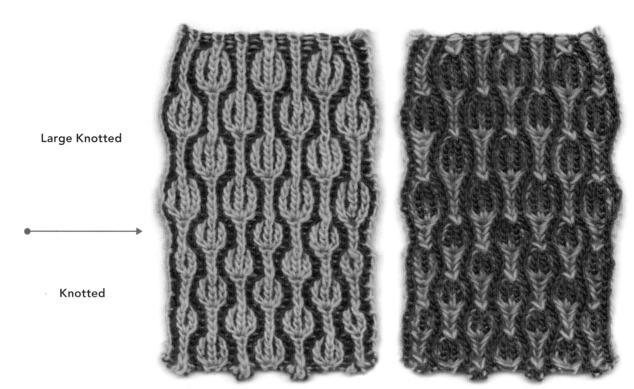

Large Knotted

Knotted

Knotted and Large Knotted

In Knotted Brioche Stitch, the decreases are worked a few rows above the increase. The motifs are worked in every other column, shifting them left and right. Note that the side edges have half motifs rather than the full motifs of the body.

Knotted Brioche Stitch
Two-Color Italian Cast-On, begin and end with LC knit st. Cast on a multiple of 8 sts + 13. For the sample shown, I cast on 29 sts.

Set-Up Row DS LC: p1, *sl1yo, p1; rep from * to end. Do *not* turn, slide.
Set-Up Row DS DC: sl1, *brk1, sl1yo; rep from * to last 2 sts, brk1, sl1. Turn.

Row 1 LS LC: k1, sl1yo, brLsl dec, sl1yo, *br4st inc, sl1yo, br4st dec, sl1yo; rep from * to last 7 sts, br4st inc, sl1yo, brRsl dec, sl1yo, k1. Do *not* turn, slide.
Row 1 LS DC: sl1, brp1, sl1yo, brp1, *[sl1yo, p1] twice, [sl1yo, brp1] twice; rep from * to last st, sl1. Turn.

Row 2 DS LC and all DS LC rows: p1, *sl1yo, brp1; rep from * to last 2 sts, sl1yo, p1. Do *not* turn, slide.

Row 2 DS DC and all DS DC rows: sl1, *brk1, sl1yo; rep from * to last 2 sts, brk1, sl1. Turn.

Row 3 LS LC: k1, sl1yo, *brk1, sl1yo; rep from * to last st, k1. Do *not* turn, slide.
Row 3 LS DC: sl1, brp1, *sl1yo, brp1; rep from * to last st, sl1. Turn.

Row 5 LS LC: k1, sl1yo, brkyobrk, sl1yo, *br4st dec, sl1yo, br4st inc, sl1yo; rep from * to last 9 sts, br4st dec, sl1yo, brkyobrk, sl1yo, k1. Do *not* turn, slide.
Row 5 LS DC: sl1, brp1, sl1yo, p1, sl1yo, brp1, *sl1yo, brp1, [sl1yo, p1] twice, sl1yo, brp1; rep from * to last 7 sts, sl1yo, brp1, sl1yo, p1, sl1yo, brp1, sl1. Turn.

Row 7 LS LC: as Row 3 LS LC.
Row 7 LS DC: as Row 3 LS DC.

After working last set of DS rows, rep from Row 1 LS LC. ∎

Knotted Brioche Stitch has been elongated by adding rows in between to create Large Knotted Brioche Stitch. The edge motifs match the inner motifs, and the edge treatment creates a nice undulating effect.

Large Knotted Brioche Stitch

Using Two-Color Italian Cast-On, begin and end with LC knit st. Cast on a multiple of 8 sts + 5. For the sample shown, I cast on 29 sts.

Set-Up Row DS LC: p1, *sl1yo, p1; rep from * to end. Do *not* turn, slide.
Set-Up Row DS DC: sl1, *brk1, sl1yo; rep from * to last 2 sts, brk1, sl1. Turn.

Row 1 LS LC: k1, sl1yo, *br4st inc, sl1yo, br4st dec, sl1yo; rep from * to last 3 sts, br4st inc, sl1yo, k1. Do *not* turn, slide.
Row 1 LS DC: sl1, brp1, *[sl1yo, p1] twice, [sl1yo, brp1] twice; rep from * to last 7 sts, [sl1yo, p1] twice, sl1yo, brp1, sl1. Turn.

Row 2 DS LC and all DS LC rows: p1, *sl1yo, brp1; rep from * to last 2 sts, sl1yo, p1. Do *not* turn, slide.
Row 2 DS DC and all DS DC rows: sl1, *brk1, sl1yo; rep from * to last 2 sts, brk1, sl1. Turn.

Row 3 LS LC: k1, sl1yo, *brk1, sl1yo; rep from * to last st, k1. Do *not* turn, slide.
Row 3 LS DC: sl1, brp1, *sl1yo, brp1; rep from * to last st, sl1. Turn.

Row 5 LS LC: as Row 3 LS LC.
Row 5 LS DC: as Row 3 LS DC.

Row 7 LS LC: k1, sl1yo, *br4st dec, sl1yo, br4st inc, sl1yo; rep from * to last 7 sts, br4st dec, sl1yo, k1. Do *not* turn, slide.

Knotted Chart

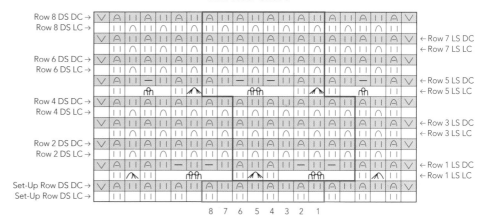

Large Knotted Chart

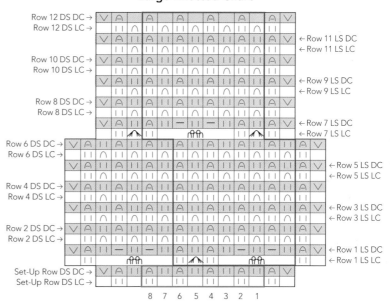

Row 7 LS DC: sl1, brp1, *sl1yo, brp1, [sl1yo, p1] twice, sl1yo, brp1; rep from * to last 3 sts, sl1yo, brp1, sl1. Turn.

Row 9 LS LC: as Row 3 LS LC.
Row 9 LS DC: as Row 3 LS DC.

Row 11 LS LC: as Row 3 LS LC.
Row 11 LS DC: as Row 3 LS DC.

After working last set of DS rows, rep from Row 1 LS LC. ∎

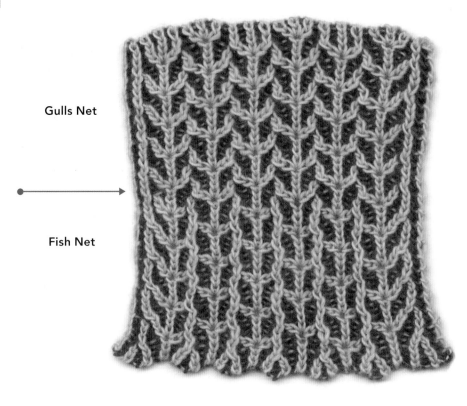

Gulls Net

Fish Net

Fish Net and Gulls Net

Note that the edges in this sample don't quite match up to the decreases in the body of the fabric. For a better match, work the edge decreases as given, in the opposite direction.

Fish Net Brioche Stitch
Using Two-Color Italian Cast-On, begin and end with LC knit st. Cast on a multiple of 12 sts + 7. For the sample shown, I cast on 43 sts.

Set-Up Row DS LC: p1, *sl1yo, p1; rep from * to end. Do *not* turn, slide.
Set-Up Row DS DC: sl1, *brk1, sl1yo; rep from * to last 2 sts, brk1, sl1. Turn.

Row 1 LS LC: k1, sl1yo, [brk1, sl1yo] twice, *brk1, sl1yo, brRsl dec, sl1yo, br4st inc, sl1yo, brLsl dec, sl1yo; rep from * to last stitch, k1. Do *not* turn, slide.
Row 1 LS DC: sl1, brp1, [sl1yo, brp1] twice, *[sl1yo, brp1] twice, [sl1yo, p1] twice, [sl1yo, brp1] twice; rep from * to last st, sl1. Turn.

Row 2 DS LC and all DS LC rows: p1, *sl1yo, brp1; rep from * to last 2 sts, sl1yo, p1. Do *not* turn, slide.
Row 2 DS DC and all DS DC rows: sl1, *brk1, sl1yo; rep from * to last 2 sts, brk1, sl1. Turn.

Row 3 LS LC: k1, sl1yo, *brRsl dec, sl1yo, br4st inc, sl1yo, brLsl dec, sl1yo, brk1, sl1yo; rep from * to last 5 sts, [brk1, sl1yo] twice, k1. Do *not* turn, slide.
Row 3 LS DC: sl1, brp1, *sl1yo, brp1, [sl1yo, p1] twice, [sl1yo, brp1] 3 times; rep from * to last 5 sts, [sl1yo, brp1] twice, sl1. Turn.

After working last set of DS rows, rep from Row 1 LS LC. ■

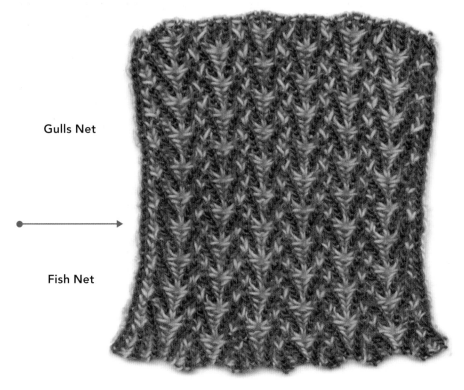

Gulls Net

Fish Net

This pattern is exactly like Fish Net Brioche Stitch, only the decreases have changed direction. Here again, the edge decreases are worked in the opposite direction from what's written. Work as given for a matching edge.

Gulls Net Brioche Stitch
Using Two-Color Italian Cast-On, begin and end with LC knit st. Cast on a multiple of 12 sts + 7. For the sample shown, I cast on 43 sts.

Set-Up Row DS LC: p1, *sl1yo, p1; rep from * to end. Do *not* turn, slide.
Set-Up Row DS DC: sl1, *brk1, sl1yo; rep from * to last 2 sts, brk1, sl1. Turn.

Row 1 LS LC: k1, sl1yo, [brk1, sl1yo] twice, *brk1, sl1yo, brLsl dec, sl1yo, br4st inc, sl1yo, brRsl dec, sl1yo; rep from * to last stitch, k1. Do *not* turn, slide.
Row 1 LS DC: sl1, brp1, [sl1yo, brp1] twice, *[sl1yo, brp1] twice, [sl1yo, p1] twice, [sl1yo, brp1] twice; rep from * to last st, sl1. Turn.

Row 2 DS LC and all DS LC rows: p1, *sl1yo, brp1; rep from * to last 2 sts, sl1yo, p1. Do *not* turn, slide.
Row 2 DS DC and all DS DC rows: sl1, *brk1, sl1yo; rep from * to last 2 sts, brk1, sl1. Turn.

Row 3 LS LC: k1, sl1yo, *brLsl dec, sl1yo, br4st inc, sl1yo, brRsl dec, sl1yo, brk1, sl1yo; rep from * to last 5 sts, [brk1, sl1yo] twice, k1. Do *not* turn, slide.
Row 3 LS DC: sl1, brp1, *sl1yo, brp1, [sl1yo, p1] twice, [sl1yo, brp1] 3 times; rep from * to last 5 sts, [sl1yo, brp1] twice, sl1. Turn.

After working last set of DS rows, rep from Row 1 LS LC. ∎

Fish Net

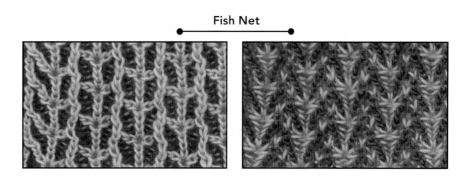

Fish Net Chart

Gulls Net

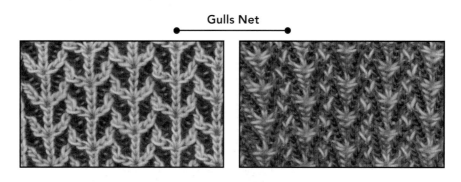

Gulls Net Chart

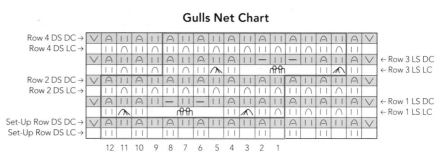

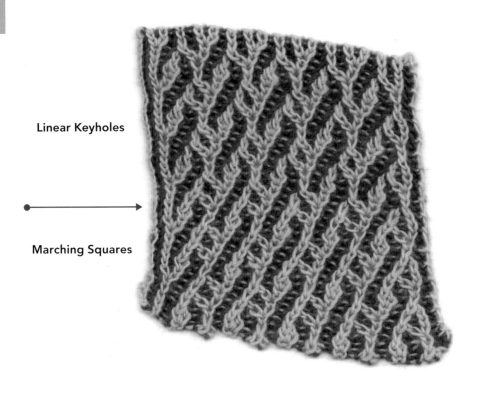

Linear Keyholes

Marching Squares

Marching Squares and Linear Keyholes

Marching Squares Brioche Stitch

Using Two-Color Italian Cast-On, begin and end with LC knit st. Cast on a multiple of 6 sts + 5. For the sample shown, I cast on 35 sts.

Set-Up Row DS LC: p1, *sl1yo, p1; rep from * to end. Do *not* turn, slide.
Set-Up Row DS DC: sl1, *brk1, sl1yo; rep from * to last 2 sts, brk1, sl1. Turn.

Row 1 LS LC: k1, sl1yo, *brRsl dec, sl1yo, brkyobrk, sl1yo; rep from * to last 3 sts, brk1, sl1yo, k1. Do *not* turn, slide.
Row 1 LS DC: sl1, brp1, *sl1yo, brp1, sl1yo, p1, sl1yo, brp1; rep from * to last 3 sts, sl1yo, brp1, sl1. Turn.

Row 2 DS LC and all DS LC rows: p1, *sl1yo, brp1; rep from * to last 2 sts, sl1yo, p1. Do *not* turn, slide.
Row 2 DS DC and all DS DC rows: sl1, *brk1, sl1yo; rep from * to last 2 sts, brk1, sl1. Turn.

Row 3 LS LC: k1, sl1yo, *brkyobrk, sl1yo, brRsl dec, sl1yo; rep from * to last 3 sts, brk1, sl1yo, k1. Do *not* turn, slide.
Row 3 LS DC: sl1, brp1, *sl1yo, p1, [sl1yo, brp1] twice; rep from * to last 3 sts, sl1yo, brp1, sl1. Turn.

Row 5 LS LC: k1, sl1yo, brk1, sl1yo, *brRsl dec, sl1yo, brkyobrk, sl1yo; rep from * to last st, k1. Do *not* turn, slide.
Row 5 LS DC: sl1, brp1, sl1yo, brp1, *sl1yo, brp1, sl1yo, p1, sl1yo brp1; rep from * to last st, sl1. Turn.

After working last set of DS rows, rep from Row 1 LS LC. ∎

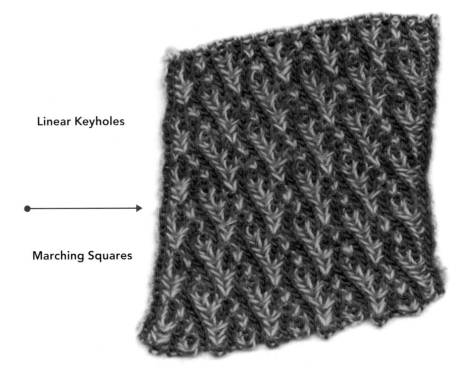

Linear Keyholes

Marching Squares

Linear Keyholes Brioche Stitch

Using Two-Color Italian Cast-On, begin and end with LC knit st. Cast on a multiple of 6 sts + 5. For the sample shown, I cast on 35 sts.

Set-Up Row DS LC: p1, *sl1yo, p1; rep from * to end. Do *not* turn, slide.
Set-Up Row DS DC: sl1, *brk1, sl1yo; rep from * to last 2 sts, brk1, sl1. Turn.

Row 1 LS LC: k1, sl1yo, *brLsl dec, sl1yo, brkyobrk, sl1yo; rep from * to last 3 sts, brk1, sl1yo, k1. Do *not* turn, slide.
Row 1 LS DC: sl1, brp1, *sl1yo, brp1, sl1yo, p1, sl1yo, brp1; rep from * to last 3 sts, sl1yo, brp1, sl1. Turn.

Row 2 DS LC and all DS LC rows: p1, *sl1yo, brp1; rep from * to last 2 sts, sl1yo, p1. Do *not* turn, slide.
Row 2 DS DC and all DS DC rows: sl1, *brk1, sl1yo; rep from * to last 2 sts, brk1, sl1. Turn.

Row 3 LS LC: k1, sl1yo, *brkyobrk, sl1yo, brLsl dec, sl1yo; rep from * to last 3 sts, brk1, sl1yo, k1. Do *not* turn, slide.
Row 3 LS DC: sl1, brp1, *sl1yo, p1, [sl1yo, brp1] twice; rep from * to last 3 sts, sl1yo, brp1, sl1. Turn.

Row 5 LS LC: k1, sl1yo, brk1, sl1yo, *brLsl dec, sl1yo, brkyobrk, sl1yo; rep from * to last st, k1. Do *not* turn, slide.
Row 5 LS DC: sl1, brp1, sl1yo, brp1, *sl1yo, brp1, sl1yo, p1, sl1yo brp1; rep from * to last st, sl1. Turn.

After working last set of DS rows, rep from Row 1 LS LC. ∎

Marching Squares

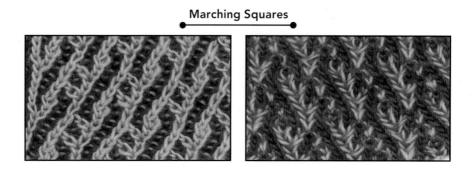

Marching Squares Chart

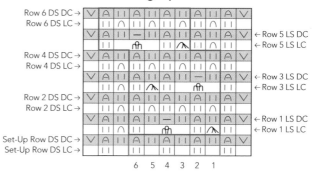

Linear Keyholes

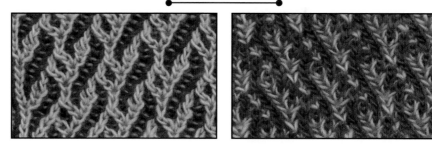

Linear Keyholes Chart

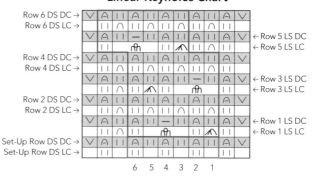

Wavy Buds

Wavy Buds Brioche Stitch
Using Two-Color Italian Cast-On, begin and end with LC knit st. Cast on a multiple of 6 sts + 3. For the sample shown, I cast on 27 sts.

Set-Up Row DS LC: p1, *sl1yo, p1; rep from * to end. Do *not* turn, slide.
Set-Up Row DS DC: sl1, *brk1, sl1yo; rep from * to last 2 sts, brk1, sl1. Turn.

Row 1 LS LC: k1, sl1yo, *brkyobrk, sl1yo, brLsl dec, sl1yo; rep from * to last st, k1. Do *not* turn, slide.
Row 1 LS DC: sl1, brp1, *sl1yo, p1, [sl1yo, brp1] twice; rep from * to last st, sl1. Turn.

Row 2 DS LC and all DS LC rows: p1, *sl1yo, brp1; rep from * to last 2 sts, sl1yo, p1. Do *not* turn, slide.
Row 2 DS DC and all DS DC rows: sl1, *brk1, sl1yo; rep from * to last 2 sts, brk1, sl1. Turn.

Row 3 LS LC: as Row 1 LS LC.
Row 3 LS DC: as Row 1 LS DC.

Row 5 LS LC: k1, sl1yo, *brk1, sl1yo; rep from * to last st, k1. Do *not* turn, slide.
Row 5 LS DC: sl1, brp1, *sl1yo, brp1; rep from * to last st, sl1. Turn.

Row 7 LS LC: k1, sl1yo, *brRsl dec, sl1yo, brkyobrk, sl1yo; rep from * to last st, k1. Do *not* turn, slide.

Row 7 LS DC: sl1, brp1, *sl1yo, brp1, sl1yo, p1, sl1yo, brp1; rep from * to last st, sl1. Turn.

Row 9 LS LC: as Row 7 LS LC.
Row 9 LS DC: as Row 7 LS DC.

Row 11 LS LC: as Row 5 LS LC.
Row 11 LS DC: as Row 5 LS DC.

After working last set of DS rows, rep from Row 1 LS LC. ∎

Wavy Buds Chart

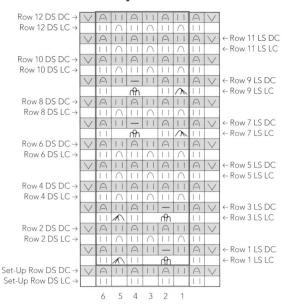

Crossing Paths

This pattern was created by working increases in Rows 1 and 7, then working their complementary decreases in Rows 5 and 11.

Crossing Paths Brioche Stitch
Using Two-Color Italian Cast-On, begin and end with LC knit st. Cast on a multiple of 4 sts (at least 8) + 3. For the sample shown, I cast on 27 sts.

Set-Up Row DS LC: p1, *sl1yo, p1; rep from * to end. Do *not* turn, slide.
Set-Up Row DS DC: sl1, *brk1, sl1yo; rep from * to last 2 sts, brk1, sl1. Turn.

Row 1 LS LC: k1, sl1yo, *brkyobrk, sl1yo, brk1, sl1yo; rep from * to last st, k1. Do *not* turn, slide.
Row 1 LS DC: sl1, brp1, *sl1yo, p1, [sl1yo, brp1] twice; rep from * to last st, sl1. Turn.

Row 2 DS LC and all DS LC rows: p1, *sl1yo, brp1; rep from * to last 2 sts, sl1yo, p1. Do *not* turn, slide.
Row 2 DS DC and all DS DC rows: sl1, *brk1, sl1yo; rep from * to last 2 sts, brk1, sl1. Turn.

Row 3 LS LC: k1, sl1yo, *brk1, sl1yo; rep from * to last st, k1. Do *not* turn, slide.
Row 3 LS DC: sl1, brp1, *sl1yo, brp1; rep from * to last st, sl1. Turn.

Row 5 LS LC: k1, sl1yo, *brk1, sl1yo, brLsl dec, sl1yo; rep from * to last st, k1. Do *not* turn, slide.
Row 5 LS DC: as Row 3 LS DC.

Row 7 LS LC: k1, sl1yo, * brk1, sl1yo, brkyobrk, sl1yo; rep from * to last 5 sts, [brk1, sl1yo] twice, k1. Do *not* turn, slide.

Row 7 LS DC: sl1, brp1, *sl1yo, brp1, sl1yo, p1, sl1yo, brp1; rep from * to last 5 sts, [sl1yo, brp1] twice, sl1. Turn.

Row 9 LS LC: as Row 3 LS LC.
Row 9 LS DC: as Row 3 LS DC.

Row 11 LS LC: k1, sl1yo, brk1, sl1yo, *brk1, sl1yo, brLsl dec, sl1yo; rep from * to last 3 sts, brk1, sl1yo, k1. Do *not* turn, slide.
Row 11 LS DC: as Row 3 LS DC.

After working last set of DS rows, rep from Row 1 LS LC. ∎

Crossing Paths Chart

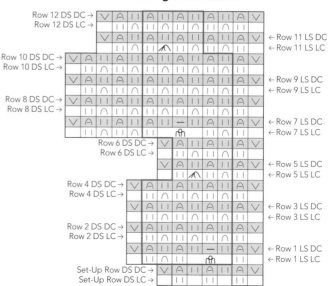

Stag

For this sweet little pattern, the increases and decreases have been grouped together. Note that the edge decreases are 2-stitch, while those on the inside are 4-stitch decreases.

Stag Brioche Stitch

Using Two-Color Italian Cast-On, begin and end with LC knit st. Cast on a multiple of 8 sts + 13. For the sample shown, I cast on 29 sts.

Set-Up Row DS LC: p1, *sl1yo, p1; rep from * to end. Do *not* turn, slide.
Set-Up Row DS DC: sl1, *brk1, sl1yo; rep from * to last 2 sts, brk1, sl1. Turn.

Row 1 LS LC: k1, sl1yo, brRsl dec, sl1yo, *br4st inc, sl1yo, br4st dec, sl1yo; rep from * to last 7 sts, br4st inc, sl1yo, brLsl dec, sl1yo, k1. Do *not* turn, slide.
Row 1 LS DC: sl1, brp1, sl1yo, brp1, *[sl1yo, p1] twice, [sl1yo, brp1] twice; rep from * to last st, sl1. Turn.

Row 2 DS LC and all DS LC rows: p1, *sl1yo, brp1; rep from * to last 2 sts, sl1yo, p1. Do *not* turn, slide.
Row 2 DS DC and all DS DC rows: sl1, *brk1, sl1yo; rep from * to last 2 sts, brk1, sl1. Turn.

Row 3 LS LC: k1, sl1yo, *brk1, sl1yo; rep from * to last st, k1. Do *not* turn, slide.
Row 3 LS DC: sl1, brp1, *sl1yo, brp1; rep from * to last st, sl1. Turn.

After working last set of DS rows, rep from Row 1 LS LC. ∎

Stag Chart

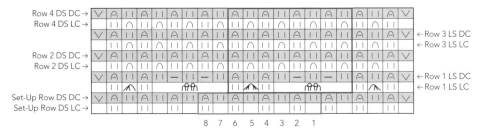

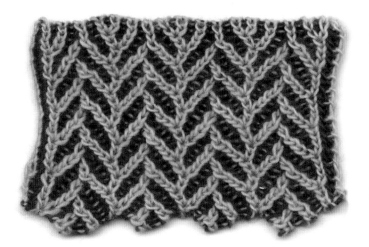

Herringbone

Herringbone Brioche Stitch
Using Two-Color Italian Cast-On, begin and end with LC knit st. Cast on a multiple of 8 sts + 13. For the sample shown, I cast on 37 sts.

Set-Up Row DS LC: p1, *sl1yo, p1; rep from * to end. Do *not* turn, slide.
Set-Up Row DS DC: sl1, *brk1, sl1yo; rep from * to last 2 sts, brk1, sl1. Turn.

Row 1 LS LC: k1, sl1yo, [brk1, sl1yo] twice, *brRsl dec, sl1yo, brkyobrk, sl1yo, brk1, sl1yo; rep from * to last 7 sts, brRsl dec, sl1yo, brkyobrk, sl1yo, k1. Do *not* turn, slide.

Row 1 LS DC: sl1, brp1, [sl1yo, brp1] twice *sl1yo, brp1, sl1yo, p1, [sl1yo, brp1] twice; rep from * to last 7 sts, sl1yo, brp1, sl1yo, p1, sl1yo, brp1, sl1. Turn.

Row 2 DS LC and all DS LC rows: p1, *sl1yo, brp1; rep from * to last 2 sts, sl1yo, p1. Do *not* turn, slide.
Row 2 DS DC and all DS DC rows: sl1, *brk1, sl1yo; rep from * to last 2 sts, brk1, sl1. Turn.

Row 3 LS LC: k1, sl1yo, brkyobrk, sl1yo, *brLsl dec, sl1yo, brk1, sl1yo, brkyobrk, sl1yo; rep from * to last 9 sts, brLsl dec, sl1yo, [brk1, sl1yo] twice, k1. Do *not* turn, slide.

Row 3 LS DC: sl1, brp1, sl1yo, p1, sl1yo, brp1, *[sl1yo, brp1] twice, sl1yo, p1, sl1yo, brp1; rep from * to last 7 sts, [sl1yo, brp1] 3 times, sl1. Turn.

After working last set of DS rows, rep from Row 1 LS LC. ∎

Herringbone Chart

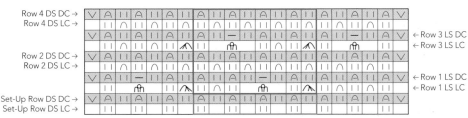

Straight-Edge Ribs

Scalloped-Edge Ribs

Straight-Edge Ribs

Scalloped-Edge Ribs

Scalloped-Edge Ribs and Straight-Edge Ribs

Scalloped-Edge Ribs Brioche Stitch
Using Two-Color Italian Cast-On, begin and end with LC knit st.
Cast on a multiple of 18 sts + 3. For the sample shown, I cast on 39 sts.

Set-Up Row DS LC: p1, *sl1yo, p1; rep from * to end. Do *not* turn, slide.
Set-Up Row DS DC: sl1, *brk1, sl1yo; rep from * to last 2 sts, brk1, sl1. Turn.

Row 1 LS LC: k1, sl1yo, *brRsl dec, sl1yo, [brk1, sl1yo] twice, br4st inc, sl1yo, [brk1, sl1yo] twice, brLsl dec, sl1yo; rep from * to last st, k1.
Do *not* turn, slide.
Row 1 LS DC: sl1, brp1, *[sl1yo, brp1] 3 times, [sl1yo, p1] twice, [sl1yo, brp1] 4 times; rep from * to last st, sl1. Turn.

Row 2 DS LC and all DS LC rows: p1, *sl1yo, brp1; rep from * to last 2 sts, sl1yo, p1. Do *not* turn, slide.
Row 2 DS DC and all DS DC rows: sl1, *brk1, sl1yo; rep from * to last 2 sts, brk1, sl1. Turn.

Row 3 LS LC: k1, sl1yo, *brk1, sl1yo; rep from * to last st, k1. Do *not* turn, slide.
Row 3 LS DC: sl1, brp1, *sl1yo, brp1; rep from * to last st, sl1. Turn.

After working last set of DS rows, rep from Row 1 LS LC. ■

This pattern is exactly like Scalloped-Edge Ribs Brioche Stitch, except the decreases slant in the opposite direction. This creates a straight column, rather than fluted, at the edges of the motif.

Straight-Edge Ribs Brioche Stitch
Using Two-Color Italian Cast-On, begin and end with LC knit st. Cast on a multiple of 18 sts + 3. For the sample shown, I cast on 39 sts.

Set-Up Row DS LC: p1, *sl1yo, p1; rep from * to end. Do *not* turn, slide.
Set-Up Row DS DC: sl1, *brk1, sl1yo; rep from * to last 2 sts, brk1, sl1. Turn.

Row 1 LS LC: k1, sl1yo, *brLsl dec, sl1yo, [brk1, sl1yo] twice, br4st inc, sl1yo, [brk1, sl1yo] twice, brRsl dec, sl1yo; rep from * to last st, k1. Do *not* turn, slide.
Row 1 LS DC: sl1, brp1, *[sl1yo, brp1] 3 times, [sl1yo, p1] twice, [sl1yo, brp1] 4 times; rep from * to last st, sl1. Turn.

Row 2 DS LC and all DS LC rows: p1, *sl1yo, brp1; rep from * to last 2 sts, sl1yo, p1. Do *not* turn, slide.
Row 2 DS DC and all DS DC rows: sl1, *brk1, sl1yo; rep from * to last 2 sts, brk1, sl1. Turn.

Row 3 LS LC: k1, sl1yo, *brk1, sl1yo; rep from * to last st, k1. Do *not* turn, slide.
Row 3 LS DC: sl1, brp1, *sl1yo, brp1; rep from * to last st, sl1. Turn.

After working last set of DS rows, rep from Row 1 LS LC. ■

Scalloped-Edge Ribs

Scalloped-Edge Ribs Chart

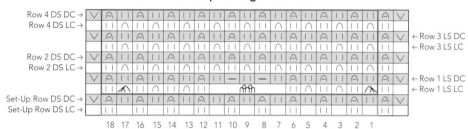

Straight-Edge Ribs

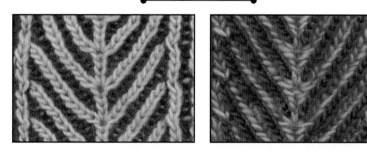

Straight-Edge Ribs Chart

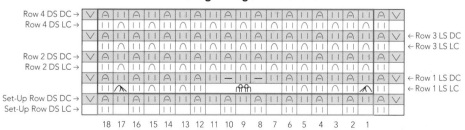

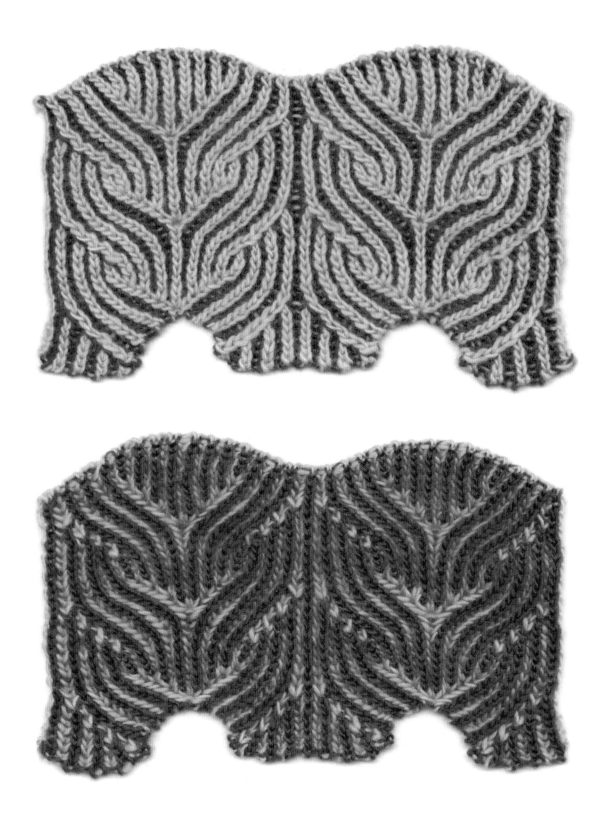

Staghorn

Staghorn is similar to Wide Flat Cables (page 115). However, for this stitch pattern, the cables were mirrored and meshed together.

Staghorn Brioche Stitch
Using Two-Color Italian Cast-On, begin and end with LC knit st. Cast on a multiple of 30 sts + 3. For the sample shown, I cast on 63 sts.

Set-Up Row DS LC: p1, *sl1yo, p1; rep from * to end. Do *not* turn, slide.
Set-Up Row DS DC: sl1, *brk1, sl1yo; rep from * to last 2 sts, brk1, sl1. Turn.

Row 1 LS LC: k1, sl1yo, *[brk1, sl1yo] 3 times, brRsl dec, sl1yo, [brk1, sl1yo] twice, br4st inc, sl1yo, [brk1, sl1yo] twice, brLsl dec, sl1yo, [brk1, sl1yo] 3 times; rep from * to last st, k1. Do *not* turn, slide.
Row 1 LS DC: sl1, brp1, *[sl1yo, brp1] 6 times, [sl1yo, p1] twice, [sl1yo, brp1] 7 times; rep from * to last st, sl1. Turn.

Row 2 DS LC and all DS LC rows: p1, *sl1yo, brp1; rep from * to last 2 sts, sl1yo, p1. Do *not* turn, slide.
Row 2 DS DC and all DS DC rows: sl1, *brk1, sl1yo; rep from * to last 2 sts, brk1, sl1. Turn.

Row 3 LS LC: k1, sl1yo, *[brk1, sl1yo] twice, brRsl dec, sl1yo, [brk1, sl1yo] twice, brkyobrk, sl1yo, brk1, sl1yo, brkyobrk, sl1yo, [brk1, sl1yo] twice, brLsl dec, sl1yo, [brk1, sl1yo] twice; rep from * to last st, k1. Do *not* turn, slide.
Row 3 LS DC: sl1, brp1, *[sl1yo, brp1] 5 times, sl1yo, p1, [sl1yo, brp1] twice, sl1yo, p1, [sl1yo, brp1] 6 times; rep from * to last st, sl1. Turn.

Row 5 LS LC: k1, sl1yo, *brk1, sl1yo, brRsl dec, sl1yo, [brk1, sl1yo] twice, brkyobrk, sl1yo, [brk1, sl1yo] 3 times, brkyobrk, sl1yo, [brk1, sl1yo] twice, brLsl dec, sl1yo, brk1, sl1yo; rep from * to last st, k1. Do *not* turn, slide.
Row 5 LS DC: sl1, brp1, *[sl1yo, brp1] 4 times, sl1yo, p1, [sl1yo, brp1] 4 times, sl1yo, p1, [sl1yo, brp1] 5 times; rep from * to last st, sl1. Turn.

Row 7 LS LC: k1, sl1yo, *brRsl dec, sl1yo, [brk1, sl1yo] twice, brkyobrk, sl1yo, [brk1, sl1yo] 5 times, brkyobrk, sl1yo, [brk1,sl1yo] twice, brLsl dec, sl1yo; rep from * to last st, k1. Do *not* turn, slide.
Row 7 LS DC: sl1, brp1, *[sl1yo, brp1] 3 times, sl1yo, p1, [sl1yo, brp1] 6 times, sl1yo, p1, [sl1yo, brp1] 4 times; rep from * to last st, sl1. Turn.

Row 9 LS LC: k1, sl1yo, *brk1, sl1yo; rep from * to last st, k1. Do *not* turn, slide.
Row 9 LS DC: sl1, brp1, *sl1yo, brp1; rep from * to last st, sl1. Turn.

After working last set of DS rows, rep from Row 1 LS LC. ∎

Staghorn Chart

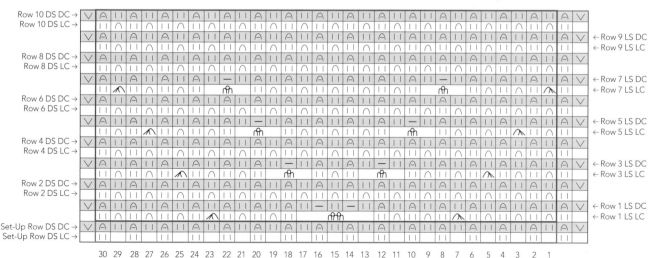

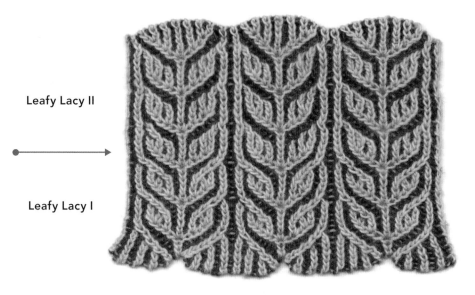

Leafy Lacy II

→

Leafy Lacy I

Leafy Lacy I and Leafy Lacy II

This pretty little sample shows how using a different decrease can create a subtly different stitch pattern. (See page 146 for Leafy Lacy III.)

Leafy Lacy I Brioche Stitch

Using Two-Color Italian Cast-On, begin and end with LC knit st. Cast on a multiple of 18 sts + 3. For the sample shown, I cast on 57 sts.

Set-Up Row DS LC: p1, *sl1yo, p1; rep from * to end. Do *not* turn, slide.
Set-Up Row DS DC: sl1, *brk1, sl1yo; rep from * to last 2 sts, brk1, sl1. Turn.

Row 1 LS LC: k1, sl1yo, *[brk1, sl1yo] twice, brRsl dec, sl1yo, br4st inc, sl1yo, brLsl dec, sl1yo, [brk1, sl1yo] twice; rep from * to last st, k1. Do *not* turn, slide.
Row 1 LS DC: sl1, brp1, *[sl1yo, brp1] 3 times, [sl1yo, p1] twice, [sl1yo, brp1] 4 times; rep from * to last st, sl1. Turn.

Row 2 DS LC and all DS LC rows: p1, *sl1yo, brp1; rep from * to last 2 sts, sl1yo, p1. Do *not* turn, slide.
Row 2 DS DC and all DS DC rows: sl1, *brk1, sl1yo; rep from * to last 2 sts, brk1, sl1. Turn.

Row 3 LS LC: k1, sl1yo, *brk1, sl1yo, brRsl dec, sl1yo, brkyobrk, sl1yo, brk1, sl1yo, brkyobrk, sl1yo, brLsl dec, sl1yo, brk1, sl1yo; rep from * to last st, k1. Do *not* turn, slide.
Row 3 LS DC: sl1, brp1, *[sl1yo, brp1] twice, sl1yo, p1, [sl1yo, brp1] twice, sl1yo, p1, [sl1yo, brp1] 3 times; rep from * to last st, sl1. Turn.

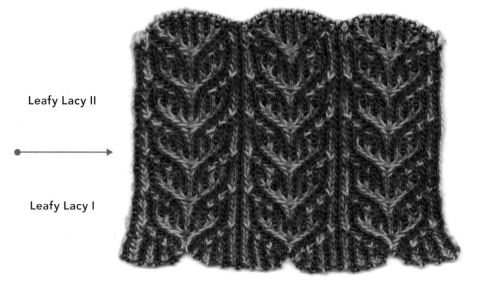

Leafy Lacy II

→

Leafy Lacy I

Row 5 LS LC: k1, sl1yo, *brRsl dec, sl1yo, brkyobrk, sl1yo, [brk1, sl1yo] 3 times, brkyobrk, sl1yo, brLsl dec, sl1yo; rep from * to last st, k1. Do *not* turn, slide.

Row 5 LS DC: sl1, brp1, *sl1yo, brp1, sl1yo, p1, [sl1yo, brp1] 4 times, sl1yo, p1, [sl1yo, brp1] twice; rep from * to last st, sl1. Turn.

After working last set of DS rows, rep from Row 1 LS LC. ∎

Leafy Lacy I Chart

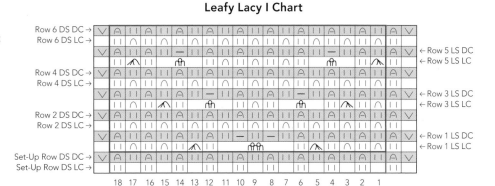

This is exactly like Leafy Lacy I, except the direction of the decreases has been changed.

Leafy Lacy II Brioche Stitch

Using Two-Color Italian Cast-On, begin and end with LC knit st. Cast on a multiple of 18 sts + 3. For the sample shown, I cast on 57 sts.

Set-Up Row DS LC: p1, *sl1yo, p1; rep from * to end. Do *not* turn, slide.
Set-Up Row DS DC: sl1, *brk1, sl1yo; rep from * to last 2 sts, brk1, sl1. Turn.

Row 1 LS LC: k1, sl1yo, *[brk1, sl1yo] twice, brLsl dec, sl1yo, br4st inc, sl1yo, brRsl dec, sl1yo, [brk1, sl1yo] twice; rep from * to last st, k1. Do *not* turn, slide.
Row 1 LS DC: sl1, brp1, *[sl1yo, brp1] 3 times, [sl1yo, p1] twice, [sl1yo, brp1] 4 times; rep from * to last st, sl1. Turn.

Leafy Lacy II Chart

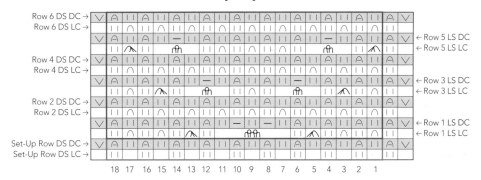

Row 2 DS LC and all DS LC rows: p1, *sl1yo, brp1; rep from * to last 2 sts, sl1yo, p1. Do *not* turn, slide.
Row 2 DS DC and all DS DC rows: sl1, *brk1, sl1yo; rep from * to last 2 sts, brk1, sl1. Turn.

Row 3 LS LC: k1, sl1yo, *brk1, sl1yo, brLsl dec, sl1yo, brkyobrk, sl1yo, brk1, sl1yo, brkyobrk, sl1yo, brRsl dec, sl1yo, brk1, sl1yo; rep from * to last st, k1. Do *not* turn, slide.
Row 3 LS DC: sl1, brp1, *[sl1yo, brp1] twice, sl1yo, p1, [sl1yo, brp1] twice, sl1yo, p1, [sl1yo, brp1] 3 times; rep from * to last st, sl1. Turn.

Row 5 LS LC: k1, sl1yo, *brLsl dec, sl1yo, brkyobrk, sl1yo, [brk1, sl1yo] 3 times, brkyobrk, sl1yo, brRsl dec, sl1yo; rep from * to last st, k1. Do *not* turn, slide.
Row 5 LS DC: sl1, brp1, *sl1yo, brp1, sl1yo, p1, [sl1yo, brp1] 4 times, sl1yo, p1, [sl1yo, brp1] twice; rep from * to last st, sl1. Turn.

After working last set of DS rows, rep from Row 1 LS LC. ∎

Divided Herringbone

Divided Herringbone Brioche Stitch
Using Two-Color Italian Cast-On, begin and end with LC knit st. Cast on a multiple of 10 sts + 3. For the sample shown, I cast on 33 sts.

Set-Up Row DS LC: p1, *sl1yo, p1; rep from * to end. Do *not* turn, slide.
Set-Up Row DS DC: sl1, *brk1, sl1yo; rep from * to last 2 sts, brk1, sl1. Turn.

Row 1 LS LC: k1, sl1yo, *[brk1, sl1yo] twice, brRsl dec, sl1yo, brkyobrk, sl1yo; rep from * to last st, k1. Do *not* turn, slide.
Row 1 LS DC: sl1, brp1, *[sl1yo, brp1] 3 times, sl1yo, p1, sl1yo, brp1; rep from * to last st, sl1. Turn.

Row 2 DS LC and all DS LC rows: p1, *sl1yo, brp1; rep from * to last 2 sts, sl1yo, p1. Do *not* turn, slide.
Row 2 DS DC and all DS DC rows: sl1, *brk1, sl1yo; rep from * to last 2 sts, brk1, sl1. Turn.

Row 3 LS LC: k1, sl1yo, *brkyobrk, sl1yo, brLsl dec, sl1yo, [brk1, sl1yo] twice; rep from * to last st, k1. Do *not* turn, slide.
Row 3 LS DC: sl1, brp1, *sl1yo, p1, [sl1yo, brp1] 4 times; rep from * to last st, sl1. Turn.

After working last set of DS rows, rep from Row 1 LS LC. ■

Divided Herringbone Chart

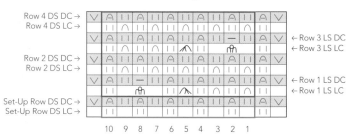

Row 4 DS DC →
Row 4 DS LC →
← Row 3 LS DC
← Row 3 LS LC
Row 2 DS DC →
Row 2 DS LC →
← Row 1 LS DC
← Row 1 LS LC
Set-Up Row DS DC →
Set-Up Row DS LC →

10 9 8 7 6 5 4 3 2 1

Smiling Fox

Smiling Fox Brioche Stitch

Using Two-Color Italian Cast-On, begin and end with LC knit st. Cast on a multiple of 18 sts + 3. For the sample shown, I cast on 57 sts.

Set-Up Row DS LC: p1, *sl1yo, p1; rep from * to end. Do *not* turn, slide.
Set-Up Row DS DC: sl1, *brk1, sl1yo; rep from * to last 2 sts, brk1, sl1. Turn.

Row 1 LS LC: k1, sl1yo, *[brk1, sl1yo] twice, brRsl dec, sl1yo, br4st inc, sl1yo, brLsl dec, sl1yo, [brk1, sl1yo] twice; rep from * to last st, k1. Do *not* turn, slide.
Row 1 LS DC: sl1, brp1, *[sl1yo, brp1] 3 times, [sl1yo, p1] twice, [sl1yo, brp1] 4 times; rep from * to last st, sl1. Turn.

Row 2 DS LC and all DS LC rows: p1, *sl1yo, brp1; rep from * to last 2 sts, sl1yo, p1. Do *not* turn, slide.
Row 2 DS DC and all DS DC rows: sl1, *brk1, sl1yo; rep from * to last 2 sts, brk1, sl1. Turn.

Row 3 LS LC: k1, sl1yo, *brk1, sl1yo, brRsl dec, sl1yo, brkyobrk, sl1yo, brk1, sl1yo, brkyobrk, sl1yo, brLsl dec, sl1yo, brk1, sl1yo; rep from * to last st, k1. Do *not* turn, slide.
Row 3 LS DC: sl1, brp1, *[sl1yo, brp1] twice, sl1yo, p1, [sl1yo, brp1] twice, sl1yo, p1, [sl1yo, brp1] 3 times; rep from * to last st, sl1. Turn.

Row 5 LS LC: k1, sl1yo, *brRsl dec, sl1yo, brkyobrk, sl1yo, [brk1, sl1yo] 3 times, brkyobrk, sl1yo, brLsl dec, sl1yo; rep from * to last st, k1. Do *not* turn, slide.
Row 5 LS DC: sl1, brp1, *sl1yo, brp1, sl1yo, p1, [sl1yo, brp1] 4 times, sl1yo, p1, [sl1yo, brp1] twice; rep from * to last st, sl1. Turn.

Row 7 LS LC: as Row 3 LS LC.
Row 7 LS DC: as Row 3 LS DC.

After working last set of DS rows, rep from Row 1 LS LC. ■

Smiling Fox Chart

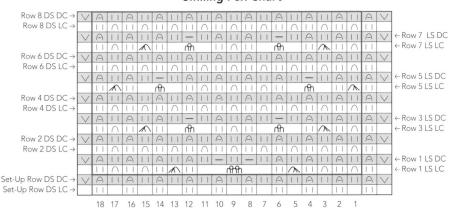

Budding Columns

This highly undulated bottom edge occurs in Budding Columns because 4 increases and 4 decreases are worked sequentially in Row 1 LS LC. This forces the fabric to drastically distort.

Budding Columns Brioche Stitch
Using Two-Color Italian Cast-On, begin and end with LC knit st. Cast on a multiple of 24 sts + 3. For the sample shown, I cast on 51 sts.

Set-Up Row DS LC: p1, *sl1yo, p1; rep from * to end. Do *not* turn, slide.
Set-Up Row DS DC: sl1, *brk1, sl1yo; rep from * to last 2 sts, brk1, sl1. Turn.

Row 1 LS LC: k1, sl1yo, *[brRsl dec, sl1yo] twice, [brkyobrk, sl1yo] 4 times, [brLsl dec, sl1yo] twice; rep from * to last st, k1. Do *not* turn, slide.
Row 1 LS DC: sl1, brp1, *[sl1yo, brp1] twice, [sl1yo, p1, sl1yo, brp1] 4 times, [sl1yo, brp1] twice; rep from * to last st, sl1. Turn.

Row 2 DS LC and all DS LC rows: p1, *sl1yo, brp1; rep from * to last 2 sts, sl1yo, p1. Do *not* turn, slide.
Row 2 DS DC and all DS DC rows: sl1, *brk1, sl1yo; rep from * to last 2 sts, brk1, sl1. Turn.

Row 3 LS LC: k1, sl1yo, *brk1, sl1yo; rep from * to last st, k1. Do *not* turn, slide.
Row 3 LS DC: sl1, brp1, *sl1yo, brp1; rep from * to last st, sl1. Turn.

After working last set of DS rows, rep from Row 1 LS LC. ∎

Budding Columns Chart

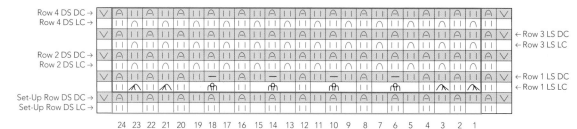

Aliens

As with Budding Columns, Aliens also increases and decreases 8 stitches in Row 1 LS LC. However, the new stitches all stem from one stitch.

Aliens Brioche Stitch
Using Two-Color Italian Cast-On, begin and end with LC knit st. Cast on a multiple of 18 sts + 3. For the sample shown, I cast on 39 sts.

Set-Up Row DS LC: p1, *sl1yo, p1; rep from * to end. Do *not* turn, slide.
Set-Up Row DS DC: sl1, *brk1, sl1yo; rep from * to last 2 sts, brk1, sl1. Turn.

Row 1 LS LC: k1, sl1yo, *[brRsl dec, sl1yo] twice, br8st inc, sl1yo, [brLsl dec, sl1yo] twice; rep from * to last st, k1. Do *not* turn, slide.
Row 1 LS DC: sl1, brp1, *[sl1yo, brp1] twice, [sl1yo, p1] 4 times, [sl1yo, brp1] 3 times; rep from * to last st, sl1. Turn.

Row 2 DS LC and all DS LC rows: p1, *sl1yo, brp1; rep from * to last 2 sts, sl1yo, p1. Do *not* turn, slide.
Row 2 DS DC and all DS DC rows: sl1, *brk1, sl1yo; rep from * to last 2 sts, brk1, sl1. Turn.

Row 3 LS LC: k1, sl1yo, *brk1, sl1yo; rep from * to last st, k1. Do *not* turn, slide.
Row 3 LS DC: sl1, brp1, *sl1yo, brp1; rep from * to last st, sl1. Turn.

After working last set of DS rows, rep from Row 1 LS LC. ∎

Aliens Chart

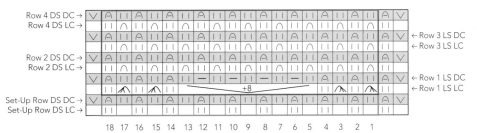

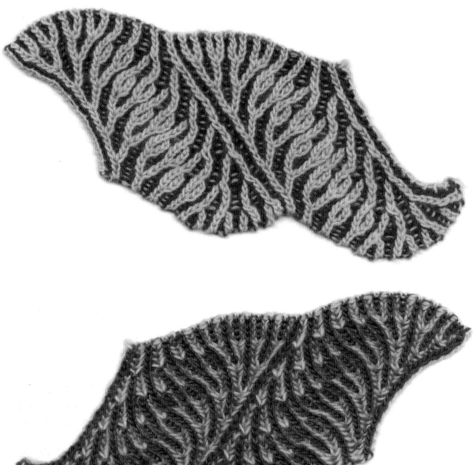

Feathery and Fanny

Feathery and Fanny Brioche Stitch
Using Two-Color Italian Cast-On, begin and end with LC knit st. Cast on a multiple of 24 sts + 3. For the sample shown, I cast on 51 sts.

Set-Up Row DS LC: p1, *sl1yo, p1; rep from * to end. Do *not* turn, slide.
Set-Up Row DS DC: sl1, *brk1, sl1yo; rep from * to last 2 sts, brk1, sl1. Turn.

Row 1 LS LC: k1, sl1yo, *[brLsl dec, sl1yo] twice, [brRsl dec, sl1yo] twice, [brkyobrk, sl1yo] 4 times; rep from * to last st, k1. Do *not* turn, slide.
Row 1 LS DC: sl1, brp1, *[sl1yo, brp1] 4 times, [sl1yo, p1, sl1yo, brp1] 4 times; rep from * to last st, sl1. Turn.

Row 2 DS LC and all DS LC rows: p1, *sl1yo, brp1; rep from * to last 2 sts, sl1yo, p1. Do *not* turn, slide.
Row 2 DS DC and all DS DC rows: sl1, *brk1, sl1yo; rep from * to last 2 sts, brk1, sl1. Turn.

Row 3 LS LC: k1, sl1yo, *brk1, sl1yo; rep from * to last st, k1. Do *not* turn, slide.
Row 3 LS DC: sl1, brp1, *sl1yo, brp1; rep from * to last st, sl1. Turn.

After working last set of DS rows, rep from Row 1 LS LC. ■

Feathery and Fanny Chart

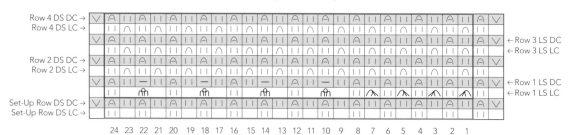

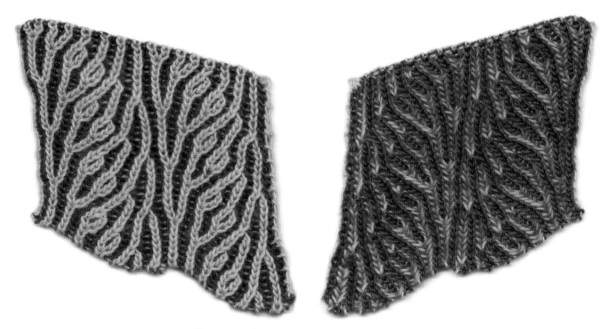

All Paths Lead to One

The construction of this stitch is similar to Wide Flat Cables Brioche Stitch (page 115), except that I switched the position of the increases and decreases.

All Paths Lead to One Brioche Stitch
Using Two-Color Italian Cast-On, begin and end with LC knit st. Cast on a multiple of 16 sts + 3. For the sample shown, I cast on 35 sts.

Set-Up Row DS LC: p1, *sl1yo, p1; rep from * to end. Do *not* turn, slide.

Set-Up Row DS DC: sl1, *brk1, sl1yo; rep from * to last 2 sts, brk1, sl1. Turn.

Row 1 LS LC: k1, sl1yo, *brRsl dec, sl1yo, [brk1, sl1yo] twice, brkyobrk, sl1yo, [brk1, sl1yo] 3 times; rep from * to last st, k1. Do *not* turn, slide.
Row 1 LS DC: sl1, brp1, *[sl1yo, brp1] 3 times, sl1yo, p1, [sl1yo, brp1] 4 times; rep from * to last st, sl1. Turn.

Row 2 DS LC and all DS LC rows: p1, *sl1yo, brp1; rep from * to last 2 sts, sl1yo, p1. Do *not* turn, slide.

Row 2 DS DC and all DS DC rows: sl1, *brk1, sl1yo; rep from * to last 2 sts, brk1, sl1. Turn.

Row 3 LS LC: k1, sl1yo, *brk1, sl1yo, brRsl dec, sl1yo, [brk1, sl1yo] twice, brkyobrk, sl1yo, [brk1, sl1yo] twice; rep from * to last st, k1. Do *not* turn, slide.
Row 3 LS DC: sl1, brp1, *[sl1yo, brp1] 4 times, sl1yo, p1, [sl1yo, brp1] 3 times; rep from * to last st, sl1. Turn.

Row 5 LS LC: k1, sl1yo, *[brk1, sl1yo] twice, brRsl dec, sl1yo, [brk1, sl1yo] twice, brkyobrk, sl1yo, brk1, sl1yo; rep from * to last st, k1. Do *not* turn, slide.
Row 5 LS DC: sl1, brp1, *[sl1yo, brp1] 5 times, sl1yo, p1, [sl1yo, brp1] twice; rep from * to last st, sl1. Turn.

Row 7 LS LC: k1, sl1yo, *[brk1, sl1yo] 3 times, brRsl dec, sl1yo, [brk1, sl1yo] twice, brkyobrk, sl1yo; rep from * to last st, k1. Do *not* turn, slide.
Row 7 LS DC: sl1, brp1, *[sl1yo, brp1] 6 times, sl1yo, p1, sl1yo, brp1; rep from * to last st, sl1. Turn.

After working last set of DS rows, rep from Row 1 LS LC. ■

All Paths Lead to One Chart

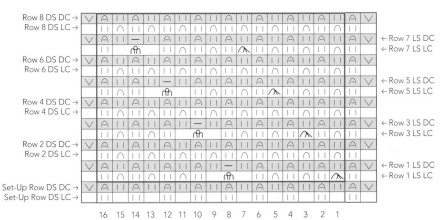

Speed Knitter

Miriam Tegels holds the Guinness title as the World's Fastest Knitter. She made a dress from this pattern, in lace-weight yarn, in record speed.

Speed Knitter Brioche Stitch
Using Two-Color Italian Cast-On, begin and end with LC knit st. Cast on a multiple of 22 sts + 3. For the sample shown, I cast on 47 sts.

Set-Up Row DS LC: p1, *sl1yo, p1; rep from * to end. Do *not* turn, slide.
Set-Up Row DS DC: sl1, *brk1, sl1yo; rep from * to last 2 sts, brk1, sl1. Turn.

Row 1 LS LC: k1, sl1yo, *[brk1, sl1yo] 5 times, br4st inc, sl1yo, [brk1, sl1yo] 5 times; rep from * to last st, k1. Do *not* turn, slide.
Row 1 LS DC: sl1, brp1, *[sl1yo, brp1] 5 times, [sl1yo, p1] twice, [sl1yo, brp1] 6 times; rep from * to last st, sl1. Turn.

Row 2 DS LC and all DS LC rows: p1, *sl1yo, brp1; rep from * to last 2 sts, sl1yo, p1. Do *not* turn, slide.
Row 2 DS DC and all DS DC rows: sl1, *brk1, sl1yo; rep from * to last 2 sts, brk1, sl1. Turn.

Row 3 LS LC: k1, sl1yo, *[brk1, sl1yo] 4 times, brRsl dec, sl1yo, brk1, sl1yo, brLsl dec, sl1yo, [brk1, sl1yo] 4 times; rep from * to last st, k1. Do *not* turn, slide.
Row 3 LS DC: sl1, brp1, *sl1yo, brp1; rep from * to last st, sl1. Turn.

Row 5 LS LC: as Row 1 LS LC.
Row 5 LS DC: as Row 1 LS DC.

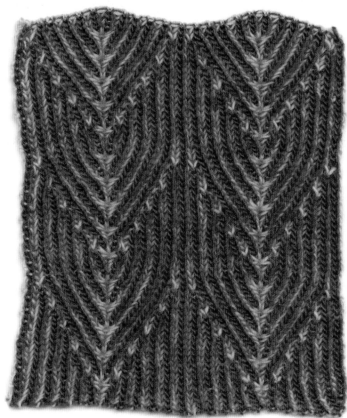

Speed Knitter Chart

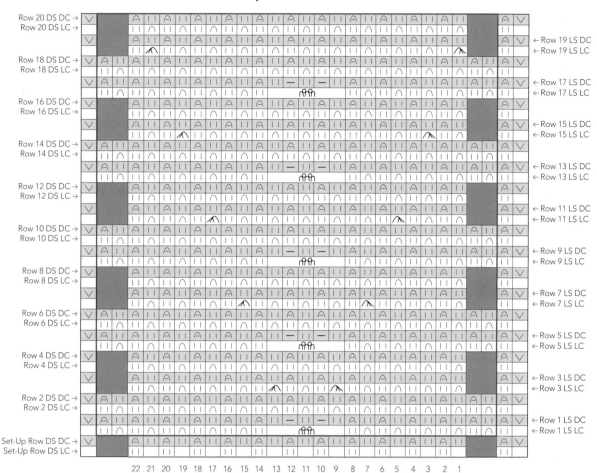

Row 20 DS DC →
Row 20 DS LC →
← Row 19 LS DC
← Row 19 LS LC
Row 18 DS DC →
Row 18 DS LC →
← Row 17 LS DC
← Row 17 LS LC
Row 16 DS DC →
Row 16 DS LC →
← Row 15 LS DC
← Row 15 LS LC
Row 14 DS DC →
Row 14 DS LC →
← Row 13 LS DC
← Row 13 LS LC
Row 12 DS DC →
Row 12 DS LC →
← Row 11 LS DC
← Row 11 LS LC
Row 10 DS DC →
Row 10 DS LC →
← Row 9 LS DC
← Row 9 LS LC
Row 8 DS DC →
Row 8 DS LC →
← Row 7 LS DC
← Row 7 LS LC
Row 6 DS DC →
Row 6 DS LC →
← Row 5 LS DC
← Row 5 LS LC
Row 4 DS DC →
Row 4 DS LC →
← Row 3 LS DC
← Row 3 LS LC
Row 2 DS DC →
Row 2 DS LC →
← Row 1 LS DC
← Row 1 LS LC
Set-Up Row DS DC →
Set-Up Row DS LC →

22 21 20 19 18 17 16 15 14 13 12 11 10 9 8 7 6 5 4 3 2 1

Row 7 LS LC: k1, sl1yo, *[brk1, sl1yo] 3 times, brRsl dec, sl1yo, [brk1, sl1yo] 3 times, brLsl dec, sl1yo, [brk1, sl1yo] 3 times; rep from * to last st, k1. Do *not* turn, slide.
Row 7 LS DC: as Row 3 LS DC.

Row 9 LS LC: as Row 1 LS LC.
Row 9 LS DC: as Row 1 LS DC.

Row 11 LS LC: k1, sl1yo, *[brk1, sl1yo] twice, brRsl dec, sl1yo, [brk1, sl1yo] 5 times, brLsl dec, sl1yo, [brk1, sl1yo] twice; rep from * to last st, k1. Do *not* turn, slide.
Row 11 LS DC: as Row 3 LS DC.

Row 13 LS LC: as Row 1 LS LC.
Row 13 LS DC: as Row 1 LS DC.

Row 15 LS LC: k1, sl1yo, *brk1, sl1yo, brRsl dec, sl1yo, [brk1, sl1yo] 7 times, brLsl dec, sl1yo, brk1, sl1yo; rep from * to last st, k1. Do *not* turn, slide.
Row 15 LS DC: as Row 3 LS DC.

Row 17 LS LC: as Row 1 LS LC.
Row 17 LS DC: as Row 1 LS DC.

Row 19 LS LC: k1, sl1yo, *brRsl dec, sl1yo, [brk1, sl1yo] 9 times, brLsl dec, sl1yo; rep from * to last st, k1. Do *not* turn, slide.

Row 19 LS DC: as Row 3 LS DC.

After working last set of DS rows, rep from Row 1 LS LC. ■

Optic Waves I

Optic Waves I Brioche Stitch

Using Two-Color Italian Cast-On, begin and end with LC knit st. Cast on a multiple of 16 sts + 3. For the sample shown, I cast on 51 sts.

Set-Up Row DS LC: p1, *sl1yo, p1; rep from * to end. Do *not* turn, slide.
Set-Up Row DS DC: sl1, *brk1, sl1yo; rep from * to last 2 sts, brk1, sl1. Turn.

Row 1 LS LC: k1, sl1yo, *[brk1, sl1yo] 4 times, brRsl dec, sl1yo, brk1, sl1yo, brkyobrk, sl1yo; rep from * to last st, k1. Do *not* turn, slide.
Row 1 LS DC: sl1, brp1, *[sl1yo, brp1] 6 times, sl1yo, p1, sl1yo, brp1; rep from * to last st, sl1. Turn.

Row 2 DS LC and all DS LC rows: p1, *sl1yo, brp1; rep from * to last 2 sts, sl1yo, p1. Do *not* turn, slide.
Row 2 DS DC and all DS DC rows: sl1, *brk1, sl1yo; rep from * to last 2 sts, brk1, sl1. Turn.

Row 3 LS LC: k1, sl1yo, *[brk1, sl1yo] 3 times, brRsl dec, sl1yo, brk1, sl1yo, brkyobrk, sl1yo, brk1, sl1yo; rep from * to last st, k1. Do *not* turn, slide.
Row 3 LS DC: sl1, brp1, *[sl1yo, brp1] 5 times, sl1yo, p1, [sl1yo, brp1] twice; rep from * to last st, sl1. Turn.

Row 5 LS LC: k1, sl1yo, *[brk1, sl1yo] twice, brRsl dec, sl1yo, brk1, sl1yo, brkyobrk, sl1yo, [brk1, sl1yo] twice; rep from * to last st, k1. Do *not* turn, slide.
Row 5 LS DC: sl1, brp1, *[sl1yo, brp1] 4 times, sl1yo, p1, [sl1yo, brp1] 3 times; rep from * to last st, sl1. Turn.

Row 7 LS LC: k1, sl1yo, *brk1, sl1yo, brRsl dec, sl1yo, brk1, sl1yo, brkyobrk, sl1yo, [brk1, sl1yo] 3 times; rep from * to last st, k1. Do *not* turn, slide.
Row 7 LS DC: sl1, brp1, *[sl1yo, brp1] 3 times, sl1yo, p1, [sl1yo, brp1] 4 times; rep from * to last st, sl1. Turn.

Row 9 LS LC: k1, sl1yo, *brRsl dec, sl1yo, brk1, sl1yo, brkyobrk, sl1yo, [brk1, sl1yo] 4 times; rep from * to last st, k1. Do *not* turn, slide.
Row 9 LS DC: sl1, brp1, *[sl1yo, brp1] twice, sl1yo, p1, [sl1yo, brp1] 5 times; rep from * to last st, sl1. Turn.

Row 11 LS LC: k1, sl1yo, *brk1, sl1yo; rep from * to last st, k1. Do *not* turn, slide.
Row 11 LS DC: sl1, brp1, *sl1yo, brp1; rep from * to last st, sl1. Turn.

Row 13 LS LC: k1, sl1yo, *brkyobrk, sl1yo, brk1, sl1yo, brLsl dec, sl1yo, [brk1, sl1yo] 4 times; rep from * to last st, k1. Do *not* turn, slide.
Row 13 LS DC: sl1, brp1, *sl1yo, p1, [sl1yo, brp1] 7 times; rep from * to last st, sl1. Turn.

Row 15 LS LC: k1, sl1yo, *brk1, sl1yo, brkyobrk, sl1yo, brk1, sl1yo, brLsl dec, sl1yo, [brk1, sl1yo] 3 times; rep from * to last st, k1. Do *not* turn, slide.
Row 15 LS DC: sl1, brp1, *sl1yo, brp1, sl1yo, p1, [sl1yo, brp1] 6 times; rep from * to last st, sl1. Turn.

Row 17 LS LC: k1, sl1yo, *[brk1, sl1yo] twice, brkyobrk, sl1yo, brk1, sl1yo, brLsl dec, sl1yo, [brk1, sl1yo] twice; rep from * to last st, k1. Do *not* turn, slide.
Row 17 LS DC: sl1, brp1, *[sl1yo, brp1] twice, sl1yo, p1, [sl1yo, brp1] 5 times; rep from * to last st, sl1. Turn.

Optic Waves I Chart

Row 24 DS DC →
Row 24 DS LC →
Row 22 DS DC →
Row 22 DS LC →
Row 20 DS DC →
Row 20 DS LC →
Row 18 DS DC →
Row 18 DS LC →
Row 16 DS DC →
Row 16 DS LC →
Row 14 DS DC →
Row 14 DS LC →
Row 12 DS DC →
Row 12 DS LC →
Row 10 DS DC →
Row 10 DS LC →
Row 8 DS DC →
Row 8 DS LC →
Row 6 DS DC →
Row 6 DS LC →
Row 4 DS DC →
Row 4 DS LC →
Row 2 DS DC →
Row 2 DS LC →
Set-Up Row DS DC →
Set-Up Row DS LC →

← Row 23 LS DC
← Row 23 LS LC
← Row 21 LS DC
← Row 21 LS LC
← Row 19 LS DC
← Row 19 LS LC
← Row 17 LS DC
← Row 17 LS LC
← Row 15 LS DC
← Row 15 LS LC
← Row 13 LS DC
← Row 13 LS LC
← Row 11 LS DC
← Row 11 LS LC
← Row 9 LS DC
← Row 9 LS LC
← Row 7 LS DC
← Row 7 LS LC
← Row 5 LS DC
← Row 5 LS LC
← Row 3 LS DC
← Row 3 LS LC
← Row 1 LS DC
← Row 1 LS LC

16 15 14 13 12 11 10 9 8 7 6 5 4 3 2 1

Row 19 LS LC: k1, sl1yo, *[brk1, sl1yo] 3 times, brkyobrk, sl1yo, brk1, sl1yo, brLsl dec, sl1yo, brk1, sl1yo; rep from * to last st, k1. Do *not* turn, slide.
Row 19 LS DC: sl1, brp1, *[sl1yo, brp1] 3 times, sl1yo, p1, [sl1yo, brp1] 4 times; rep from * to last st, sl1. Turn.

Row 21 LS LC: k1, sl1yo, *[brk1, sl1yo] 4 times, brkyobrk, sl1yo, brk1, sl1yo, brLsl dec, sl1yo; rep from * to last st, k1. Do *not* turn, slide.

Row 21 LS DC: sl1, brp1, *[sl1yo, brp1] 4 times, sl1yo, p1, [sl1yo, brp1] 3 times; rep from * to last st, sl1. Turn.

Row 23 LS LC: as Row 11 LS LC.
Row 23 LS DC: as Row 11 LS DC.

After working last set of DS rows, rep from Row 1 LS LC. ∎

Optic Waves II

This stitch pattern is derived from Optic Waves I, using fewer columns between the increases and decreases and offsetting the zigzags.

Optic Waves II Brioche Stitch
Using Two-Color Italian Cast-On, begin and end with LC knit st. Cast on a multiple of 26 sts + 3. For the sample shown, I cast on 55 sts.

Set-Up Row DS LC: p1, *sl1yo, p1; rep from * to end. Do *not* turn, slide.
Set-Up Row DS DC: sl1, *brk1, sl1yo; rep from * to last 2 sts, brk1, sl1. Turn.

Row 1 LS LC: k1, sl1yo, *[brk1, sl1yo] 9 times, brkyobrk, sl1yo, brLsl dec, sl1yo, brk1, sl1yo; rep from * to last st, k1. Do *not* turn, slide.
Row 1 LS DC: sl1, brp1, *[sl1yo, brp1] 9 times, sl1yo, p1, [sl1yo, brp1] 3 times; rep from * to last st, sl1. Turn.

Row 2 DS LC and all DS LC rows: p1, *sl1yo, brp1; rep from * to last 2 sts, sl1yo, p1. Do *not* turn, slide.
Row 2 DS DC and all DS DC rows: sl1, *brk1, sl1yo; rep from * to last 2 sts, brk1, sl1. Turn.

Row 3 LS LC: k1, sl1yo, *[brk1, sl1yo] 4 times, brRsl dec, sl1yo, brkyobrk, sl1yo, [brk1, sl1yo] 3 times, brkyobrk, sl1yo, brLsl dec, sl1yo; rep from * to last st, k1. Do *not* turn, slide.
Row 3 LS DC: sl1, brp1, *[sl1yo, brp1] 5 times, sl1yo, p1, [sl1yo, brp1] 4 times, sl1yo, p1, [sl1yo, brp1] twice; rep from * to last st, sl1. Turn.

Optic Waves II Chart

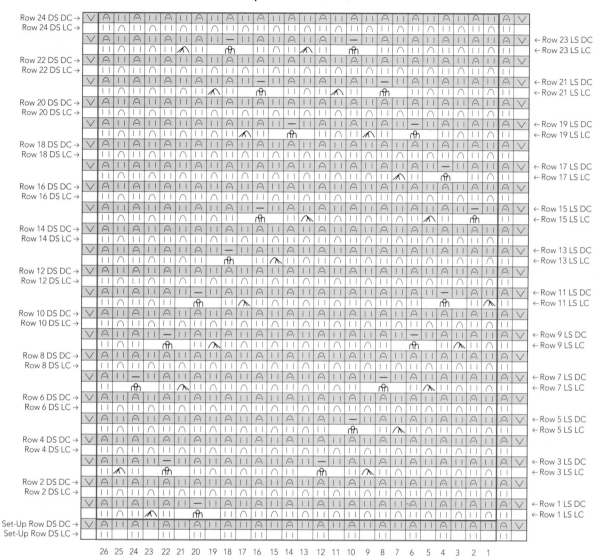

Row 24 DS DC →
Row 24 DS LC →
Row 22 DS DC →
Row 22 DS LC →
Row 20 DS DC →
Row 20 DS LC →
Row 18 DS DC →
Row 18 DS LC →
Row 16 DS DC →
Row 16 DS LC →
Row 14 DS DC →
Row 14 DS LC →
Row 12 DS DC →
Row 12 DS LC →
Row 10 DS DC →
Row 10 DS LC →
Row 8 DS DC →
Row 8 DS LC →
Row 6 DS DC →
Row 6 DS LC →
Row 4 DS DC →
Row 4 DS LC →
Row 2 DS DC →
Row 2 DS LC →
Set-Up Row DS DC →
Set-Up Row DS LC →

← Row 23 LS DC
← Row 23 LS LC
← Row 21 LS DC
← Row 21 LS LC
← Row 19 LS DC
← Row 19 LS LC
← Row 17 LS DC
← Row 17 LS LC
← Row 15 LS DC
← Row 15 LS LC
← Row 13 LS DC
← Row 13 LS LC
← Row 11 LS DC
← Row 11 LS LC
← Row 9 LS DC
← Row 9 LS LC
← Row 7 LS DC
← Row 7 LS LC
← Row 5 LS DC
← Row 5 LS LC
← Row 3 LS DC
← Row 3 LS LC
← Row 1 LS DC
← Row 1 LS LC

26 25 24 23 22 21 20 19 18 17 16 15 14 13 12 11 10 9 8 7 6 5 4 3 2 1

Row 5 LS LC: k1, sl1yo, *[brk1, sl1yo] 3 times, brRsl dec, sl1yo, brkyobrk, sl1yo, [brk1, sl1yo] 7 times; rep from * to last st, k1. Do *not* turn, slide.
Row 5 LS DC: sl1, brp1, *[sl1yo, brp1] 4 times, sl1yo, p1, [sl1yo, brp1] 8 times; rep from * to last st, sl1. Turn.

Row 7 LS LC: k1, sl1yo, *[brk1, sl1yo] twice, brRsl dec, sl1yo, brkyobrk, sl1yo, [brk1, sl1yo] 5 times, brRsl dec, sl1yo, brkyobrk, sl1yo; rep from * to last st, k1. Do *not* turn, slide.
Row 7 LS DC: sl1, brp1, *[sl1yo, brp1] 3 times, sl1yo, p1, [sl1yo, brp1] 7 times, sl1yo, p1, sl1yo, brp1; rep from * to last st, sl1. Turn.

Row 9 LS LC: k1, sl1yo, *brk1, sl1yo, brRsl dec, sl1yo, brkyobrk, sl1yo, [brk1, sl1yo] 5 times, brRsl dec, sl1yo, brkyobrk, sl1yo, brk1, sl1yo; rep from * to last st, k1. Do *not* turn, slide.
Row 9 LS DC: sl1, brp1, *[sl1yo, brp1] twice, sl1yo, p1, [sl1yo, brp1] 7 times, sl1yo, p1, [sl1yo, brp1] twice; rep from * to last st, sl1. Turn.

Row 11 LS LC: k1, sl1yo, *brRsl dec, sl1yo, brkyobrk, sl1yo, [brk1, sl1yo] 5 times, brRsl dec, sl1yo, brkyobrk, sl1yo, [brk1, sl1yo] twice; rep from * to last st, k1. Do *not* turn, slide.
Row 11 LS DC: sl1, brp1, *sl1yo, brp1, sl1yo, p1, [sl1yo, brp1] 7 times, sl1yo, p1, [sl1yo, brp1] 3 times; rep from * to last st, sl1. Turn.

Row 13 LS LC: k1, sl1yo, *[brk1, sl1yo] 7 times, brRsl dec, sl1yo, brkyobrk, sl1yo, [brk1, sl1yo] 3 times; rep from * to last st, k1. Do *not* turn, slide.
Row 13 LS DC: sl1, brp1, *[sl1yo, brp1] 8 times, sl1yo, p1, [sl1yo, brp1] 4 times; rep from * to last st, sl1. Turn.

Row 15 LS LC: k1, sl1yo, *brkyobrk, sl1yo, brLsl dec, sl1yo, [brk1, sl1yo] 3 times, brRsl dec, sl1yo, brkyobrk, sl1yo, [brk1, sl1yo] 4 times; rep from * to last st, k1. Do *not* turn, slide.
Row 15 LS DC: sl1, brp1, *sl1yo, p1, [sl1yo, brp1] 6 times, sl1yo, p1, [sl1yo, brp1] 5 times; rep from * to last st, sl1. Turn.

Row 17 LS LC: k1, sl1yo, *brk1, sl1yo, brkyobrk, sl1yo, brLsl dec, sl1yo, [brk1, sl1yo] 9 times; rep from * to last st, k1. Do *not* turn, slide.
Row 17 LS DC: sl1, brp1, *sl1yo, brp1, sl1yo, p1, [sl1yo, brp1] 11 times; rep from * to last st, sl1. Turn.

Row 19 LS LC: k1, sl1yo, *[brk1, sl1yo] twice, brkyobrk, sl1yo, brLsl dec, sl1yo, brk1, sl1yo, brkyobrk, sl1yo, brLsl dec, sl1yo, [brk1, sl1yo] 4 times; rep from * to last st, k1. Do *not* turn, slide.
Row 19 LS DC: sl1, brp1, *[sl1yo, brp1] twice, sl1yo, p1, [sl1yo, brp1] 3 times, sl1yo, p1, [sl1yo, brp1] 6 times; rep from * to last st, sl1. Turn.

Row 21 LS LC: k1, sl1yo, *[brk1, sl1yo] 3 times, brkyobrk, sl1yo, brLsl dec, sl1yo, brk1, sl1yo, brkyobrk, sl1yo, brLsl dec, sl1yo, [brk1, sl1yo] 3 times; rep from * to last st, k1. Do *not* turn, slide.
Row 21 LS DC: sl1, brp1, *[sl1yo, brp1] 3 times, sl1yo, p1, [sl1yo, brp1] 3 times, sl1yo, p1, [sl1yo, brp1] 5 times; rep from * to last st, sl1. Turn.

Row 23 LS LC: k1, sl1yo, *[brk1, sl1yo] 4 times, brkyobrk, sl1yo, brLsl dec, sl1yo, brk1, sl1yo, brkyobrk, sl1yo, brLsl dec, sl1yo, [brk1, sl1yo] twice; rep from * to last st, k1. Do *not* turn, slide.
Row 23 LS DC: sl1, brp1, *[sl1yo, brp1] 4 times, sl1yo, p1, [sl1yo, brp1] 3 times, sl1yo, p1, [sl1yo, brp1] 4 times; rep from * to last st, sl1. Turn.

After working last set of DS rows, rep from Row 1 LS LC. ∎

Ocean Waves

Ocean Waves Brioche Stitch

Using Two-Color Italian Cast-On, begin and end with LC knit st. Cast on a multiple of 14 sts + 3. For the sample shown, I cast on 45 sts.

Set-Up Row DS LC: p1, *sl1yo, p1; rep from * to end. Do *not* turn, slide.
Set-Up Row DS DC: sl1, *brk1, sl1yo; rep from * to last 2 sts, brk1, sl1. Turn.

Row 1 LS LC: k1, sl1yo, *[brk1, sl1yo] 4 times, brRsl dec, sl1yo, brkyobrk, sl1yo; rep from * to last st, k1. Do *not* turn, slide.
Row 1 LS DC: sl1, brp1, *[sl1yo, brp1] 5 times, sl1yo, p1, sl1yo, brp1; rep from * to last st, sl1. Turn.

Row 2 DS LC and all DS LC rows: p1, *sl1yo, brp1; rep from * to last 2 sts, sl1yo, p1. Do *not* turn, slide.
Row 2 DS DC and all DS DC rows: sl1, *brk1, sl1yo; rep from * to last 2 sts, brk1, sl1. Turn.

Row 3 LS LC: k1, sl1yo, *[brk1, sl1yo] 3 times, brRsl dec, sl1yo, brk1, sl1yo, brkyobrk, sl1yo; rep from * to last st, k1. Do *not* turn, slide.
Row 3 LS DC: as Row 1 LS DC.

Row 5 LS LC: k1, sl1yo, *[brk1, sl1yo] twice, brRsl dec, sl1yo, [brk1, sl1yo] twice, brkyobrk, sl1yo; rep from * to last st, k1. Do *not* turn, slide.
Row 5 LS DC: as Row 1 LS DC.

Row 7 LS LC: k1, sl1yo, *brk1, sl1yo, brRsl dec, sl1yo, [brk1, sl1yo] 3 times, brkyobrk, sl1yo; rep from * to last st, k1. Do *not* turn, slide.
Row 7 LS DC: as Row 1 LS DC.

Row 9 LS LC: k1, sl1yo, *brRsl dec, sl1yo, [brk1, sl1yo] 4 times, brkyobrk, sl1yo; rep from * to last st, k1. Do *not* turn, slide.
Row 9 LS DC: as Row 1 LS DC.

After working last set of DS rows, rep from Row 1 LS LC. ■

Ocean Waves Chart

Undulating Hourglass

Undulating Hourglass Brioche Stitch
Using Two-Color Italian Cast-On, begin and end with LC knit st. Cast on a multiple of 28 sts + 3. For the sample shown, I cast on 59 sts.

Set-Up Row DS LC: p1, *sl1yo, p1; rep from * to end. Do *not* turn, slide.
Set-Up Row DS DC: sl1, *brk1, sl1yo; rep from * to last 2 sts, brk1, sl1. Turn.

Row 1 LS LC: k1, sl1yo, *brkyobrk, sl1yo, brLsl dec, sl1yo, [brk1, sl1yo] 8 times, brRsl dec, sl1yo, brkyobrk, sl1yo; rep from * to last st, k1. Do *not* turn, slide.
Row 1 LS DC: sl1, brp1, *sl1yo, p1, [sl1yo, brp1] 11 times, sl1yo, p1, sl1yo, brp1; rep from * to last st, sl1. Turn.

Row 2 DS LC and all DS LC rows: p1, *sl1yo, brp1; rep from * to last 2 sts, sl1yo, p1. Do *not* turn, slide.
Row 2 DS DC and all DS DC rows: sl1, *brk1, sl1yo; rep from * to last 2 sts, brk1, sl1. Turn.

Row 3 LS LC: k1, sl1yo, *brk1, sl1yo, brkyobrk, sl1yo, brLsl dec, sl1yo, [brk1, sl1yo] 6 times, brRsl dec, sl1yo, brkyobrk, sl1yo, brk1, sl1yo; rep from * to last st, k1. Do *not* turn, slide.
Row 3 LS DC: sl1, brp1, *sl1yo, brp1, sl1yo, p1, [sl1yo, brp1] 9 times, sl1yo, p1, [sl1yo, brp1] twice; rep from * to last st, sl1. Turn.

Row 5 LS LC: k1, sl1yo, *[brk1, sl1yo] twice, brkyobrk, sl1yo, brLsl dec, sl1yo, [brk1, sl1yo] 4 times, brRsl dec, sl1yo, brkyobrk, sl1yo, [brk1, sl1yo] twice; rep from * to last st, k1. Do *not* turn, slide.
Row 5 LS DC: sl1, brp1, *[sl1yo, brp1] twice, sl1yo, p1, [sl1yo, brp1] 7 times, sl1yo, p1, [sl1yo, brp1] 3 times; rep from * to last st, sl1. Turn.

Row 7 LS LC: k1, sl1yo, *[brk1, sl1yo] 3 times, brkyobrk, sl1yo, brLsl dec, sl1yo, [brk1, sl1yo] twice, brRsl dec, sl1yo, brkyobrk, sl1yo, [brk1, sl1yo] 3 times; rep from * to last st, k1. Do *not* turn, slide.
Row 7 LS DC: sl1, brp1, *[sl1yo, brp1] 3 times, sl1yo, p1, [sl1yo, brp1] 5 times, sl1yo, p1, [sl1yo, brp1] 4 times; rep from * to last st, sl1. Turn.

Row 9 LS LC: k1, sl1yo, *[brk1, sl1yo] 4 times, brkyobrk, sl1yo, brLsl dec, sl1yo, brRsl dec, sl1yo, brkyobrk, sl1yo, [brk1, sl1yo] 4 times; rep from * to last st, k1. Do *not* turn, slide.
Row 9 LS DC: sl1, brp1, *[sl1yo, brp1] 4 times, sl1yo, p1, [sl1yo, brp1] 3 times, sl1yo, p1, [sl1yo, brp1] 5 times; rep from * to last st, sl1. Turn.

Row 11 LS LC: k1, sl1yo, *brk1, sl1yo; rep from * to last st, k1. Do *not* turn, slide.
Row 11 LS DC: sl1, brp1, *sl1yo, brp1; rep from * to last st, sl1. Turn.

Row 13 LS LC: k1, sl1yo, *[brk1, sl1yo] 4 times, brRsl dec, sl1yo, [brkyobrk, sl1yo] twice, brLsl dec, sl1yo, [brk1, sl1yo] 4 times; rep from * to last st, k1. Do *not* turn, slide.
Row 13 LS DC: sl1, brp1, *[sl1yo, brp1] 5 times, sl1yo, p1, sl1yo, brp1, sl1yo, p1, [sl1yo, brp1] 6 times; rep from * to last st, sl1. Turn.

Row 15 LS LC: k1, sl1yo, *[brk1, sl1yo] 3 times, brRsl dec, sl1yo, brkyobrk, sl1yo, [brk1, sl1yo] twice, brkyobrk, sl1yo, brLsl dec, sl1yo, [brk1, sl1yo] 3 times; rep from * to last st, k1. Do *not* turn, slide.
Row 15 LS DC: sl1, brp1, *[sl1yo, brp1] 4 times, sl1yo, p1, [sl1yo, brp1] 3 times, sl1yo, p1, [sl1yo, brp1] 5 times; rep from * to last st, sl1. Turn.

Row 17 LS LC: k1, sl1yo, *[brk1, sl1yo] twice, brRsl dec, sl1yo, brkyobrk, sl1yo, [brk1, sl1yo] 4 times, brkyobrk, sl1yo, brLsl dec, sl1yo, [brk1, sl1yo] twice; rep from * to last st, k1. Do *not* turn, slide.
Row 17 LS DC: sl1, brp1, *[sl1yo, brp1] 3 times, sl1yo, p1, [sl1yo, brp1] 5 times, sl1yo, p1, [sl1yo, brp1] 4 times; rep from * to last st, sl1. Turn.

Row 19 LS LC: k1, sl1yo, *brk1, sl1yo, brRsl dec, sl1yo, brkyobrk, sl1yo, [brk1, sl1yo] 6 times, brkyobrk, sl1yo, brLsl dec, sl1yo, brk1, sl1yo; rep from * to last st, k1. Do *not* turn, slide.
Row 19 LS DC: sl1, brp1, *[sl1yo, brp1] twice, sl1yo, p1, [sl1yo, brp1] 7 times, sl1yo, p1, [sl1yo, brp1] 3 times; rep from * to last st, sl1. Turn.

Row 21 LS LC: k1, sl1yo, *brRsl dec, sl1yo, brkyobrk, sl1yo, [brk1, sl1yo] 8 times, brkyobrk, sl1yo, brLsl dec, sl1yo; rep from * to last st, k1. Do *not* turn, slide.
Row 21 LS DC: sl1, brp1, *sl1yo, brp1, sl1yo, p1, [sl1yo, brp1] 9 times, sl1yo, p1, [sl1yo, brp1] twice; rep from * to last st, sl1. Turn.

Row 23 LS LC: as Row 11 LS LC.
Row 23 LS DC: as Row 11 LS DC.

After working last set of DS rows, rep from Row 1 LS LC. ■

Undulating Hourglass Chart

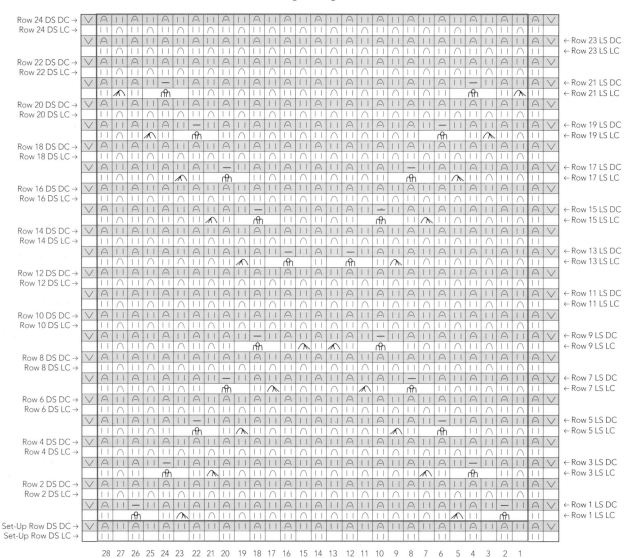

Row 24 DS DC →
Row 24 DS LC →
← Row 23 LS DC
← Row 23 LS LC
Row 22 DS DC →
Row 22 DS LC →
← Row 21 LS DC
← Row 21 LS LC
Row 20 DS DC →
Row 20 DS LC →
← Row 19 LS DC
← Row 19 LS LC
Row 18 DS DC →
Row 18 DS LC →
← Row 17 LS DC
← Row 17 LS LC
Row 16 DS DC →
Row 16 DS LC →
← Row 15 LS DC
← Row 15 LS LC
Row 14 DS DC →
Row 14 DS LC →
← Row 13 LS DC
← Row 13 LS LC
Row 12 DS DC →
Row 12 DS LC →
← Row 11 LS DC
← Row 11 LS LC
Row 10 DS DC →
Row 10 DS LC →
← Row 9 LS DC
← Row 9 LS LC
Row 8 DS DC →
Row 8 DS LC →
← Row 7 LS DC
← Row 7 LS LC
Row 6 DS DC →
Row 6 DS LC →
← Row 5 LS DC
← Row 5 LS LC
Row 4 DS DC →
Row 4 DS LC →
← Row 3 LS DC
← Row 3 LS LC
Row 2 DS DC →
Row 2 DS LC →
← Row 1 LS DC
← Row 1 LS LC
Set-Up Row DS DC →
Set-Up Row DS LC →

28 27 26 25 24 23 22 21 20 19 18 17 16 15 14 13 12 11 10 9 8 7 6 5 4 3 2 1

Crossing Arms

For this sample I worked Beginning Rows 1 and 2, then Rows 1–12 twice, then Finishing Rows 1–12.

Crossing Arms Brioche Stitch

Using Two-Color Italian Cast-On, begin and end with LC knit st. Cast on a multiple of 26 sts + 3. For the sample shown, I cast on 55 sts.

Set-Up Row DS LC: p1, *sl1yo, p1; rep from * to end. Do *not* turn, slide.
Set-Up Row DS DC: sl1, *brk1, sl1yo; rep from * to last 2 sts, brk1, sl1. Turn.

Beginning Row 1 LS LC: k1, sl1yo, *[brk1, sl1yo] 3 times, brRsl dec, sl1yo, brkyobrk, sl1yo, [brk1, sl1yo] 7 times; rep from * to last st, k1. Do *not* turn, slide.
Beginning Row 1 LS DC: sl1, brp1, *[sl1yo, brp1] 4 times, sl1yo, p1, [sl1yo, brp1] 8 times; rep from * to last st, sl1. Turn.

Beginning Row 2 DS LC and all DS LC rows: p1, *sl1yo, brp1; rep from * to last 2 sts, sl1yo, p1. Do *not* turn, slide.
Beginning Row 2 DS DC and all DS DC rows: sl1, *brk1, sl1yo; rep from * to last 2 sts, brk1, sl1. Turn.

Row 1 LS LC: k1, sl1yo, *[brk1, sl1yo] twice, brRsl dec, sl1yo, brkyobrk, sl1yo, brkyobrk, sl1yo, brLsl dec, sl1yo, [brk1, sl1yo] 5 times; rep from * to last st, k1. Do *not* turn, slide.
Row 1 LS DC: sl1, brp1, *[sl1yo, brp1] 3 times, sl1yo, p1, sl1yo, brp1, sl1yo, p1, [sl1yo, brp1] 7 times; rep from * to last st, sl1. Turn.

Row 3 LS LC: k1, sl1yo, *brk1, sl1yo, brRsl dec, sl1yo, brkyobrk, sl1yo, [brk1, sl1yo] twice, brkyobrk, sl1yo, brLsl dec, sl1yo, [brk1, sl1yo] 4 times; rep from * to last st, k1. Do *not* turn, slide.
Row 3 LS DC: sl1, brp1, *[sl1yo, brp1] twice, sl1yo, p1, [sl1yo, brp1] 3 times, sl1yo, p1, [sl1yo, brp1] 6 times; rep from * to last st, sl1. Turn.

Row 5 LS LC: k1, sl1yo, *brRsl dec, sl1yo, brkyobrk, sl1yo, [brk1, sl1yo] 4 times, brkyobrk, sl1yo, brLsl dec, sl1yo, [brk1, sl1yo] 3 times; rep from * to last st, k1. Do *not* turn, slide.
Row 5 LS DC: sl1, brp1, *sl1yo, brp1, sl1yo, p1, [sl1yo, brp1] 5 times, sl1yo, p1, [sl1yo, brp1] 5 times; rep from * to last st, sl1. Turn.

Row 7 LS LC: k1, sl1yo, *[brk1, sl1yo] 5 times, brRsl dec, sl1yo, brkyobrk, sl1yo, brkyobrk, sl1yo, brLsl dec, sl1yo, [brk1, sl1yo] twice; rep from * to last st, k1. Do *not* turn, slide.
Row 7 LS DC: sl1, brp1, *[sl1yo, brp1] 6 times, sl1yo, p1, sl1yo, brp1, sl1yo, p1, [sl1yo, brp1] 4 times; rep from * to last st, sl1. Turn.

Row 9 LS LC: k1, sl1yo, *[brk1, sl1yo] 4 times, brRsl dec, sl1yo, brkyobrk, sl1yo, [brk1, sl1yo] twice, brkyobrk, sl1yo, brLsl dec, sl1yo, brk1, sl1yo; rep from * to last st, k1. Do *not* turn, slide.
Row 9 LS DC: sl1, brp1, *[sl1yo, brp1] 5 times, sl1yo, p1, [sl1yo, brp1] 3 times, sl1yo, p1, [sl1yo, brp1] 3 times; rep from * to last st, sl1. Turn.

Row 11 LS LC: k1, sl1yo, *[brk1, sl1yo] 3 times, brRsl dec, sl1yo, brkyobrk, sl1yo, [brk1, sl1yo] 4 times, brkyobrk, sl1yo, brLsl dec, sl1yo; rep from * to last st, k1. Do *not* turn, slide.
Row 11 LS DC: sl1, brp1, *[sl1yo, brp1] 4 times, sl1yo, p1, [sl1yo, brp1] 5 times, sl1yo, p1, [sl1yo, brp1] twice; rep from * to last st, sl1. Turn.

After working last set of DS rows, rep from Row 1 LS LC until ready to finish.

Crossing Arms Chart

Finishing Row 12 DS DC →
Finishing Row 12 DS LC →
Finishing Row 10 DS DC →
Finishing Row 10 DS LC →
Finishing Row 8 DS DC →
Finishing Row 8 DS LC →
Finishing Row 6 DS DC →
Finishing Row 6 DS LC →
Finishing Row 4 DS DC →
Finishing Row 4 DS LC →
Finishing Row 2 DS DC →
Finishing Row 2 DS LC →
Row 12 DS DC →
Row 12 DS LC →
Row 10 DS DC →
Row 10 DS LC →
Row 8 DS DC →
Row 8 DS LC →
Row 6 DS DC →
Row 6 DS LC →
Row 4 DS DC →
Row 4 DS LC →
Row 2 DS DC →
Row 2 DS LC →
Beginning Row 2 DS DC →
Beginning Row 2 DS LC →
Set-Up Row DS DC →
Set-Up Row DS LC →

← Finishing Row 11 LS DC
← Finishing Row 11 LS LC
← Finishing Row 9 LS DC
← Finishing Row 9 LS LC
← Finishing Row 7 LS DC
← Finishing Row 7 LS LC
← Finishing Row 5 LS DC
← Finishing Row 5 LS LC
← Finishing Row 3 LS DC
← Finishing Row 3 LS LC
← Finishing Row 1 LS DC
← Finishing Row 1 LS LC
← Row 11 LS DC
← Row 11 LS LC
← Row 9 LS DC
← Row 9 LS LC
← Row 7 LS DC
← Row 7 LS LC
← Row 5 LS DC
← Row 5 LS LC
← Row 3 LS DC
← Row 3 LS LC
← Row 1 LS DC
← Row 1 LS LC
← Beginning Row 1 LS DC
← Beginning Row 1 LS LC

26 25 24 23 22 21 20 19 18 17 16 15 14 13 12 11 10 9 8 7 6 5 4 3 2 1

Finishing Row 1 LS LC: as Row 1 LS LC.
Finishing Row 1 LS DC: as Row 1 LS DC.

Finishing Row 3 LS LC: as Row 3 LS LC.
Finishing Row 3 LS DC: as Row 3 LS DC.

Finishing Row 5 LS LC: as Row 5 LS LC.
Finishing Row 5 LS DC: as Row 5 LS DC
.

Finishing Row 7 LS LC: k1, sl1yo, *[brk1, sl1yo] 8 times, brkyobrk, sl1yo, brLsl dec, sl1yo, [brk1, sl1yo] twice; rep from * to last st, k1. Do *not* turn, slide.

Finishing Row 7 LS DC: sl1, brp1, *[sl1yo, brp1] 8 times, sl1yo, p1, [sl1yo, brp1] 4 times; rep from * to last st, sl1. Turn.

Finishing Row 9 LS LC: k1, sl1yo, *[brk1, sl1yo] 9 times, brkyobrk, sl1yo, brLsl dec, sl1yo, brk1, sl1yo; rep from * to last st, k1. Do *not* turn, slide.

Finishing Row 9 LS DC: sl1, brp1, *[sl1yo, brp1] 9 times, sl1yo, p1, [sl1yo, brp1] 3 times; rep from * to last st, sl1. Turn.

Finishing Row 11 LS LC: k1, sl1yo, *[brk1, sl1yo] 10 times, brkyobrk, sl1yo, brLsl dec, sl1yo; rep from * to last st, k1. Do *not* turn, slide.

Finishing Row 11 LS DC: sl1, brp1, *[sl1yo, brp1] 10 times, sl1yo, p1, [sl1yo, brp1] twice; rep from * to last st, sl1. Turn.

Bind off after working last set of DS rows. ■

Branching Paths

This stitch was created by mirroring the All Paths Lead to One Brioche Stitch (page 83), creating a wider pattern.

Branching Paths Brioche Stitch
Using Two-Color Italian Cast-On, begin and end with LC knit st. Cast on a multiple of 32 sts + 3. For the sample shown, I cast on 35 sts.

Set-Up Row DS LC: p1, *sl1yo, p1; rep from * to end. Do *not* turn, slide.
Set-Up Row DS DC: sl1, *brk1, sl1yo; rep from * to last 2 sts, brk1, sl1. Turn.

Row 1 LS LC: k1, sl1yo, *brLsl dec, sl1yo, [brk1, sl1yo] twice, brkyobrk, sl1yo, [brk1, sl1yo] 6 times, brkyobrk, sl1yo, [brk1, sl1yo] twice, brRsl dec, sl1yo; rep from * to last st, k1. Do *not* turn, slide.
Row 1 LS DC: sl1, brp1, *[sl1yo, brp1] 3 times, sl1yo, p1, [sl1yo, brp1] 7 times, sl1yo, p1, [sl1yo, brp1] 4 times; rep from * to last st, sl1. Turn.

Row 2 DS LC and all DS LC rows: p1, *sl1yo, brp1; rep from * to last 2 sts, sl1yo, p1. Do *not* turn, slide.
Row 2 DS DC and all DS DC rows: sl1, *brk1, sl1yo; rep from * to last 2 sts, brk1, sl1. Turn.

Row 3 LS LC: k1, sl1yo, *brk1, sl1yo, brLsl dec, sl1yo, [brk1, sl1yo] twice, brkyobrk, sl1yo, [brk1, sl1yo] 4 times, brkyobrk, sl1yo, [brk1, sl1yo] twice, brRsl dec, sl1yo, brk1, sl1yo; rep from * to last st, k1. Do *not* turn, slide.
Row 3 LS DC: sl1, brp1, *[sl1yo, brp1] 4 times, sl1yo, p1, [sl1yo, brp1] 5 times, sl1yo, p1, [sl1yo, brp1] 5 times; rep from * to last st, sl1. Turn.

Row 5 LS LC: k1, sl1yo, *[brk1, sl1yo] twice, brLsl dec, sl1yo, [brk1, sl1yo] twice, brkyobrk, sl1yo, [brk1, sl1yo] twice, brkyobrk, sl1yo, [brk1, sl1yo] twice, brRsl dec, sl1yo, [brk1, sl1yo] twice; rep from * to last st, k1. Do *not* turn, slide.
Row 5 LS DC: sl1, brp1, *[sl1yo, brp1] 5 times, sl1yo, p1, [sl1yo, brp1] 3 times, sl1yo, p1, [sl1yo, brp1] 6 times; rep from * to last st, sl1. Turn.

Row 7 LS LC: k1, sl1yo, *[brk1, sl1yo] 3 times, brLsl dec, sl1yo, [brk1, sl1yo] twice, brkyobrk, sl1yo, brkyobrk, sl1yo, [brk1, sl1yo] twice, brRsl dec, sl1yo, [brk1, sl1yo] 3 times; rep from * to last st, k1. Do *not* turn, slide.
Row 7 LS DC: sl1, brp1, *[sl1yo, brp1] 6 times, sl1yo, p1, sl1yo, brp1, sl1yo, p1, [sl1yo, brp1] 7 times; rep from * to last st, sl1. Turn.

After working last set of DS rows, rep from Row 1 LS LC. ■

Branching Paths Chart

Row 8 DS DC →	
Row 8 DS LC →	
	← Row 7 LS DC
	← Row 7 LS LC
Row 6 DS DC →	
Row 6 DS LC →	
	← Row 5 LS DC
	← Row 5 LS LC
Row 4 DS DC →	
Row 4 DS LC →	
	← Row 3 LS DC
	← Row 3 LS LC
Row 2 DS DC →	
Row 2 DS LC →	
	← Row 1 LS DC
	← Row 1 LS LC
Set-Up Row DS DC →	
Set-Up Row DS LC →	

32 31 30 29 28 27 26 25 24 23 22 21 20 19 18 17 16 15 14 13 12 11 10 9 8 7 6 5 4 3 2 1

Double Line Chevron

Double Line Chevron Brioche Stitch
Using Two-Color Italian Cast-On, begin and end with LC knit st. Cast on a multiple of 26 sts + 3. For the sample shown, I cast on 55 sts.

Set-Up Row DS LC: p1, *sl1yo, p1; rep from * to end. Do *not* turn, slide.
Set-Up Row DS DC: sl1, *brk1, sl1yo; rep from * to last 2 sts, brk1, sl1. Turn.

Beginning Row 1 LS LC: k1, sl1yo, *brk1, sl1yo; rep from * to last st, k1. Do *not* turn, slide.
Beginning Row 1 LS DC: sl1, brp1, *sl1yo, brp; rep from * to last st, sl1. Turn.

Beginning Row 2 DS LC: p1, *sl1yo, brp1; rep from * to last 2 sts, sl1yo, p1. Do *not* turn, slide.
Beginning Row 2 DS DC: sl1, *brk1, sl1yo; rep from * to last 2 sts, brk1, sl1. Turn.

Row 1 LS LC: k1, sl1yo, *[brk1, sl1yo] 4 times, brRsl dec, sl1yo, br4st inc, sl1yo, brLsl dec, sl1yo, [brk1, sl1yo] 4 times; rep from * to last st, k1. Do *not* turn, slide.
Row 1 LS DC: sl1, brp1, *[sl1yo, brp1] 5 times, [sl1yo, p1] twice, [sl1yo, brp1] 6 times; rep from * to last st, sl1. Turn.

Row 2 DS LC and all DS LC rows: p1, *sl1yo, brp1; rep from * to last 2 sts, sl1yo, p1. Do *not* turn, slide.
Row 2 DS DC and all DS DC rows: sl1, *brk1, sl1yo; rep from * to last 2 sts, brk1, sl1. Turn.

Double Line Chevron Chart

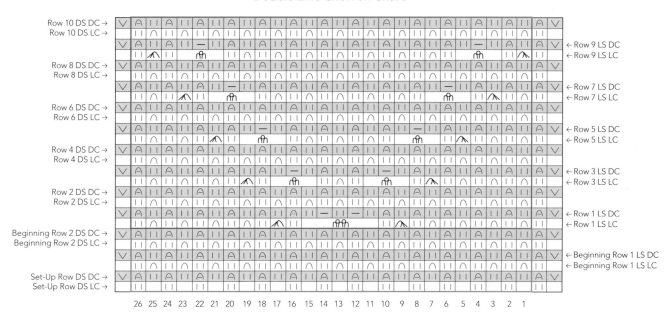

Row 10 DS DC →
Row 10 DS LC →

Row 8 DS DC →
Row 8 DS LC →

Row 6 DS DC →
Row 6 DS LC →

Row 4 DS DC →
Row 4 DS LC →

Row 2 DS DC →
Row 2 DS LC →

Beginning Row 2 DS DC →
Beginning Row 2 DS LC →

Set-Up Row DS DC →
Set-Up Row DS LC →

← Row 9 LS DC
← Row 9 LS LC

← Row 7 LS DC
← Row 7 LS LC

← Row 5 LS DC
← Row 5 LS LC

← Row 3 LS DC
← Row 3 LS LC

← Row 1 LS DC
← Row 1 LS LC

← Beginning Row 1 LS DC
← Beginning Row 1 LS LC

26 25 24 23 22 21 20 19 18 17 16 15 14 13 12 11 10 9 8 7 6 5 4 3 2 1

Row 3 LS LC: k1, sl1yo, *[brk1, sl1yo] 3 times, brRsl dec, sl1yo, brkyobrk, sl1yo, brk1, sl1yo, brkyobrk, sl1yo, brLsl dec, sl1yo, [brk1, sl1yo] 3 times; rep from * to last st, k1. Do *not* turn, slide.
Row 3 LS DC: sl1, brp1, *[sl1yo, brp1] 4 times, sl1yo, p1, [sl1yo, brp1] twice, sl1yo, p1, [sl1yo, brp1] 5 times; rep from * to last st, sl1. Turn.

Row 5 LS LC: k1, sl1yo, *[brk1, sl1yo] twice, brRsl dec, sl1yo, brkyobrk, sl1yo, [brk1, sl1yo] 3 times, brkyobrk, sl1yo, brLsl dec, sl1yo, [brk1, sl1yo] twice; rep from * to last st, k1. Do *not* turn, slide.
Row 5 LS DC: sl1, brp1, *[sl1yo, brp1] 3 times, sl1yo, p1, [sl1yo, brp1] 4 times, sl1yo, p1, [sl1yo, brp1] 4 times; rep from * to last st, sl1. Turn.

Row 7 LS LC: k1, sl1yo, *brk1, sl1yo, brRsl dec, sl1yo, brkyobrk, sl1yo, [brk1, sl1yo] 5 times, brkyobrk, sl1yo, brLsl dec, sl1yo, brk1, sl1yo; rep from * to last st, k1. Do *not* turn, slide.
Row 7 LS DC: sl1, brp1, *[sl1yo, brp1] twice, sl1yo, p1, [sl1yo, brp1] 6 times, sl1yo, p1, [sl1yo, brp1] 3 times; rep from * to last st, sl1. Turn.

Row 9 LS LC: k1, sl1yo, *brRsl dec, sl1yo, brkyobrk, sl1yo, [brk1, sl1yo] 7 times, brkyobrk, sl1yo, brLsl dec, sl1yo; rep from * to last st, k1. Do *not* turn, slide.
Row 9 LS DC: sl1, brp1, *sl1yo, brp1, sl1yo, p1, [sl1yo, brp1] 8 times, sl1yo, p1, [sl1yo, brp1] twice; rep from * to last st, sl1. Turn.

After working last set of DS rows, rep from Row 1 LS LC. ■

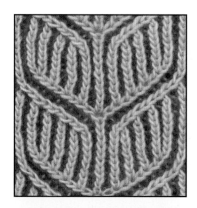

Rick Rack

Rick Rack Brioche Stitch
Using Two-Color Italian Cast-On, begin and end with LC knit st. Cast on a multiple of 12 sts + 3. For the sample shown, I cast on 39 sts.

Set-Up Row DS LC: p1, *sl1yo, p1; rep from * to end. Do *not* turn, slide.
Set-Up Row DS DC: sl1, *brk1, sl1yo; rep from * to last 2 sts, brk1, sl1. Turn.

Row 1 LS LC: k1, sl1yo, *brRsl dec, sl1yo, [brk1, sl1yo] 3 times, brkyobrk, sl1yo; rep from * to last st, k1. Do *not* turn, slide.
Row 1 LS DC: sl1, brp1, *[sl1yo, brp1] 4 times, sl1yo, p1, sl1yo, brp1; rep from * to last st, sl1. Turn.

Row 2 DS LC and all DS LC rows: p1, *sl1yo, brp1; rep from * to last 2 sts, sl1yo, p1. Do *not* turn, slide.
Row 2 DS DC and all DS DC rows: sl1, *brk1, sl1yo; rep from * to last 2 sts, brk1, sl1. Turn.

Rows 3, 5, 7 and 9 LS LC: as Row 1 LS LC.
Rows 3, 5, 7 and 9 LS DC: as Row 1 LC DC.

Row 11 LS LC: k1, sl1yo, *brk1, sl1yo; rep from * to last st, k1. Do *not* turn, slide.

Row 11 LS DC: sl1, brp1, *sl1yo, brp1; rep from * to last st, sl1. Turn.

Row 13 LS LC: k1, sl1yo, *brkyobrk, sl1yo, [brk1, sl1yo] 3 times, brLsl dec, sl1yo; rep from * to last st, k1. Do *not* turn, slide.

Row 13 LS DC: sl1, brp1, *sl1yo, p1, [sl1yo, brp1] 5 times; rep from * to last st, sl1. Turn.

Rows 15, 17, 19 and 21 LS LC: as Row 13 LS LC.
Rows 15, 17, 19 and 21 LS DC: as Row 13 LC DC.

Row 23 LS LC: as Row 11 LS LC.
Row 23 LS DC: as Row 11 LC DC.

After working last set of DS rows, rep from Row 1 LS LC. ■

Rick Rack Chart

Row 24 DS DC →
Row 24 DS LC →
← Row 23 LS DC
← Row 23 LS LC
Row 22 DS DC →
Row 22 DS LC →
← Row 21 LS DC
← Row 21 LS LC
Row 20 DS DC →
Row 20 DS LC →
← Row 19 LS DC
← Row 19 LS LC
Row 18 DS DC →
Row 18 DS LC →
← Row 17 LS DC
← Row 17 LS LC
Row 16 DS DC →
Row 16 DS LC →
← Row 15 LS DC
← Row 15 LS LC
Row 14 DS DC →
Row 14 DS LC →
← Row 13 LS DC
← Row 13 LS LC
Row 12 DS DC →
Row 12 DS LC →
← Row 11 LS DC
← Row 11 LS LC
Row 10 DS DC →
Row 10 DS LC →
← Row 9 LS DC
← Row 9 LS LC
Row 8 DS DC →
Row 8 DS LC →
← Row 7 LS DC
← Row 7 LS LC
Row 6 DS DC →
Row 6 DS LC →
← Row 5 LS DC
← Row 5 LS LC
Row 4 DS DC →
Row 4 DS LC →
← Row 3 LS DC
← Row 3 LS LC
Row 2 DS DC →
Row 2 DS LC →
← Row 1 LS DC
← Row 1 LS LC
Set-Up Row DS DC →
Set-Up Row DS LC →

12 11 10 9 8 7 6 5 4 3 2 1

101

Under Dutch Skies

Under Dutch Skies Brioche Stitch
Using Two-Color Italian Cast-On, begin and end with LC knit st. Cast on a multiple of 24 sts + 29. For the sample shown, I cast on 53 sts.

Set-Up Row DS LC: p1, *sl1yo, p1; rep from * to end. Do *not* turn, slide.
Set-Up Row DS DC: sl1, *brk1, sl1yo; rep from * to last 2 sts, brk1, sl1. Turn.

Row 1 LS LC: k1, sl1yo, brkyobrk, sl1yo, *brLsl dec, sl1yo, [brk1, sl1yo] 7 times, brRsl dec, sl1yo, br4st inc, sl1yo; rep from * to last 25 sts, brLsl dec, sl1yo, [brk1, sl1yo] 7 times, brRsl dec, sl1yo, brkyobrk, sl1yo, k1. Do *not* turn, slide.
Row 1 LS DC: sl1, brp1, sl1yo, p1, sl1yo, brp1, *[sl1yo, brp1] 9 times, [sl1yo, p1] twice, sl1yo, brp1; rep from * to last 23 sts, [sl1yo, brp1] 9 times, sl1yo, p1, sl1yo, brp1, sl1. Turn.

Row 2 DS LC and all DS LC rows: p1, *sl1yo, brp1; rep from * to last 2 sts, sl1yo, p1. Do *not* turn, slide.
Row 2 DS DC and all DS DC rows: sl1, *brk1, sl1yo; rep from * to last 2 sts, brk1, sl1. Turn.

Row 3 LS LC: k1, sl1yo, brkyobrk, sl1yo, *brk1, sl1yo, brLsl dec, sl1yo, [brk1, sl1yo] 5 times, brRsl dec, sl1yo, brk1, sl1yo, br4st inc, sl1yo; rep from * to last 25 sts, brk1, sl1yo, brLsl dec, sl1yo, [brk1, sl1yo] 5 times, brRsl dec, sl1yo, brk1, sl1yo, brkyobrk, sl1yo, k1. Do *not* turn, slide.
Row 3 LS DC: as Row 1 LS DC.

Under Dutch Skies Chart: Left Side

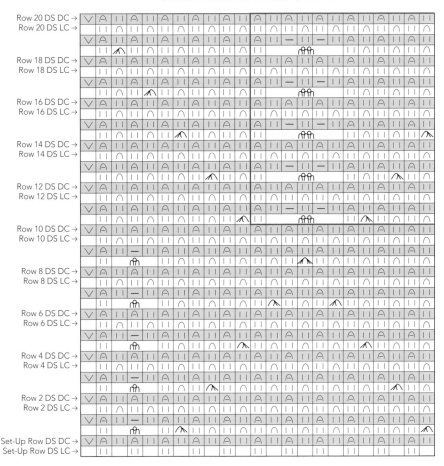

Row 20 DS DC →
Row 20 DS LC →

Row 18 DS DC →
Row 18 DS LC →

Row 16 DS DC →
Row 16 DS LC →

Row 14 DS DC →
Row 14 DS LC →

Row 12 DS DC →
Row 12 DS LC →

Row 10 DS DC →
Row 10 DS LC →

Row 8 DS DC →
Row 8 DS LC →

Row 6 DS DC →
Row 6 DS LC →

Row 4 DS DC →
Row 4 DS LC →

Row 2 DS DC →
Row 2 DS LC →

Set-Up Row DS DC →
Set-Up Row DS LC →

Row 5 LS LC: k1, sl1yo, brkyobrk, sl1yo, *[brk1, sl1yo] twice, brLsl dec, sl1yo, [brk1, sl1yo] 3 times, brRsl dec, sl1yo, [brk1, sl1yo] twice, br4st inc, sl1yo; rep from * to last 25 sts, [brk1, sl1yo] twice, brLsl dec, sl1yo, [brk1, sl1yo] 3 times, brRsl dec, sl1yo, [brk1, sl1yo] twice, brkyobrk, sl1yo, k1. Do *not* turn, slide.
Row 5 LS DC: as Row 1 LS DC.

Row 7 LS LC: k1, sl1yo, brkyobrk, sl1yo, *[brk1, sl1yo] 3 times, brLsl dec, sl1yo, brk1, sl1yo, brRsl dec, sl1yo, [brk1, sl1yo] 3 times, br4st inc, sl1yo; rep from * to last 25 sts, [brk1, sl1yo] 3 times, brLsl dec, sl1yo, brk1, sl1yo, brRsl dec, sl1yo, [brk1, sl1yo] 3 times, brkyobrk, sl1yo, k1. Do *not* turn, slide.
Row 7 LS DC: as Row 1 LS DC.

Row 9 LS LC: k1, sl1yo, brkyobrk, sl1yo, *[brk1, sl1yo] 4 times, br4st dec, sl1yo, [brk1, sl1yo] 4 times, br4st inc, sl1yo; rep from * to last 25 sts, [brk1, sl1yo] 4 times, br4st dec, sl1yo, [brk1, sl1yo] 4 times, brkyobrk, sl1yo, k1. Do *not* turn, slide.
Row 9 LS DC: as Row 1 LS DC.

Row 11 LS LC: k1, sl1yo, [brk1, sl1yo] 4 times, brRsl dec, sl1yo, br4st inc, sl1yo, *brLsl dec, sl1yo, [brk1, sl1yo] 7 times, brRsl dec, sl1yo, br4st inc, sl1yo; rep from * to last 13 sts, brLsl dec, sl1yo, [brk1, sl1yo] 4 times, k1. Do *not* turn, slide.
Row 11 LS DC: sl1, [brp1, sl1yo] 6 times, [p1, sl1yo] twice, brp1 *[sl1yo, brp1] 9 times, [sl1yo, p1] twice, sl1yo, brp1; rep from * to last 11 sts, [sl1yo, brp1] 5 times, sl1. Turn.

Row 13 LS LC: k1, sl1yo, [brk1, sl1yo] 3 times, brRsl dec, sl1yo, brk1, sl1yo, br4st inc, sl1yo, *[brk1, sl1yo] twice, brLsl dec, sl1yo, [brk1, sl1yo] 5 times, brRsl dec, sl1yo, brk1, sl1yo, br4st inc, sl1yo; rep from * to last 13 sts, brk1, sl1yo, brLsl dec, sl1yo, [brk1, sl1yo] 3 times, k1. Do *not* turn, slide.
Row 13 LS DC: as Row 11 LS DC.

Row 15 LS LC: k1, sl1yo, [brk1, sl1yo] twice, brRsl dec, sl1yo, [brk1, sl1yo] twice, br4st inc, sl1yo, *[brk1, sl1yo] twice, brLsl dec, sl1yo, [brk1, sl1yo] 3 times, brRsl dec, sl1yo, [brk1, sl1yo] twice, br4st inc, sl1yo; rep from * to last 13 sts, [brk1, sl1yo] twice, brLsl dec, sl1yo, [brk1, sl1yo] twice, k1. Do *not* turn, slide.
Row 15 LS DC: as Row 11 LS DC.

Under Dutch Skies Chart: Right Side

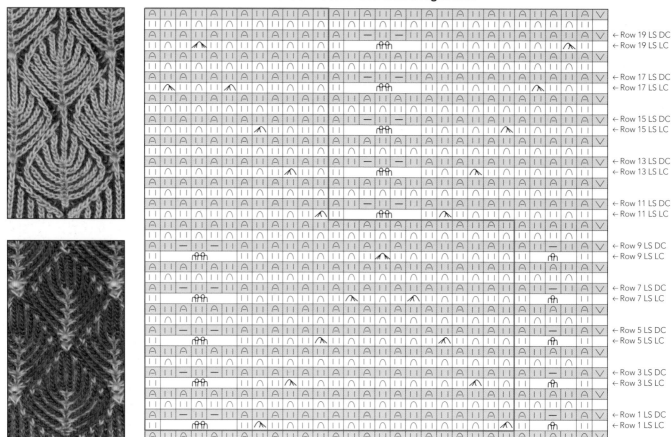

← Row 19 LS DC
← Row 19 LS LC
← Row 17 LS DC
← Row 17 LS LC
← Row 15 LS DC
← Row 15 LS LC
← Row 13 LS DC
← Row 13 LS LC
← Row 11 LS DC
← Row 11 LS LC
← Row 9 LS DC
← Row 9 LS LC
← Row 7 LS DC
← Row 7 LS LC
← Row 5 LS DC
← Row 5 LS LC
← Row 3 LS DC
← Row 3 LS LC
← Row 1 LS DC
← Row 1 LS LC

24 23 22 21 20 19 18 17 16 15 14 13 12 11 10 9 8 7 6 5 4 3 2 1

■ To more easily follow this chart, make a copy of both left and right sides.
Cut them out and tape them together to make a complete chart.

Row 17 LS LC: k1, sl1yo, brk1, sl1yo, brRsl dec, sl1yo, [brk1, sl1yo] 3 times, br4st inc, sl1yo, *[brk1, sl1yo] 3 times, brLsl dec, sl1yo, brk1, sl1yo, brRsl dec, sl1yo, [brk1, sl1yo] 3 times, br4st inc, sl1yo; rep from * to last 13 sts, [brk1, sl1yo] 3 times, brLsl dec, sl1yo, brk1, sl1yo, k1. Do *not* turn, slide.
Row 17 LS DC: as Row 11 LS DC.

Row 19 LS LC: k1, sl1yo, brRsl dec, sl1yo, [brk1, sl1yo] 4 times, br4st inc, sl1yo, *[brk1, sl1yo] 4 times, br4st dec, sl1yo, [brk1, sl1yo] 4 times, br4st inc, sl1yo; rep from * to last 13 sts, [brk1, sl1yo] 4 times, brLsl dec, sl1yo, k1. Do *not* turn, slide.
Row 19 LS DC: as Row 11 LS DC.

After working last set of DS rows, rep from Row 1 LS LC. ■

Sushi Ushi Revisited

I designed the original Sushi Ushi pattern many years ago with rather complicated increases and decreases. This revisited version looks almost the same and is much more intuitive.

Sushi Ushi Revisited Brioche Stitch
Using Two-Color Italian Cast-On, begin and end with LC knit st. Cast on a multiple of 12 sts + 3. For the sample shown, I cast on 39 sts.

Set-Up Row DS LC: p1, *sl1yo, p1; rep from * to end. Do *not* turn, slide.
Set-Up Row DS DC: sl1, *brk1, sl1yo; rep from * to last 2 sts, brk1, sl1. Turn.

Row 1 LS LC: k1, sl1yo, *brkyobrk, sl1yo, [brk1, sl1yo] 3 times, brRsl dec, sl1yo; rep from * to last st, k1. Do *not* turn, slide.
Row 1 LS DC: sl1, brp1, *sl1yo, p1, [sl1yo, brp1] 5 times; rep from * to last st, sl1. Turn.

Row 2 DS LC and all DS LC rows: p1, *sl1yo, brp1; rep from * to last 2 sts, sl1yo, p1. Do *not* turn, slide.
Row 2 DS DC and all DS DC rows: sl1, *brk1, sl1yo; rep from * to last 2 sts, brk1, sl1. Turn.

Row 3 LS LC: k1, sl1yo, *brk1, sl1yo, brkyobrk, sl1yo, [brk1, sl1yo] twice, brRsl dec, sl1yo; rep from * to last st, k1. Do *not* turn, slide.
Row 3 LS DC: sl1, brp1, *sl1yo, brp1, sl1yo, p1, [sl1yo, brp1] 4 times; rep from * to last st, sl1. Turn.

Row 5 LS LC: k1, sl1yo, *[brk1, sl1yo] twice, brkyobrk, sl1yo, brk1, sl1yo, brRsl dec, sl1yo; rep from * to last st, k1. Do *not* turn, slide.
Row 5 LS DC: sl1, brp1, *[sl1yo, brp1] twice, sl1yo, p1, [sl1yo, brp1] 3 times; rep from * to last st, sl1. Turn.

Row 7 LS LC: k1, sl1yo, *[brk1, sl1yo] 3 times, brkyobrk, sl1yo, brRsl dec, sl1yo; rep from * to last st, k1. Do *not* turn, slide.
Row 7 LS DC: sl1, brp1, *[sl1yo, brp1] 3 times, sl1yo, p1, [sl1yo, brp1] twice; rep from * to last st, sl1. Turn.

Row 9 LS LC: k1, sl1yo, *brLsl dec, sl1yo, [brk1, sl1yo] 3 times, brkyobrk, sl1yo; rep from * to last st, k1. Do *not* turn, slide.

Row 9 LS DC: sl1, brp1, *[sl1yo, brp1] 4 times, sl1yo, p1, sl1yo, brp1; rep from * to last st, sl1. Turn.

Row 11 LS LC: k1, sl1yo, *brLsl dec, sl1yo, [brk1, sl1yo] twice, brkyobrk, sl1yo, brk1, sl1yo; rep from * to last st, k1. Do *not* turn, slide.

Row 11 LS DC: sl1, brp1, *[sl1yo, brp1] 3 times, sl1yo, p1, [sl1yo, brp1] twice; rep from * to last st, sl1. Turn.

Row 13 LS LC: k1, sl1yo, *brLsl dec, sl1yo, brk1, sl1yo, brkyobrk, sl1yo, [brk1, sl1yo] twice; rep from * to last st, k1. Do *not* turn, slide.

Row 13 LS DC: sl1, brp1, *[sl1yo, brp1] twice, sl1yo, p1, [sl1yo, brp1] 3 times; rep from * to last st, sl1. Turn.

Row 15 LS LC: k1, sl1yo, *brLsl dec, sl1yo, brkyobrk, sl1yo, [brk1, sl1yo] 3 times; rep from * to last st, k1. Do *not* turn, slide.

Row 15 LS DC: sl1, brp1, *sl1yo, brp1, sl1yo, p1, [sl1yo, brp1] 4 times; rep from * to last st, sl1. Turn.

After working last set of DS rows, rep from Row 1 LS LC. ∎

Sushi Ushi Revisited Chart

Mr. Flood's

I made a small scarf using this, one of my first stitch patterns. I appreciated Mr. Flood's admiration of the pattern and wound up giving him the scarf.

Mr. Flood's Brioche Stitch
Using Two-Color Italian Cast-On, begin and end with LC knit st. Cast on a multiple of 10 sts + 5. For the sample shown, I cast on 35 sts.

Set-Up Row DS LC: p1, *sl1yo, p1; rep from * to end. Do *not* turn, slide.
Set-Up Row DS DC: sl1, *brk1, sl1yo; rep from * to last 2 sts, brk1, sl1. Turn.

Row 1 LS LC: k1, sl1yo, brk1, sl1yo, *brk1, sl1yo, brkyobrk, sl1yo, [brk1, sl1yo] 3 times; rep from * to last st, k1. Do *not* turn, slide.
Row 1 LS DC: sl1, brp1, sl1yo, brp1, *sl1yo, brp1, sl1yo, p1, [sl1yo, brp1] 4 times; rep from * to last st, sl1. Turn.

Row 2 DS LC and all DS LC rows: p1, *sl1yo, brp1; rep from * to last 2 sts, sl1yo, p1. Do *not* turn, slide.
Row 2 DS DC and all DS DC rows: sl1, *brk1, sl1yo; rep from * to last 2 sts, brk1, sl1. Turn.

Row 3 LS LC: k1, sl1yo, brk1, sl1yo, *brk1, sl1yo, brkyobrk, sl1yo, brLsl dec, sl1yo, [brk1, sl1yo] twice; rep from * to last st, k1. Do *not* turn, slide.
Row 3 LS DC: as Row 1 LS DC.

Row 5 LS LC: k1, sl1yo, brk1, sl1yo, *brk1, sl1yo, brkyobrk, sl1yo, brk1, sl1yo, brLsl dec, sl1yo, brk1, sl1yo; rep from * to last st, k1. Do *not* turn, slide.
Row 5 LS DC: as Row 1 LS DC.

Row 7 LS LC: k1, sl1yo, brk1, sl1yo, *[brk1, sl1yo] 4 times, brLsl dec, sl1yo; rep from * to last st, k1. Do *not* turn, slide.
Row 7 LS DC: sl1, *brp1, sl1yo; rep from * to last 2 sts, brp1, sl1. Turn.

Row 9 LS LC: k1, sl1yo, *[brk1, sl1yo] 3 times, brkyobrk, sl1yo, brk1, sl1yo; rep from * to last 3 sts, brk1, sl1yo, k1. Do *not* turn, slide.
Row 9 LS DC: sl1, brp1, *[sl1yo, brp1] 3 times, sl1yo, p1, [sl1yo, brp1] twice; rep from * to last 3 sts, sl1yo, brp1, sl1. Turn.

Row 11 LS LC: k1, sl1yo, *[brk1, sl1yo] twice, brRsl dec, sl1yo, brkyobrk, sl1yo, brk1, sl1yo; rep from * to last 3 sts, brk1, sl1yo, k1. Do *not* turn, slide.
Row 11 LS DC: as Row 9 LS DC.

Row 13 LS LC: k1, sl1yo, *brk1, sl1yo, brRsl dec, sl1yo, brk1, sl1yo, brkyobrk, sl1yo, brk1, sl1yo; rep from * to last 3 sts, brk1, sl1yo, k1. Do *not* turn, slide.
Row 13 LS DC: as Row 9 LS DC.

Row 15 LS LC: k1, sl1yo, * brRsl dec, sl1yo, [brk1, sl1yo] 4 times; rep from * to last 3 sts, brk1, sl1yo, k1. Do *not* turn, slide.
Row 15 LS DC: as Row 7 LS DC.

After working last set of DS rows, rep from Row 1 LS LC. ∎

Mr. Flood's Chart

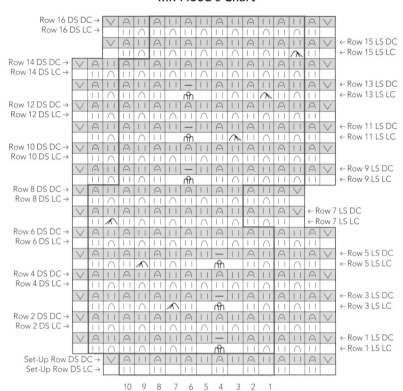

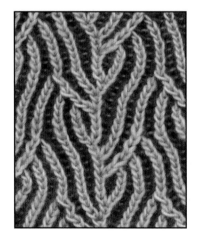

Pear Leaf

Pear Leaf Brioche Stitch

Using Two-Color Italian Cast-On, begin and end with LC knit st. Cast on a multiple of 12 sts + 3. For the sample shown, I cast on 39 sts.

Set-Up Row DS LC: p1, *sl1yo, p1; rep from * to end. Do *not* turn, slide.
Set-Up Row DS DC: sl1, *brk1, sl1yo; rep from * to last 2 sts, brk1, sl1. Turn.

Row 1 LS LC: k1, sl1yo, *brk1, sl1yo, brkyobrk, sl1yo, [brk1, sl1yo] 4 times; rep from * to last st, k1. Do *not* turn, slide.
Row 1 LS DC: sl1, brp1, *sl1yo, brp1, sl1yo, p1, [sl1yo, brp1] 5 times; rep from * to last st, sl1. Turn.

Row 2 DS LC and all DS LC rows: p1, *sl1yo, brp1; rep from * to last 2 sts, sl1yo, p1. Do *not* turn, slide.
Row 2 DS DC and all DS DC rows: sl1, *brk1, sl1yo; rep from * to last 2 sts, brk1, sl1. Turn.

Row 3 LS LC: k1, sl1yo, *brk1, sl1yo, brkyobrk, sl1yo, brLsl dec, sl1yo, [brk1, sl1yo] 3 times; rep from * to last st, k1. Do *not* turn, slide.
Row 3 LS DC: as Row 1 LC DC.

Row 5 LS LC: k1, sl1yo, *[brk1, sl1yo] twice, brkyobrk, sl1yo, brLsl dec, sl1yo, [brk1, sl1yo] twice; rep from * to last st, k1. Do *not* turn, slide.
Row 5 LS DC: sl1, brp1, *[sl1yo, brp1] twice, sl1yo, p1, [sl1yo, brp1] 4 times; rep from * to last st, sl1. Turn.

Row 7 LS LC: k1, sl1yo, *[brk1, sl1yo] twice, brkyobrk, sl1yo, brk1, sl1yo, brLsl dec, sl1yo, brk1, sl1yo; rep from * to last st, k1. Do *not* turn, slide.
Row 7 LS DC: as Row 5 LC DC.

Row 9 LS LC: k1, sl1yo, *[brk1, sl1yo] 5 times, brLsl dec, sl1yo; rep from * to last st, k1. Do *not* turn, slide.
Row 9 LS DC: sl1, brp1, *sl1yo, brp1; rep from * to last st, sl1. Turn.

After working last set of DS rows, rep from Row 1 LS LC. ■

Pear Leaf Chart

Row 10 DS DC →
Row 10 DS LC →
← Row 9 LS DC
← Row 9 LS LC
Row 8 DS DC →
Row 8 DS LC →
← Row 7 LS DC
← Row 7 LS LC
Row 6 DS DC →
Row 6 DS LC →
← Row 5 LS DC
← Row 5 LS LC
Row 4 DS DC →
Row 4 DS LC →
← Row 3 LS DC
← Row 3 LS LC
Row 2 DS DC →
Row 2 DS LC →
← Row 1 LS DC
← Row 1 LS LC
Set-Up Row DS DC →
Set-Up Row DS LC →

12 11 10 9 8 7 6 5 4 3 2 1

Double Pear Leaf

For this pattern, I designed Beginning Rows 1–4 and Finishing Rows 1–10 just to make the finished swatch a little prettier. I suggest placing a marker between each repeat. I also placed a marker on Row 1 each time I worked it, so I could count up and see which row I needed to work next.

Double Pear Leaf Brioche Stitch
Using Two-Color Italian Cast-On, begin and end with LC knit st. Cast on a multiple of 20 sts + 3. For the sample shown, I cast on 43 sts.

Set-Up Row DS LC: p1, *sl1yo, p1; rep from * to end. Do *not* turn, slide.
Set-Up Row DS DC: sl1, *brk1, sl1yo; rep from * to last 2 sts, brk1, sl1. Turn.

BEGINNING PATTERN ROWS
Beginning Row 1 LS LC: k1, sl1yo, *[brk1, sl1yo] 5 times, brkyobrk, sl1yo, [brk1, sl1yo] 4 times; rep from * to last st, k1. Do *not* turn, slide.
Beginning Row 1 LS DC: sl1, brp1, *[sl1yo, brp1] 5 times, sl1yo, p1, [sl1yo, brp1] 5 times; rep from * to last st, sl1. Turn.

Beginning Row 2 DS LC and all DS LC rows: p1, *sl1yo, brp1; rep from * to last 2 sts, sl1yo, p1. Do *not* turn, slide.
Beginning Row 2 DS DC and all DS DC rows: sl1, *brk1, sl1yo; rep from * to last 2 sts, brk1, sl1. Turn.

Double Pear Leaf Chart

Finishing Row 10 DS DC →
Finishing Row 10 DS LC →
Finishing Row 8 DS DC →
Finishing Row 8 DS LC →
Finishing Row 6 DS DC →
Finishing Row 6 DS LC →
Finishing Row 4 DS DC →
Finishing Row 4 DS LC →
Finishing Row 2 DS DC →
Finishing Row 2 DS LC →
Row 10 DS DC →
Row 10 DS LC →
Row 8 DS DC →
Row 8 DS LC →
Row 6 DS DC →
Row 6 DS LC →
Row 4 DS DC →
Row 4 DS LC →
Row 2 DS DC →
Row 2 DS LC →
Beginning Row 4 DS DC →
Beginning Row 4 DS LC →
Beginning Row 2 DS DC →
Beginning Row 2 DS LC →
Set-Up Row DS DC →
Set-Up Row DS LC →

← Finishing Row 9 LS DC
← Finishing Row 9 LS LC
← Finishing Row 7 LS DC
← Finishing Row 7 LS LC
← Finishing Row 5 LS DC
← Finishing Row 5 LS LC
← Finishing Row 3 LS DC
← Finishing Row 3 LS LC
← Finishing Row 1 LS DC
← Finishing Row 1 LS LC
← Row 9 LS DC
← Row 9 LS LC
← Row 7 LS DC
← Row 7 LS LC
← Row 5 LS DC
← Row 5 LS LC
← Row 3 LS DC
← Row 3 LS LC
← Row 1 LS DC
← Row 1 LS LC
← Beginning Row 3 LS DC
← Beginning Row 3 LS LC
← Beginning Row 1 LS DC
← Beginning Row 1 LS LC

20 19 18 17 16 15 14 13 12 11 10 9 8 7 6 5 4 3 2 1

111

Beginning Row 3 LS LC: k1, sl1yo, *[brk1, sl1yo] 5 times, brkyobrk, sl1yo, brLsl dec, sl1yo, [brk1, sl1yo] 3 times; rep from * to last st, k1. Do *not* turn, slide.
Beginning Row 3 LS DC: as Beginning Row 1 LS DC.

MAIN PATTERN ROWS
Row 1 LS LC: k1, sl1yo, *[brk1, sl1yo] 4 times, brkyobrk, sl1yo, brk1, sl1yo, brkyobrk, sl1yo, brLsl dec, sl1yo, [brk1, sl1yo] twice; rep from * to last st, k1. Do *not* turn, slide.
Row 1 LS DC: sl1, brp1, *[sl1yo, brp1] 4 times, sl1yo, p1, [sl1yo, brp1] twice, sl1yo, p1, [sl1yo, brp1] 4 times; rep from * to last st, sl1. Turn.

Row 3 LS LC: k1, sl1yo, *[brk1, sl1yo] 3 times, brRsl dec, sl1yo, brkyobrk, sl1yo, brk1, sl1yo, brkyobrk, sl1yo, brk1, sl1yo, brLsl dec, sl1yo, brk1, sl1yo; rep from * to last st, k1. Do *not* turn, slide.
Row 3 LS DC: as Row 1 LS DC.

Row 5 LS LC: k1, sl1yo, *[brk1, sl1yo] twice, brRsl dec, sl1yo, brkyobrk, sl1yo, [brk1, sl1yo] 5 times, brLsl dec, sl1yo; rep from * to last st, k1. Do *not* turn, slide.
Row 5 LS DC: sl1, brp1, *[sl1yo, brp1] 3 times, sl1yo, p1, [sl1yo, brp1] 7 times; rep from * to last st, sl1. Turn.

Row 7 LS LC: k1, sl1yo, *brk1, sl1yo, brRsl dec, sl1yo, [brk1, sl1yo, brkyobrk, sl1yo] twice, [brk1, sl1yo] 4 times; rep from * to last st, k1. Do *not* turn, slide.
Row 7 LS DC: sl1, brp1, *[sl1yo, brp1] 3 times, sl1yo, p1, [sl1yo, brp1] twice, sl1yo, p1, [sl1yo, brp1] 5 times; rep from * to last st, sl1. Turn.

Row 9 LS LC: k1, sl1yo, *brRsl dec, sl1yo, [brk1, sl1yo] 4 times, brkyobrk, sl1yo, brLsl dec, sl1yo, [brk1, sl1yo] 3 times; rep from * to last st, k1. Do *not* turn, slide.
Row 9 LS DC: sl1, brp1, *[sl1yo, brp1] 5 times, sl1yo, p1, [sl1yo, brp1] 5 times; rep from * to last st, sl1. Turn.

After working last set of DS rows, rep from Main Pattern Row 1 LS LC until ready to finish.

FINISHING PATTERN ROWS
Finishing Row 1 LS LC–Finishing Row 6 DS DC: as (Main Pattern) Row 1 LS LC–Row 6 DS DC.

Finishing Row 7 LS LC: k1, sl1yo, *brk1, sl1yo, brRsl dec, sl1yo, brk1, sl1yo, brkyobrk, sl1yo, [brk1, sl1yo] 6 times; rep from * to last st, k1. Do *not* turn, slide.
Finishing Row 7 LS DC: sl1, brp1, *[sl1yo, brp1] 3 times, sl1yo, p1, [sl1yo, brp1] 7 times; rep from * to last st, sl1. Turn.

Finishing Row 9 LS LC: k1, sl1yo, *brRsl dec, sl1yo, [brk1, sl1yo] 9 times; rep from * to last st, k1. Do *not* turn, slide.
Finishing Row 9 LS DC: sl1, brp1, *sl1yo, brp1; rep from * to last st, sl1. Turn.

Bind off after working last set of DS rows.■

Narrow Flat Cables

For the sample shown, an extra set of plain two-color brioche rows (see page 22) was worked after the Set-Up Rows and before starting with Row 1 LS LC.

Narrow Flat Cables Brioche Stitch
Using Two-Color Italian Cast-On, begin and end with LC knit st. Cast on a multiple of 16 sts + 3. For the sample shown, I cast on 35 sts.

Set-Up Row DS LC: p1, *sl1yo, p1; rep from * to end. Do *not* turn, slide.
Set-Up Row DS DC: sl1, *brk1, sl1yo; rep from * to last 2 sts, brk1, sl1. Turn.

Row 1 LS LC: k1, sl1yo, *brk1, sl1yo, brRsl dec, sl1yo, [brk1, sl1yo] 5 times; rep from * to last st, k1. Do *not* turn, slide.
Row 1 LS DC: sl1, brp1, *sl1yo, brp1; rep from * to last st, sl1. Turn.

Row 2 DS LC and all DS LC rows: p1, *sl1yo, brp1; rep from * to last 2 sts, sl1yo, p1. Do *not* turn, slide.
Row 2 DS DC and all DS DC rows: sl1, *brk1, sl1yo; rep from * to last 2 sts, brk1, sl1. Turn.

Row 3 LS LC: k1, sl1yo, *brRsl dec, sl1yo, brkyobrk, sl1yo, [brk1, sl1yo] 4 times; rep from * to last st, k1. Do *not* turn, slide.
Row 3 LS DC: sl1, brp1, *sl1yo, brp1, sl1yo, p1, [sl1yo, brp1] 5 times; rep from * to last st, sl1. Turn.

Row 5 LS LC: k1, sl1yo, *brk1, sl1yo, brkyobrk, sl1yo, [brk1, sl1yo] 5 times; rep from * to last st, k1. Do *not* turn, slide.

Row 5 LS DC: sl1, brp1, *sl1yo, brp1, sl1yo, p1, [sl1yo, brp1] 6 times; rep from * to last st, sl1. Turn.

Row 7 LS LC: k1, sl1yo, *[brk1, sl1yo] 5 times, brRsl dec, sl1yo, brk1, sl1yo; rep from * to last st, k1. Do *not* turn, slide.

Row 7 LS DC: as Row 1 LS DC.

Row 9 LS LC: k1, sl1yo, *[brk1, sl1yo] 4 times, brRsl dec, sl1yo, brkyobrk, sl1yo; rep from * to last st, k1. Do *not* turn, slide.

Row 9 LS DC: sl1, brp1, *[sl1yo, brp1] 5 times, sl1yo, p1, sl1yo, brp1; rep from * to last st, sl1. Turn.

Row 11 LS LC: k1, sl1yo, *[brk1, sl1yo] 5 times, brkyobrk, sl1yo, brk1, sl1yo; rep from * to last st, k1. Do *not* turn, slide.

Row 11 LS DC: sl1, brp1, *[sl1yo, brp1] 5 times, sl1yo, p1, [sl1yo, brp1] twice; rep from * to last st, sl1. Turn.

After working last set of DS rows, rep from Row 1 LS LC. ■

Narrow Flat Cables Chart

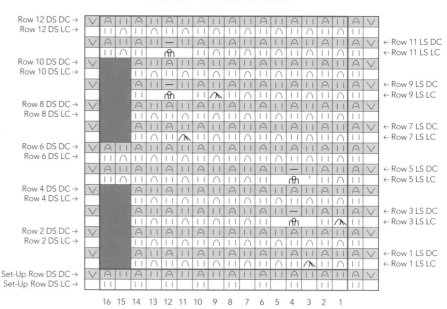

Wide Flat Cables

Wide Flat Cables Brioche Stitch
Using Two-Color Italian Cast-On, begin and end with LC knit st. Cast on a multiple of 16 sts + 3. For the sample shown, I cast on 35 sts.

Set-Up Row DS LC: p1, *sl1yo, p1; rep from * to end. Do *not* turn, slide.
Set-Up Row DS DC: sl1, *brk1, sl1yo; rep from * to last 2 sts, brk1, sl1. Turn.

Row 1 LS LC: k1, sl1yo, *brkyobrk, sl1yo, [brk1, sl1yo] twice, brLsl dec, sl1yo, [brk1, sl1yo] 3 times; rep from * to last st, k1. Do *not* turn, slide.
Row 1 LS DC: sl1, brp1, *sl1yo, p1, [sl1yo, brp1] 7 times; rep from * to last st, sl1. Turn.

Row 2 DS LC and all DS LC rows: p1, *sl1yo, brp1; rep from * to last 2 sts, sl1yo, p1. Do *not* turn, slide.
Row 2 DS DC and all DS DC rows: sl1, *brk1, sl1yo; rep from * to last 2 sts, brk1, sl1. Turn.

Row 3 LS LC: k1, sl1yo, *brk1, sl1yo, brkyobrk, sl1yo, [brk1, sl1yo] twice, brLsl dec, [brk1, sl1yo] twice; rep from * to last st, k1. Do *not* turn, slide.
Row 3 LS DC: sl1, brp1, *sl1yo, brp1, sl1yo, p1, [sl1yo, brp1] 6 times; rep from * to last st, sl1. Turn.

Row 5 LS LC: k1, sl1yo, *[brk1, sl1yo] twice, brkyobrk, sl1yo, [brk1, sl1yo] twice, brLsl dec, sl1yo, brk1, sl1yo; rep from * to last st, k1. Do *not* turn, slide.
Row 5 LS DC: sl1, brp1, *[sl1yo, brp1] twice, sl1yo, p1, [sl1yo, brp1] 5 times; rep from * to last st, sl1. Turn.

Row 7 LS LC: k1, sl1yo, *[brk1, sl1yo] 3 times, brkyobrk, sl1yo, [brk1, sl1yo] twice, brLsl dec, sl1yo; rep from * to last st, k1. Do *not* turn, slide.

Row 7 LS DC: sl1, brp1, *[sl1yo, brp1] 3 times, sl1yo, p1, [sl1yo, brp1] 4 times; rep from * to last st, sl1. Turn.

Row 9 LS LC: k1, sl1yo, *brk1, sl1yo; rep from * to last st, k1. Do *not* turn, slide.
Row 9 LS DC: sl1, brp1, *sl1yo, brp1; rep from * to last st, sl1. Turn.

After working last set of DS rows, rep from Row 1 LS LC. ∎

Wide Flat Cables Chart

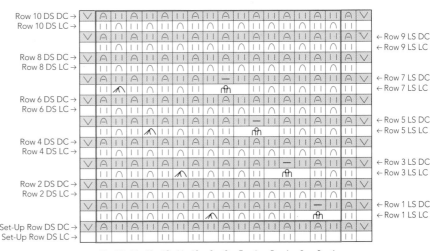

Braided Columns

Braided Columns Brioche Stitch
Using Two-Color Italian Cast-On, begin and end with LC knit st. Cast on a multiple of 24 sts + 3. For the sample shown, I cast on 51 sts.

Set-Up Row DS LC: p1, *sl1yo, p1; rep from * to end. Do *not* turn, slide.
Set-Up Row DS DC: sl1, *brk1, sl1yo; rep from * to last 2 sts, brk1, sl1. Turn.

Row 1 LS LC: k1, sl1yo, *[brk1, sl1yo] 3 times, brRsl dec, sl1yo, [brk1, sl1yo] twice, brkyobrk, sl1yo, [brk1, sl1yo] 4 times; rep from * to last st, k1. Do *not* turn, slide.
Row 1 LS DC: sl1, brp1, *[sl1yo, brp1] 6 times, sl1yo, p1, [sl1yo, brp1] 5 times; rep from * to last st, sl1. Turn.

Row 2 DS LC and all DS LC rows: p1, *sl1yo, brp1; rep from * to last 2 sts, sl1yo, p1. Do *not* turn, slide.
Row 2 DS DC and all DS DC rows: sl1, *brk1, sl1yo; rep from * to last 2 sts, brk1, sl1. Turn.

Row 3 LS LC: k1, sl1yo, *[brk1, sl1yo] twice, brRsl dec, sl1yo, [brk1, sl1yo] twice, brkyobrk, sl1yo, [brk1, sl1yo] 5 times; rep from * to last st, k1. Do *not* turn, slide.
Row 3 LS DC: sl1, brp1, *[sl1yo, brp1] 5 times, sl1yo, p1, [sl1yo, brp1] 6 times; rep from * to last st, sl1. Turn.

Row 5 LS LC: k1, sl1yo, *brk1, sl1yo, brRsl dec, sl1yo, [brk1, sl1yo] twice, brkyobrk, sl1yo, [brk1, sl1yo] 6 times; rep from * to last st, k1. Do *not* turn, slide.
Row 5 LS DC: sl1, brp1, *[sl1yo, brp1] 4 times, sl1yo, p1, [sl1yo, brp1] 7 times; rep from * to last st, sl1. Turn.

Row 7 LS LC: k1, sl1yo, *brRsl dec, sl1yo, [brk1, sl1yo] twice, brkyobrk, sl1yo, [brk1, sl1yo] 7 times; rep from * to last st, k1. Do *not* turn, slide.
Row 7 LS DC: sl1, brp1, *[sl1yo, brp1] 3 times, sl1yo, p1, [sl1yo, brp1] 8 times; rep from * to last st, sl1. Turn.

Row 9 LS LC: k1, sl1yo, *[brk1, sl1yo] 4 times, brkyobrk, sl1yo, [brk1, sl1yo] twice, brLsl dec, sl1yo, [brk1, sl1yo] 3 times; rep from * to last st, k1. Do *not* turn, slide.
Row 9 LS DC: sl1, brp1, *[sl1yo, brp1] 4 times, sl1yo, p1, [sl1yo, brp1] 7 times; rep from * to last st, sl1. Turn.

Row 11 LS LC: k1, sl1yo, *[brk1, sl1yo] 5 times, brkyobrk, sl1yo, [brk1, sl1yo] twice, brLsl dec, sl1yo, [brk1, sl1yo] twice; rep from * to last st, k1. Do *not* turn, slide.
Row 11 LS DC: sl1, brp1, *[sl1yo, brp1] 5 times, sl1yo, p1, [sl1yo, brp1] 6 times; rep from * to last st, sl1. Turn.

Row 13 LS LC: k1, sl1yo, *[brk1, sl1yo] 6 times, brkyobrk, sl1yo, [brk1, sl1yo] twice, brLsl dec, sl1yo, brk1, sl1yo; rep from * to last st, k1. Do *not* turn, slide.
Row 13 LS DC: sl1, brp1, *[sl1yo, brp1] 6 times, sl1yo, p1, [sl1yo, brp1] 5 times; rep from * to last st, sl1. Turn.

Row 15 LS LC: k1, sl1yo, *[brk1, sl1yo] 7 times, brkyobrk, sl1yo, [brk1, sl1yo] twice, brLsl dec, sl1yo; rep from * to last st, k1. Do *not* turn, slide.
Row 15 LS DC: sl1, brp1, *[sl1yo, brp1] 7 times, sl1yo, p1, [sl1yo, brp1] 4 times; rep from * to last st, sl1. Turn.

After working last set of DS rows, rep from Row 1 LS LC. ■

Braided Columns Chart

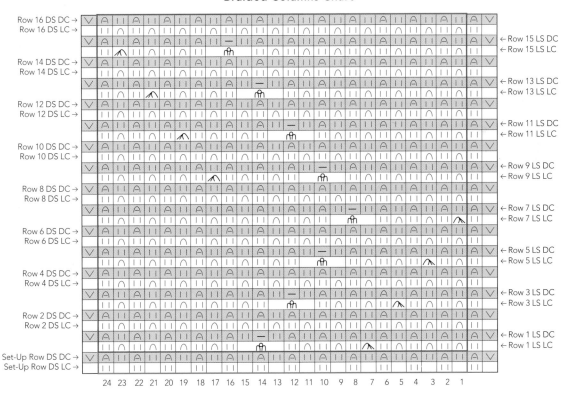

Wide Zigzag

This pattern would also be pretty with extra columns between the zigzags. See Gretchen's Zigzag (page 218) for a nice way to begin and end a scarf using the Wide Zigzag stitch.

Wide Zigzag Brioche Stitch
Using Two-Color Italian Cast-On, begin and end with LC knit st. Cast on a multiple of 26 sts + 3. For the sample shown, I cast on 55 sts.

Set-Up Row DS LC: p1, *sl1yo, p1; rep from * to end. Do *not* turn, slide.
Set-Up Row DS DC: sl1, *brk1, sl1yo; rep from * to last 2 sts, brk1, sl1. Turn.

Row 1 LS LC: k1, sl1yo, *brLsl dec, sl1yo, [brk1, sl1yo] 6 times, brkyobrk, sl1yo, [brk1, sl1yo] 4 times; rep from * to last st, k1. Do *not* turn, slide.
Row 1 LS DC: sl1, brp1, *[sl1yo, brp1] 7 times, sl1yo, p1, [sl1yo, brp1] 5 times; rep from * to last st, sl1. Turn.

Row 2 DS LC and all DS LC rows: p1, *sl1yo, brp1; rep from * to last 2 sts, sl1yo, p1. Do *not* turn, slide.
Row 2 DS DC and all DS DC rows: sl1, *brk1, sl1yo; rep from * to last 2 sts, brk1, sl1. Turn.

Row 3 LS LC: k1, sl1yo, *brLsl dec, sl1yo, [brk1, sl1yo] 5 times, brkyobrk, sl1yo, [brk1, sl1yo] 5 times; rep from * to last st, k1. Do *not* turn, slide.
Row 3 LS DC: sl1, brp1, *[sl1yo, brp1] 6 times, sl1yo, p1, [sl1yo, brp1] 6 times; rep from * to last st, sl1. Turn.

Row 5 LS LC: k1, sl1yo, *brLsl dec, sl1yo, [brk1, sl1yo] 4 times, brkyobrk, sl1yo, [brk1, sl1yo] 6 times; rep from * to last st, k1. Do *not* turn, slide.

Wide Zigzag Chart

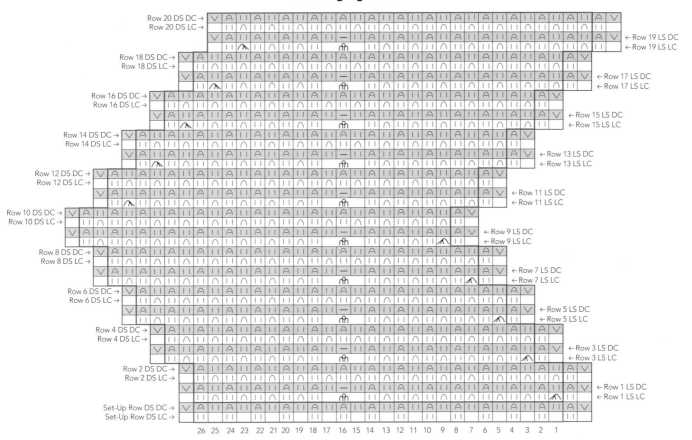

Row 20 DS DC →
Row 20 DS LC →
← Row 19 LS DC
← Row 19 LS LC
Row 18 DS DC →
Row 18 DS LC →
← Row 17 LS DC
← Row 17 LS LC
Row 16 DS DC →
Row 16 DS LC →
← Row 15 LS DC
← Row 15 LS LC
Row 14 DS DC →
Row 14 DS LC →
← Row 13 LS DC
← Row 13 LS LC
Row 12 DS DC →
Row 12 DS LC →
← Row 11 LS DC
← Row 11 LS LC
Row 10 DS DC →
Row 10 DS LC →
← Row 9 LS DC
← Row 9 LS LC
Row 8 DS DC →
Row 8 DS LC →
← Row 7 LS DC
← Row 7 LS LC
Row 6 DS DC →
Row 6 DS LC →
← Row 5 LS DC
← Row 5 LS LC
Row 4 DS DC →
Row 4 DS LC →
← Row 3 LS DC
← Row 3 LS LC
Row 2 DS DC →
Row 2 DS LC →
← Row 1 LS DC
← Row 1 LS LC
Set-Up Row DS DC →
Set-Up Row DS LC →

26 25 24 23 22 21 20 19 18 17 16 15 14 13 12 11 10 9 8 7 6 5 4 3 2 1

Row 5 LS DC: sl1, brp1, *[sl1yo, brp1] 5 times, sl1yo, p1, [sl1yo, brp1] 7 times; rep from * to last st, sl1. Turn.

Row 7 LS LC: k1, sl1yo, *brLsl dec, sl1yo, [brk1, sl1yo] 3 times, brkyobrk, sl1yo, [brk1, sl1yo] 7 times; rep from * to last st, k1. Do *not* turn, slide.
Row 7 LS DC: sl1, brp1, *[sl1yo, brp1] 4 times, sl1yo, p1, [sl1yo, brp1] 8 times; rep from * to last st, sl1. Turn.

Row 9 LS LC: k1, sl1yo, *brLsl dec, sl1yo, [brk1, sl1yo] twice, brkyobrk, sl1yo, [brk1, sl1yo] 8 times; rep from * to last st, k1. Do *not* turn, slide.
Row 9 LS DC: sl1, brp1, *[sl1yo, brp1] 3 times, sl1yo, p1, [sl1yo, brp1] 9 times; rep from * to last st, sl1. Turn.

Row 11 LS LC: k1, sl1yo, *[brk1, sl1yo] 4 times, brkyobrk, sl1yo, [brk1, sl1yo] 6 times, brRsl dec, sl1yo; rep from * to last st, k1. Do *not* turn, slide.
Row 11 LS DC: sl1, brp1, *[sl1yo, brp1] 4 times, sl1yo, p1, [sl1yo, brp1] 8 times; rep from * to last st, sl1. Turn.

Row 13 LS LC: k1, sl1yo, *[brk1, sl1yo] 5 times, brkyobrk, sl1yo, [brk1, sl1yo] 5 times, brRsl dec, sl1yo; rep from * to last st, k1. Do *not* turn, slide.
Row 13 LS DC: sl1, brp1, *[sl1yo, brp1] 5 times, sl1yo, p1, [sl1yo, brp1] 7 times; rep from * to last st, sl1. Turn.

Row 15 LS LC: k1, sl1yo, *[brk1, sl1yo] 6 times, brkyobrk, sl1yo, [brk1, sl1yo] 4 times, brRsl dec, sl1yo; rep from * to last st, k1. Do *not* turn, slide.
Row 15 LS DC: sl1, brp1, *[sl1yo, brp1] 6 times, sl1yo, p1, [sl1yo, brp1] 6 times; rep from * to last st, sl1. Turn.

Row 17 LS LC: k1, sl1yo, *[brk1, sl1yo] 7 times, brkyobrk, sl1yo, [brk1, sl1yo] 3 times, brRsl dec, sl1yo; rep from * to last st, k1. Do *not* turn, slide.
Row 17 LS DC: sl1, brp1, *[sl1yo, brp1] 7 times, sl1yo, p1, [sl1yo, brp1] 5 times; rep from * to last st, sl1. Turn.

Row 19 LS LC: k1, sl1yo, *[brk1, sl1yo] 8 times, brkyobrk, sl1yo, [brk1, sl1yo] twice, brRsl dec, sl1yo; rep from * to last st, k1. Do *not* turn, slide.
Row 19 LS DC: sl1, brp1, *[sl1yo, brp1] 8 times, sl1yo, p1, [sl1yo, brp1] 4 times; rep from * to last st, sl1. Turn.

After working last set of DS rows, rep from Row 1 LS LC. ∎

Wavy Treads

Here's a nice way to vary this stitch: repeat Rows 1–2 and Rows 9–10 several times before continuing on. The diagonal could continue across the entire width of a scarf, keeping the 2-stitch decreases at each edge.

Wavy Treads Brioche Stitch
Using Two-Color Italian Cast-On, begin and end with LC knit st. Cast on a multiple of 16 sts + 21. For the sample shown, I cast on 53 sts.

Set-Up Row DS LC: p1, *sl1yo, p1; rep from * to end. Do *not* turn, slide.
Set-Up Row DS DC: sl1, *brk1, sl1yo; rep from * to last 2 sts, brk1, sl1. Turn.

Row 1 LS LC: k1, sl1yo, brLsl dec, sl1yo, *[brk1, sl1yo] 4 times, br4st inc, sl1yo, br4st dec, sl1yo; rep from * to last 15 sts, [brk1, sl1yo] 4 times, br4st inc, sl1yo, brRsl dec, sl1yo, k1. Do *not* turn, slide.
Row 1 LS DC: sl1, brp1, sl1yo, brp1, *[sl1yo, brp1] 4 times, [sl1yo, p1] twice, [sl1yo, brp1] twice; rep from * to last st, sl1. Turn.

Row 2 DS LC and all DS LC rows: p1, *sl1yo, brp1; rep from * to last 2 sts, sl1yo, p1. Do *not* turn, slide.
Row 2 DS DC and all DS DC rows: sl1, *brk1, sl1yo; rep from * to last 2 sts, brk1, sl1. Turn.

Row 3 LS LC: k1, sl1yo, brLsl dec, sl1yo, *[brk1, sl1yo] 3 times, br4st inc, sl1yo, brk1, sl1yo, br4st dec, sl1yo; rep from * to last 15 sts, [brk1, sl1yo] 3 times, br4st inc, sl1yo, brk1, sl1yo, brRsl dec, sl1yo, k1. Do *not* turn, slide.

Wavy Treads Chart

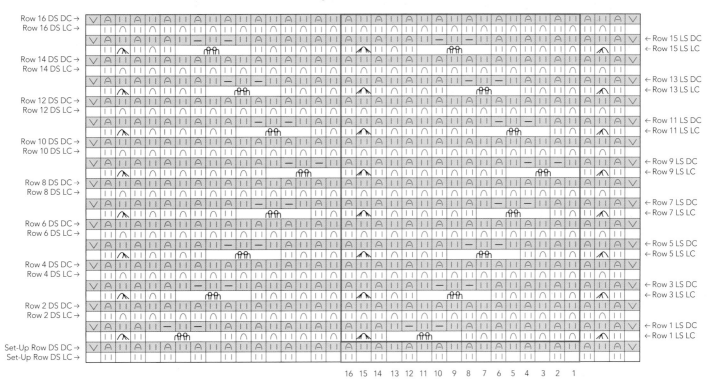

Row 16 DS DC →
Row 16 DS LC →

← Row 15 LS DC
← Row 15 LS LC

Row 14 DS DC →
Row 14 DS LC →

← Row 13 LS DC
← Row 13 LS LC

Row 12 DS DC →
Row 12 DS LC →

← Row 11 LS DC
← Row 11 LS LC

Row 10 DS DC →
Row 10 DS LC →

← Row 9 LS DC
← Row 9 LS LC

Row 8 DS DC →
Row 8 DS LC →

← Row 7 LS DC
← Row 7 LS LC

Row 6 DS DC →
Row 6 DS LC →

← Row 5 LS DC
← Row 5 LS LC

Row 4 DS DC →
Row 4 DS LC →

← Row 3 LS DC
← Row 3 LS LC

Row 2 DS DC →
Row 2 DS LC →

← Row 1 LS DC
← Row 1 LS LC

Set-Up Row DS DC →
Set-Up Row DS LC →

16 15 14 13 12 11 10 9 8 7 6 5 4 3 2 1

Row 3 LS DC: sl1, brp1, sl1yo, brp1, *[sl1yo, brp1] 3 times, [sl1yo, p1] twice, [sl1yo, brp1] 3 times; rep from * to last st, sl1. Turn.

Row 5 LS LC: k1, sl1yo, brLsl dec, sl1yo, *[brk1, sl1yo] twice, br4st inc, sl1yo, [brk1, sl1yo] twice, br4st dec, sl1yo; rep from * to last 15 sts, [brk1, sl1yo] twice, br4st inc, sl1yo, [brk1, sl1yo] twice, brRsl dec, sl1yo, k1. Do *not* turn, slide.
Row 5 LS DC: sl1, brp1, sl1yo, brp1, *[sl1yo, brp1] twice, [sl1yo, p1] twice, [sl1yo, brp1] 4 times; rep from * to last st, sl1. Turn.

Row 7 LS LC: k1, sl1yo, brLsl dec, sl1yo, *brk1, sl1yo, br4st inc, sl1yo, [brk1, sl1yo] 3 times, br4st dec, sl1yo; rep from * to last 15 sts, brk1, sl1yo, br4st inc, sl1yo, [brk1, sl1yo] 3 times, brRsl dec, sl1yo, k1. Do *not* turn, slide.
Row 7 LS DC: sl1, brp1, sl1yo, brp1, *sl1yo, brp1, [sl1yo, p1] twice, [sl1yo, brp1] 5 times; rep from * to last st, sl1. Turn.

Row 9 LS LC: k1, sl1yo, brLsl dec, sl1yo, *br4st inc, sl1yo, [brk1, sl1yo] 4 times, br4st dec, sl1yo; rep from * to last 15 sts, br4st inc, sl1yo, [brk1, sl1yo] 4 times, brRsl dec, sl1yo, k1. Do *not* turn, slide.
Row 9 LS DC: sl1, brp1, sl1yo, brp1, *[sl1yo, p1] twice, [sl1yo, brp1] 6 times; rep from * to last st, sl1. Turn.

Row 11 LS LC: as Row 7 LS LC.
Row 11 LS DC: as Row 7 LS DC.

Row 13 LS LC: as Row 5 LS LC.
Row 13 LS DC: as Row 5 LS DC.

Row 15 LS LC: as Row 3 LS LC.
Row 15 LS DC: as Row 3 LS DC.

After working last set of DS rows, rep from Row 1 LS LC. ∎

Wavy Palm Leaves

Wavy Palm Leaves Brioche Stitch
Using Two-Color Italian Cast-On, begin and end with LC knit st. Cast on a multiple of 20 sts + 25. For the sample shown, I cast on 65 sts.

Set-Up Row DS LC: p1, *sl1yo, p1; rep from * to end. Do *not* turn, slide.
Set-Up Row DS DC: sl1, *brk1, sl1yo; rep from * to last 2 sts, brk1, sl1. Turn.

Row 1 LS LC: k1, sl1yo, brLsl dec, sl1yo, *[brk1, sl1yo] 5 times, br4st inc, sl1yo, brk1, sl1yo, br4st dec, sl1yo; rep from * to last 19 sts, [brk1, sl1yo] 5 times, br4st inc, sl1yo, brk1, sl1yo, brRsl dec, sl1yo, k1. Do *not* turn, slide.
Row 1 LS DC: sl1, brp1, sl1yo, brp1, *[sl1yo, brp1] 5 times, [sl1yo, p1] twice, [sl1yo, brp1] 3 times; rep from * to last st, sl1. Turn.

Row 2 DS LC and all DS LC rows: p1, *sl1yo, brp1; rep from * to last 2 sts, sl1yo, p1. Do *not* turn, slide.
Row 2 DS DC and all DS DC rows: sl1, *brk1, sl1yo; rep from * to last 2 sts, brk1, sl1. Turn.

Rows 3, 5, 7 and 9 LS LC: as Row 1 LS LC.
Rows 3, 5, 7 and 9 LS DC: as Row 1 LC DC.

Row 11 LS LC: k1, sl1yo, brLsl dec, sl1yo, *brk1, sl1yo, br4st inc, sl1yo, [brk1, sl1yo] 5 times, br4st dec, sl1yo; rep from * to last 19 sts, brk1, sl1yo, br4st inc, sl1yo, [brk1, sl1yo] 5 times, brRsl dec, sl1yo, k1. Do *not* turn, slide.

Row 11 LS DC: sl1, brp1, sl1yo, brp1, *sl1yo, brp1, [sl1yo, p1] twice, [sl1yo, brp1] 7 times; rep from * to last st, sl1. Turn.

Rows 13, 15, 17 and 19 LS LC: as Row 11 LS LC.

Rows 13, 15, 17 and 19 LS DC: as Row 11 LC DC.

After working last set of DS rows, rep from Row 1 LS LC. ■

Wavy Palm Leaves Chart

Row 19 LS DC → · Row 19 LS LC ←
Row 17 LS DC → · Row 17 LS LC ←
Row 15 LS DC → · Row 15 LS LC ←
Row 13 LS DC → · Row 13 LS LC ←
Row 11 LS DC → · Row 11 LS LC ←
Row 9 LS DC → · Row 9 LS LC ←
Row 7 LS DC → · Row 7 LS LC ←
Row 5 LS DC → · Row 5 LS LC ←
Row 3 LS DC → · Row 3 LS LC ←
Row 1 LS DC → · Row 1 LS LC ←

Row 20 DS DC → · Row 20 DS LC →
Row 18 DS DC → · Row 18 DS LC →
Row 16 DS DC → · Row 16 DS LC →
Row 14 DS DC → · Row 14 DS LC →
Row 12 DS DC → · Row 12 DS LC →
Row 10 DS DC → · Row 10 DS LC →
Row 8 DS DC → · Row 8 DS LC →
Row 6 DS DC → · Row 6 DS LC →
Row 4 DS DC → · Row 4 DS LC →
Row 2 DS DC → · Row 2 DS LC →
Set-Up Row DS DC → · Set-Up Row DS LC →

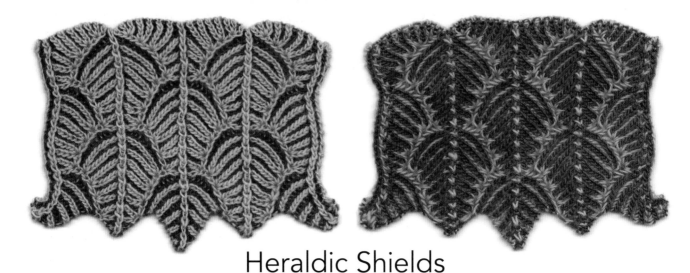

Heraldic Shields

Heraldic Shields Brioche Stitch
Using Two-Color Italian Cast-On, begin and end with LC knit st. Cast on a multiple of 32 sts + 37. For the sample shown, I cast on 69 sts.

Set-Up Row DS LC: p1, *sl1yo, p1; rep from * to end. Do *not* turn, slide.
Set-Up Row DS DC: sl1, *brk1, sl1yo; rep from * to last 2 sts, brk1, sl1. Turn.

Row 1 LS LC: k1, sl1yo, brLsl dec, sl1yo, *[brk1, sl1yo] 4 times, br4st inc, sl1yo, br4st dec, sl1yo, br4st inc, sl1yo, [brk1, sl1yo] 4 times, br4st dec, sl1yo; rep from * to last 31 sts, [brk1, sl1yo] 4 times, br4st inc, sl1yo, br4st dec, sl1yo, br4st inc, sl1yo, [brk1, sl1yo] 4 times, brRsl dec, sl1yo, k1. Do *not* turn, slide.
Row 1 LS DC: sl1, brp1, sl1yo, brp1, *[sl1yo, brp1] 4 times, [sl1yo, p1] twice, [sl1yo, brp1] twice, [sl1yo, p1] twice, [sl1yo, brp1] 6 times; rep from * to last st, sl1. Turn.

Row 2 DS LC and all DS LC rows: p1, *sl1yo, brp1; rep from * to last 2 sts, sl1yo, p1. Do *not* turn, slide.
Row 2 DS DC and all DS DC rows: sl1, *brk1, sl1yo; rep from * to last 2 sts, brk1, sl1. Turn.

Row 3 LS LC: k1, sl1yo, brLsl dec, sl1yo, *[brk1, sl1yo] 3 times, br4st inc, sl1yo, brk1, sl1yo, br4st dec, sl1yo, brk1, sl1yo, br4st inc, sl1yo, [brk1, sl1yo] 3 times, br4st dec, sl1yo; rep from * to last 31 sts, [brk1, sl1yo] 3 times, br4st inc, sl1yo, brk1, sl1yo, br4st dec, sl1yo, brk1, sl1yo, br4st inc, sl1yo, [brk1, sl1yo] 3 times, brRsl dec, sl1yo, k1. Do *not* turn, slide.
Row 3 LS DC: sl1, brp1, sl1yo, brp1, *[sl1yo, brp1] 3 times, [sl1yo, p1] twice, [sl1yo, brp1] 4 times, [sl1yo, p1] twice, [sl1yo, brp1] 5 times; rep from * to last st, sl1. Turn.

Row 5 LS LC: k1, sl1yo, brLsl dec, sl1yo, *[brk1, sl1yo] twice, br4st inc, sl1yo, [brk1, sl1yo] twice, br4st dec, sl1yo, [brk1, sl1yo] twice, br4st inc, sl1yo, [brk1, sl1yo] twice, br4st dec, sl1yo; rep from * to last 31 sts, [brk1, sl1yo] twice, br4st inc, sl1yo, [brk1, sl1yo] twice, br4st dec, sl1yo, [brk1, sl1yo] twice, br4st inc, sl1yo, [brk1, sl1yo] twice, brRsl dec, sl1yo, k1. Do *not* turn, slide.
Row 5 LS DC: sl1, brp1, sl1yo, brp1, *[sl1yo, brp1] twice, [sl1yo, p1] twice, [sl1yo, brp1] 6 times, [sl1yo, p1] twice, [sl1yo, brp1] 4 times; rep from * to last st, sl1. Turn.

Row 7 LS LC: k1, sl1yo, brLsl dec, sl1yo, *brk1, sl1yo, br4st inc, sl1yo, [brk1, sl1yo] 3 times, br4st dec, sl1yo, [brk1, sl1yo] 3 times, br4st inc, sl1yo, brk1, sl1yo, br4st dec, sl1yo; rep from * to last 31 sts, brk1, sl1yo, br4st dec, sl1yo, brk1, sl1yo, br4st inc, sl1yo, [brk1, sl1yo] 3 times, br4st dec, sl1yo; rep from * to last 31 sts, [brk1, sl1yo] 3 times, br4st inc, sl1yo, brk1, sl1yo, br4st dec, sl1yo, brk1, sl1yo, br4st inc, sl1yo, [brk1, sl1yo] 3 times, brRsl dec, sl1yo, k1. Do *not* turn, slide.
Row 3 LS DC: sl1, brp1, sl1yo, brp1, *[sl1yo, brp1] 3 times, [sl1yo, p1] twice, [sl1yo, brp1] 4 times, [sl1yo, p1] twice, [sl1yo, brp1] 5 times; rep from * to last st, sl1. Turn.

brk1, sl1yo, br4st inc, sl1yo, [brk1, sl1yo] 3 times, br4st dec, sl1yo, [brk1, sl1yo] 3 times, br4st inc, sl1yo, brk1, sl1yo, brRsl dec, sl1yo, k1. Do *not* turn, slide.
Row 7 LS DC: sl1, brp1, sl1yo, brp1, *sl1yo, brp1, [sl1yo, p1] twice, [sl1yo, brp1] 8 times, [sl1yo, p1] twice, [sl1yo, brp1] 3 times; rep from * to last st, sl1. Turn.

Row 9 LS LC: k1, sl1yo, brLsl dec, sl1yo, *br4st inc, sl1yo, [brk1, sl1yo] 4 times, br4st dec, sl1yo, [brk1, sl1yo] 4 times, br4st inc, sl1yo, br4st dec, sl1yo; rep from * to last 31 sts, br4st inc, sl1yo, [brk1, sl1yo] 4 times, br4st dec, sl1yo, [brk1, sl1yo] 4 times, br4st inc, sl1yo, brRsl dec, sl1yo, k1. Do *not* turn, slide.
Row 9 LS DC: sl1, brp1, sl1yo, brp1, *[sl1yo, p1] twice, [sl1yo, brp1] 10 times, [sl1yo, p1] twice, [sl1yo, brp1] twice; rep from * to last st, sl1. Turn.

Row 11 LS LC: as Row 7 LS LC.
Row 11 LS DC: as Row 7 LS DC.

Row 13 LS LC: as Row 5 LS LC.
Row 13 LS DC: as Row 5 LS DC.

Row 15 LS LC: as Row 3 LS LC.
Row 15 LS DC: as Row 3 LS DC.

After working last set of DS rows, rep from Row 1 LS LC. ∎

Heraldic Shields Chart: Left Side

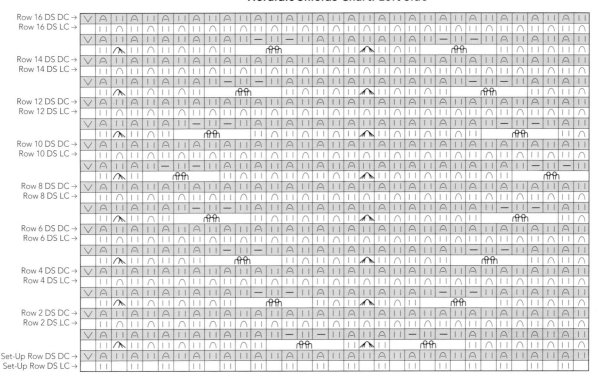

Heraldic Shields Chart: Right Side

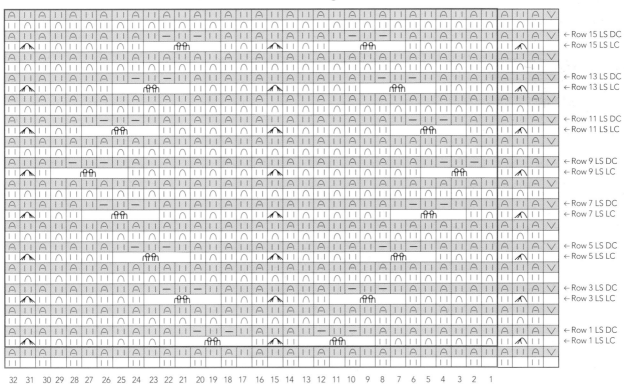

■ To more easily follow this chart, make a copy of both left and right sides.
Cut them out and tape them together to make a complete chart.

Cat's Rake

Cat's Rake Brioche Stitch

Using Two-Color Italian Cast-On, begin and end with LC knit st. Cast on a multiple of 24 sts + 3. For the sample shown, I cast on 51 sts.

Set-Up Row DS LC: p1, *sl1yo, p1; rep from * to end. Do *not* turn, slide.
Set-Up Row DS DC: sl1, *brk1, sl1yo; rep from * to last 2 sts, brk1, sl1. Turn.

Row 1 LS LC: k1, sl1yo, *brkyobrk, sl1yo, [brk1, sl1yo] 3 times, brRsl dec, sl1yo, brLsl dec, sl1yo, [brk1, sl1yo] 3 times, brkyobrk, sl1yo; rep from * to last st, k1. Do *not* turn, slide.
Row 1 LS DC: sl1, brp1, *sl1yo, p1, [sl1yo, brp1] 9 times, sl1yo, p1, sl1yo, brp1; rep from * to last st, sl1. Turn.

Row 2 DS LC and all DS LC rows: p1, *sl1yo, brp1; rep from * to last 2 sts, sl1yo, p1. Do *not* turn, slide.
Row 2 DS DC and all DS DC rows: sl1, *brk1, sl1yo; rep from * to last 2 sts, brk1, sl1. Turn.

Row 3 LS LC: k1, sl1yo, *brk1, sl1yo, brkyobrk, sl1yo, [brk1, sl1yo] twice, brRsl dec, sl1yo, brLsl dec, sl1yo, [brk1, sl1yo] twice, brkyobrk, sl1yo, brk1, sl1yo; rep from * to last st, k1. Do *not* turn, slide.
Row 3 LS DC: sl1, brp1, *sl1yo, brp1, sl1yo, p1, [sl1yo, brp1] 7 times, sl1yo, p1, [sl1yo, brp1] twice; rep from * to last st, sl1. Turn.

Cat's Rake Chart

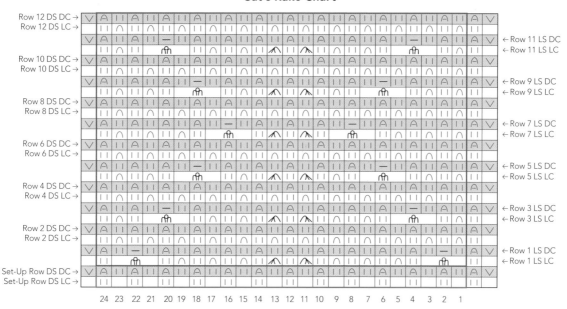

Row 12 DS DC →
Row 12 DS LC →

← Row 11 LS DC
← Row 11 LS LC

Row 10 DS DC →
Row 10 DS LC →

← Row 9 LS DC
← Row 9 LS LC

Row 8 DS DC →
Row 8 DS LC →

← Row 7 LS DC
← Row 7 LS LC

Row 6 DS DC →
Row 6 DS LC →

← Row 5 LS DC
← Row 5 LS LC

Row 4 DS DC →
Row 4 DS LC →

← Row 3 LS DC
← Row 3 LS LC

Row 2 DS DC →
Row 2 DS LC →

← Row 1 LS DC
← Row 1 LS LC

Set-Up Row DS DC →
Set-Up Row DS LC →

24 23 22 21 20 19 18 17 16 15 14 13 12 11 10 9 8 7 6 5 4 3 2 1

Row 5 LS LC: k1, sl1yo, *[brk1, sl1yo] twice, brkyobrk, sl1yo, brk1, sl1yo, brRsl dec, sl1yo, brLsl dec, sl1yo, brk1, sl1yo, brkyobrk, sl1yo, [brk1, sl1yo] twice; rep from * to last st, k1. Do *not* turn, slide.
Row 5 LS DC: sl1, brp1, *[sl1yo, brp1] twice, sl1yo, p1, [sl1yo, brp1] 5 times, sl1yo, p1, [sl1yo, brp1] 3 times; rep from * to last st, sl1. Turn.

Row 7 LS LC: k1, sl1yo, *[brk1, sl1yo] 3 times, brkyobrk, sl1yo, brRsl dec, sl1yo, brLsl dec, sl1yo, brkyobrk, sl1yo, [brk1, sl1yo] 3 times; rep from * to last st, k1. Do *not* turn, slide.
Row 7 LS DC: sl1, brp1, *[sl1yo, brp1] 3 times, sl1yo, p1, [sl1yo, brp1] 3 times, sl1yo, p1, [sl1yo, brp1] 4 times; rep from * to last st, sl1. Turn.

Row 9 LS LC: as Row 5 LS LC.
Row 9 LS DC: as Row 5 LS DC.

Row 11 LS LC: as Row 3 LS LC.
Row 11 LS DC: as Row 3 LS DC.

After working last set of DS rows, rep from Row 1 LS LC. At the end of my sample, I worked Rows 1 and 2 before binding off. ■

Waving Wheat

Waving Wheat Brioche Stitch
Using Two-Color Italian Cast-On, begin and end with LC knit st. Cast on a multiple of 26 sts + 3. For the sample shown, I cast on 55 sts.

Set-Up Row DS LC: p1, *sl1yo, p1; rep from * to end. Do *not* turn, slide.
Set-Up Row DS DC: sl1, *brk1, sl1yo; rep from * to last 2 sts, brk1, sl1. Turn.

Row 1 LS LC: k1, sl1yo, *[brk1, sl1yo] 4 times, brkyobrk, sl1yo, brk1, sl1yo, brLsl dec, sl1yo, [brk1, sl1yo] 5 times; rep from * to last st, k1. Do *not* turn, slide.
Row 1 LS DC: sl1, brp1, *[sl1yo, brp1] 4 times, sl1yo, p1, [sl1yo, brp1] 8 times; rep from * to last st, sl1. Turn.

Row 2 DS LC and all DS LC rows: p1, *sl1yo, brp1; rep from * to last 2 sts, sl1yo, p1. Do *not* turn, slide.
Row 2 DS DC and all DS DC rows: sl1, *brk1, sl1yo; rep from * to last 2 sts, brk1, sl1. Turn.

Row 3 LS LC: k1, sl1yo, *[brk1, sl1yo] 3 times, brkyobrk, sl1yo, [brk1, sl1yo] 3 times, brLsl dec, sl1yo, [brk1, sl1yo] 4 times; rep from * to last st, k1. Do *not* turn, slide.
Row 3 LS DC: sl1, brp1, *[sl1yo, brp1] 3 times, sl1yo, p1, [sl1yo, brp1] 9 times; rep from * to last st, sl1. Turn.

Row 5 LS LC: k1, sl1yo, *[brk1, sl1yo] twice, brkyobrk, sl1yo, [brk1, sl1yo] 5 times, brLsl dec, sl1yo, [brk1, sl1yo] 3 times; rep from * to last st, k1. Do *not* turn, slide.
Row 5 LS DC: sl1, brp1, *[sl1yo, brp1] twice, sl1yo, p1, [sl1yo, brp1] 10 times; rep from * to last st, sl1. Turn.

Row 7 LS LC: k1, sl1yo, *brk1, sl1yo, brkyobrk, sl1yo, [brk1, sl1yo] 7 times, brLsl dec, sl1yo, [brk1, sl1yo] twice; rep from * to last st, k1. Do *not* turn, slide.
Row 7 LS DC: sl1, brp1, *sl1yo, brp1, sl1yo, p1, [sl1yo, brp1] 11 times; rep from * to last st, sl1. Turn.

Row 9 LS LC: k1, sl1yo, *brkyobrk, sl1yo, [brk1, sl1yo] 9 times, brLsl dec, sl1yo, brk1, sl1yo; rep from * to last st, k1. Do *not* turn, slide.
Row 9 LS DC: sl1, brp1, *sl1yo, p1, [sl1yo, brp1] 12 times; rep from * to last st, sl1. Turn.

Row 11 LS LC: k1, sl1yo, *[brk1, sl1yo] 5 times, brRsl dec, sl1yo, brk1, sl1yo, brkyobrk, [brk1, sl1yo] 4 times; rep from * to last st, k1. Do *not* turn, slide.
Row 11 LS DC: sl1, brp1, *[sl1yo, brp1] 7 times, sl1yo, p1, [sl1yo, brp1] 5 times; rep from * to last st, sl1. Turn.

Row 13 LS LC: k1, sl1yo, *[brk1, sl1yo] 4 times, brRsl dec, sl1yo, [brk1, sl1yo] 3 times, brkyobrk, sl1yo, [brk1, sl1yo] 3 times; rep from * to last st, k1. Do *not* turn, slide.
Row 13 LS DC: sl1, brp1, *[sl1yo, brp1] 8 times, sl1yo, p1, [sl1yo, brp1] 4 times; rep from * to last st, sl1. Turn.

Row 15 LS LC: k1, sl1yo, *[brk1, sl1yo] 3 times, brRsl dec, sl1yo, [brk1, sl1yo] 5 times, brkyobrk, sl1yo, [brk1, sl1yo] twice; rep from * to last st, k1. Do *not* turn, slide.
Row 15 LS DC: sl1, brp1, *[sl1yo, brp1] 9 times, sl1yo, p1, [sl1yo, brp1] 3 times; rep from * to last st, sl1. Turn.

Row 17 LS LC: k1, sl1yo, *[brk1, sl1yo] twice, brRsl dec, sl1yo, [brk1, sl1yo] 7 times, brkyobrk, sl1yo, brk1, sl1yo; rep from * to last st, k1. Do *not* turn, slide.
Row 17 LS DC: sl1, brp1, *[sl1yo, brp1] 10 times, sl1yo, p1, [sl1yo, brp1] twice; rep from * to last st, sl1. Turn.

Row 19 LS LC: k1, sl1yo, *brk1, sl1yo, brRsl dec, sl1yo, [brk1, sl1yo] 9 times, brkyobrk, sl1yo; rep from * to last st, k1. Do *not* turn, slide.
Row 19 LS DC: sl1, brp1, *[sl1yo, brp1] 11 times, sl1yo, p1, sl1yo, brp1; rep from * to last st, sl1. Turn.

After working last set of DS rows, rep from Row 1 LS LC. ■

Waving Wheat Chart

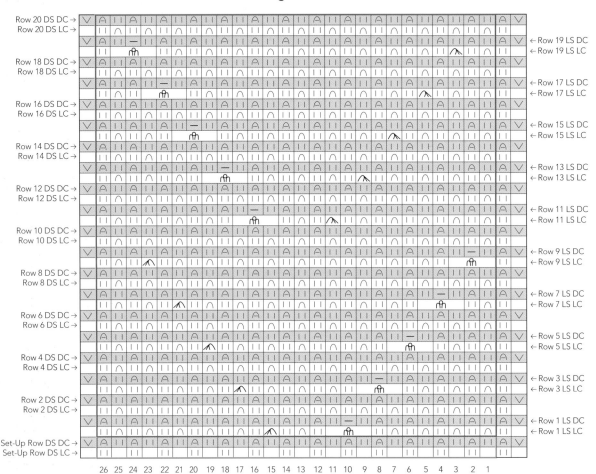

Row 20 DS DC →
Row 20 DS LC →

Row 18 DS DC →
Row 18 DS LC →

Row 16 DS DC →
Row 16 DS LC →

Row 14 DS DC →
Row 14 DS LC →

Row 12 DS DC →
Row 12 DS LC →

Row 10 DS DC →
Row 10 DS LC →

Row 8 DS DC →
Row 8 DS LC →

Row 6 DS DC →
Row 6 DS LC →

Row 4 DS DC →
Row 4 DS LC →

Row 2 DS DC →
Row 2 DS LC →

Set-Up Row DS DC →
Set-Up Row DS LC →

← Row 19 LS DC
← Row 19 LS LC

← Row 17 LS DC
← Row 17 LS LC

← Row 15 LS DC
← Row 15 LS LC

← Row 13 LS DC
← Row 13 LS LC

← Row 11 LS DC
← Row 11 LS LC

← Row 9 LS DC
← Row 9 LS LC

← Row 7 LS DC
← Row 7 LS LC

← Row 5 LS DC
← Row 5 LS LC

← Row 3 LS DC
← Row 3 LS LC

← Row 1 LS DC
← Row 1 LS LC

26 25 24 23 22 21 20 19 18 17 16 15 14 13 12 11 10 9 8 7 6 5 4 3 2 1

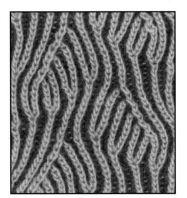

Happy Kittens

Happy Kittens

Using Two-Color Italian Cast-On, begin and end with LC knit st. Cast on a multiple of 24 sts + 29. For the sample shown, I cast on 77 sts.

Set-Up Row DS LC: p1, *sl1yo, p1; rep from * to end. Do *not* turn, slide.
Set-Up Row DS DC: sl1, *brk1, sl1yo; rep from * to last 2 sts, brk1, sl1. Turn.

Row 1 LS LC: k1, sl1yo, brk1, sl1yo, *brRsl dec, sl1yo, [brk1, sl1yo] 3 times, br4st inc, sl1yo, [brk1, sl1yo] 3 times, brLsl dec, sl1yo, brk1, sl1yo; rep from * to last st, k1. Do *not* turn, slide.
Row 1 LS DC: sl1, brp1, sl1yo, brp1, *[sl1yo, brp1] 4 times, [sl1yo, p1] twice, [sl1yo, brp1] 6 times; rep from * to last st, sl1. Turn.

Row 2 DS LC and all DS LC rows: p1, *sl1yo, brp1; rep from * to last 2 sts, sl1yo, p1. Do *not* turn, slide.
Row 2 DS DC and all DS DC rows: sl1, *brk1, sl1yo; rep from * to last 2 sts, brk1, sl1. Turn.

Row 3 LS LC: k1, sl1yo, brk1, sl1yo, *brk1, sl1yo, brRsl dec, sl1yo, [brk1, sl1yo] twice, br4st inc, sl1yo, [brk1, sl1yo] twice, brLsl dec, sl1yo, [brk1, sl1yo] twice; rep from * to last st, k1. Do *not* turn, slide.
Row 3 LS DC: as Row 1 LS DC.

Row 5 LS LC: k1, sl1yo, brk1, sl1yo, *[brk1, sl1yo] twice, brRsl dec, sl1yo, brk1, sl1yo, br4st inc, sl1yo, brk1, sl1yo, brLsl dec, sl1yo, [brk1, sl1yo] 3 times; rep from * to last st, k1. Do *not* turn, slide.
Row 5 LS DC: as Row 1 LS DC.

Row 7 LS LC: k1, sl1yo, brk1, sl1yo, *[brk1, sl1yo] 3 times, brRsl dec, sl1yo, br4st inc, sl1yo, brLsl dec, sl1yo, [brk1, sl1yo] 4 times; rep from * to last st, k1. Do *not* turn, slide.
Row 7 LS DC: as Row 1 LS DC.

Row 9 LS LC: k1, sl1yo, brkyobrk, sl1yo, [brk1, sl1yo] 3 times, brLsl dec, sl1yo, brk1, sl1yo, *brRsl dec, sl1yo, [brk1, sl1yo] 3 times, br4st inc, sl1yo, [brk1, sl1yo] 3 times, brLsl dec, sl1yo, brk1, sl1yo; rep from * to last 13 sts, brRsl dec, sl1yo, [brk1, sl1yo] 3 times, brkyobrk, sl1yo, k1. Do *not* turn, slide.
Row 9 LS DC: sl1, brp1, sl1yo, p1, [sl1yo, brp1] 6 times, *[sl1yo, brp1] 4 times, [sl1yo, p1] twice, [sl1yo, brp1] 6 times; rep from * to last 13 sts, [sl1yo, brp1] 4 times, sl1yo, p1, sl1yo, brp1, sl1. Turn.

Row 11 LS LC: k1, sl1yo, brkyobrk, sl1yo, [brk1, sl1yo] twice, brLsl dec, sl1yo, [brk1, sl1yo] twice, *brk1, sl1yo, brRsl dec, sl1yo, [brk1, sl1yo] twice, br4st inc, sl1yo, [brk1, sl1yo] twice, brLsl dec, sl1yo, [brk1, sl1yo] twice; rep from * to last 13 sts, brk1, sl1yo, brRsl dec, sl1yo, [brk1, sl1yo] twice, brkyobrk, sl1yo, k1. Do *not* turn, slide.
Row 11 LS DC: as Row 9 LS DC.

Row 13 LS LC: k1, sl1yo, brkyobrk, sl1yo, brk1, sl1yo, brLsl dec, sl1yo, [brk1, sl1yo] 3 times, *[brk1, sl1yo] twice, brRsl dec, sl1yo, brk1, sl1yo, br4st inc, sl1yo, brk1, sl1yo, brLsl dec, sl1yo, [brk1, sl1yo] 3 times; rep from * to last 13 sts, [brk1, sl1yo] twice, brRsl dec, sl1yo, brk1, sl1yo, brkyobrk, sl1yo, k1. Do *not* turn, slide.
Row 13 LS DC: as Row 9 LS DC.

Row 15 LS LC: k1, sl1yo, brkyobrk, sl1yo, brLsl dec, sl1yo, [brk1, sl1yo] 4 times, *[brk1, sl1yo] 3 times, brRsl dec, sl1yo, br4st inc, sl1yo, brLsl dec, sl1yo, [brk1, sl1yo] 4 times; rep from * to last 13 sts, [brk1, sl1yo] 3 times, brRsl dec, sl1yo, brkyobrk, sl1yo, k1. Do *not* turn, slide.
Row 15 LS DC: as Row 9 LS DC.

After working last set of DS rows, rep from Row 1 LS LC. ■

Happy Kittens Chart: Left Side

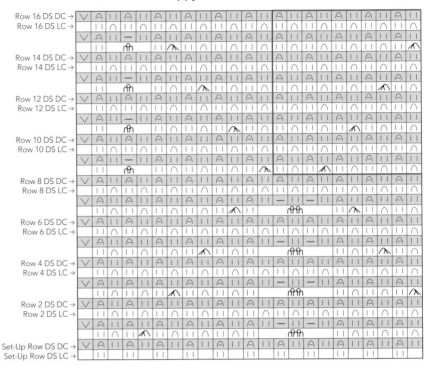

Happy Kittens Chart: Right Side

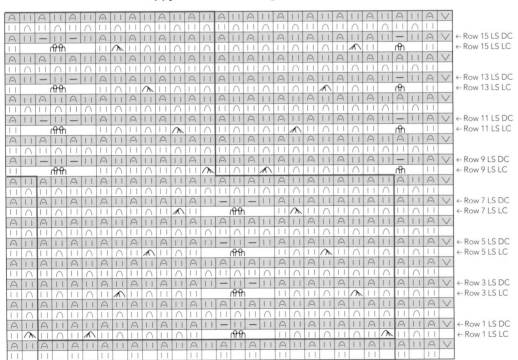

■ To more easily follow this chart, make a copy of both left and right sides. Cut them out and tape them together to make a complete chart.

Jointed Appendages
"Out"

Jointed Appendages
"In"

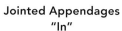

Jointed Appendages
"Out"

Jointed Appendages
"In"

Jointed Appendages "In" and Jointed Appendages "Out"

For the top half of this sample, the direction of the decrease was switched. This pattern is very similar to Dancing Arthropod Brioche Stitch (page 135).

Jointed Appendages "In" Brioche Stitch

Using Two-Color Italian Cast-On, begin and end with LC knit st. Cast on a multiple of 18 sts + 3. For the sample shown, I cast on 39 sts.

Set-Up Row DS LC: p1, *sl1yo, p1; rep from * to end. Do *not* turn, slide.
Set-Up Row DS DC: sl1, *brk1, sl1yo; rep from * to last 2 sts, brk1, sl1. Turn.

Row 1 LS LC: k1, sl1yo, *brLsl dec, sl1yo, [brk1, sl1yo] twice, br4st inc, sl1yo, [brk1, sl1yo] twice, brRsl dec, sl1yo; rep from * to last st, k1. Do *not* turn, slide.
Row 1 LS DC: sl1, brp1, *[sl1yo, brp1] 3 times, [sl1yo, p1] twice, [sl1yo, brp1] 4 times; rep from * to last st, sl1. Turn.

Row 2 DS LC and all DS LC rows: p1, *sl1yo, brp1; rep from * to last 2 sts, sl1yo, p1. Do *not* turn, slide.
Row 2 DS DC and all DS DC rows: sl1, *brk1, sl1yo; rep from * to last 2 sts, brk1, sl1. Turn.

Jointed Appendages "In" Chart

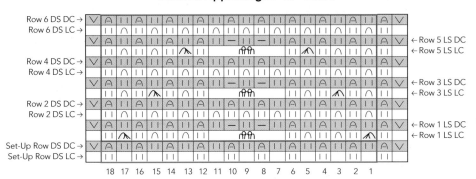

Row 6 DS DC →
Row 6 DS LC →
← Row 5 LS DC
← Row 5 LS LC
Row 4 DS DC →
Row 4 DS LC →
← Row 3 LS DC
← Row 3 LS LC
Row 2 DS DC →
Row 2 DS LC →
← Row 1 LS DC
← Row 1 LS LC
Set-Up Row DS DC →
Set-Up Row DS LC →

18 17 16 15 14 13 12 11 10 9 8 7 6 5 4 3 2 1

Row 3 LS LC: k1, sl1yo, *brk1, sl1yo, brLsl dec, sl1yo, brk1, sl1yo, br4st inc, sl1yo, brk1, sl1yo, brRsl dec, sl1yo, brk1, sl1yo; rep from * to last st, k1. Do *not* turn, slide.
Row 3 LS DC: as Row 1 LS DC.

Row 5 LS LC: k1, sl1yo, *[brk1, sl1yo] twice, brLsl dec, sl1yo, br4st inc, sl1yo, brRsl dec, sl1yo, [brk1, sl1yo] twice; rep from * to last st, k1. Do *not* turn, slide.
Row 5 LS DC: as Row 1 LS DC.

After working last set of DS rows, rep from Row 1 LS LC. ∎

Jointed Appendages "Out"
Brioche Stitch

Using Two-Color Italian Cast-On, begin and end with LC knit st. Cast on a multiple of 18 sts + 3. For the sample shown, I cast on 39 sts.

Set-Up Row DS LC: p1, *sl1yo, p1; rep from * to end. Do *not* turn, slide.
Set-Up Row DS DC: sl1, *brk1, sl1yo; rep from * to last 2 sts, brk1, sl1. Turn.

Row 1 LS LC: k1, sl1yo, *brRsl dec, sl1yo, [brk1, sl1yo] twice, br4st inc, sl1yo, [brk1, sl1yo] twice, brLsl dec, sl1yo; rep from * to last st, k1. Do *not* turn, slide.
Row 1 LS DC: sl1, brp1, *[sl1yo, brp1] 3 times, [sl1yo, p1] twice, [sl1yo, brp1] 4 times; rep from * to last st, sl1. Turn.

Row 2 DS LC and all DS LC rows: p1, *sl1yo, brp1; rep from * to last 2 sts, sl1yo, p1. Do *not* turn, slide.
Row 2 DS DC and all DS DC rows: sl1, *brk1, sl1yo; rep from * to last 2 sts, brk1, sl1. Turn.

Row 3 LS LC: k1, sl1yo, *brk1, sl1yo, brRsl dec, sl1yo, brk1, sl1yo, br4st inc, sl1yo, brk1, sl1yo, brLsl dec, sl1yo, brk1, sl1yo; rep from * to last st, k1. Do *not* turn, slide.
Row 3 LS DC: as Row 1 LS DC.

Row 5 LS LC: k1, sl1yo, *[brk1, sl1yo] twice, brRsl dec, sl1yo, br4st inc, sl1yo, brLsl dec, sl1yo, [brk1, sl1yo] twice; rep from * to last st, k1. Do *not* turn, slide.
Row 5 LS DC: as Row 1 LS DC.

After working last set of DS rows, rep from Row 1 LS LC. ∎

Jointed Appendages "Out" Chart

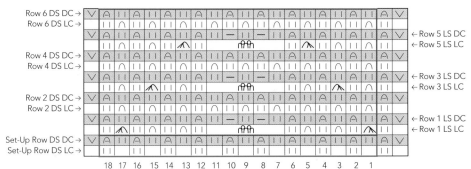

Row 6 DS DC →
Row 6 DS LC →
← Row 5 LS DC
← Row 5 LS LC
Row 4 DS DC →
Row 4 DS LC →
← Row 3 LS DC
← Row 3 LS LC
Row 2 DS DC →
Row 2 DS LC →
← Row 1 LS DC
← Row 1 LS LC
Set-Up Row DS DC →
Set-Up Row DS LC →

18 17 16 15 14 13 12 11 10 9 8 7 6 5 4 3 2 1

Dancing Arthropod

Dancing Arthropod Brioche Stitch
Using Two-Color Italian Cast-On, begin and end with LC knit st. Cast on a multiple of 22 sts + 3. For the sample shown, I cast on 47 sts.

Set-Up Row DS LC: p1, *sl1yo, p1; rep from * to end. Do *not* turn, slide.
Set-Up Row DS DC: sl1, *brk1, sl1yo; rep from * to last 2 sts, brk1, sl1. Turn.

Row 1 LS LC: k1, sl1yo, *brRsl dec, sl1yo, [brk1, sl1yo] 3 times, br4st inc, sl1yo, [brk1, sl1yo] 3 times, brLsl dec, sl1yo; rep from * to last st, k1. Do *not* turn, slide.
Row 1 LS DC: sl1, brp1, *[sl1yo, brp1] 4 times, [sl1yo, p1] twice, [sl1yo, brp1] 5 times; rep from * to last st, sl1. Turn.

Row 2 DS LC and all DS LC rows: p1, *sl1yo, brp1; rep from * to last 2 sts, sl1yo, p1. Do *not* turn, slide.
Row 2 DS DC and all DS DC rows: sl1, *brk1, sl1yo; rep from * to last 2 sts, brk1, sl1. Turn.

Row 3 LS LC: as Row 1 LS LC.
Row 3 LS DC: as Row 1 LS DC.

Row 5 LS LC: k1, sl1yo, *brk1, sl1yo, brRsl dec, sl1yo, [brk1, sl1yo] twice, br4st inc, sl1yo, [brk1, sl1yo] twice, brLsl dec, sl1yo, brk1, sl1yo; rep from * to last st, k1. Do *not* turn, slide.
Row 5 LS DC: as Row 1 LS DC.

Dancing Arthropod Chart

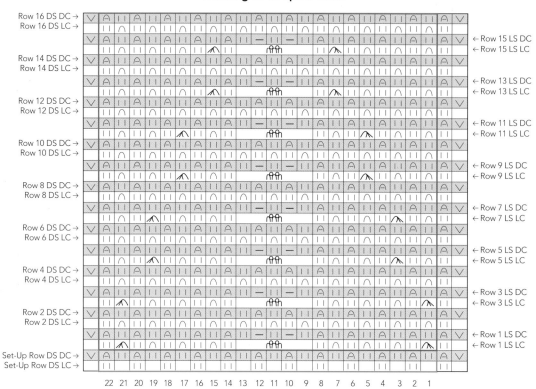

Row 16 DS DC →
Row 16 DS LC →
Row 14 DS DC →
Row 14 DS LC →
Row 12 DS DC →
Row 12 DS LC →
Row 10 DS DC →
Row 10 DS LC →
Row 8 DS DC →
Row 8 DS LC →
Row 6 DS DC →
Row 6 DS LC →
Row 4 DS DC →
Row 4 DS LC →
Row 2 DS DC →
Row 2 DS LC →
Set-Up Row DS DC →
Set-Up Row DS LC →

← Row 15 LS DC
← Row 15 LS LC
← Row 13 LS DC
← Row 13 LS LC
← Row 11 LS DC
← Row 11 LS LC
← Row 9 LS DC
← Row 9 LS LC
← Row 7 LS DC
← Row 7 LS LC
← Row 5 LS DC
← Row 5 LS LC
← Row 3 LS DC
← Row 3 LS LC
← Row 1 LS DC
← Row 1 LS LC

22 21 20 19 18 17 16 15 14 13 12 11 10 9 8 7 6 5 4 3 2 1

Row 7 LS LC: as Row 5 LS LC.
Row 7 LS DC: as Row 1 LS DC.

Row 9 LS LC: k1, sl1yo, *[brk1, sl1yo] twice, brRsl dec, sl1yo, brk1, sl1yo, br4st inc, sl1yo, brk1, sl1yo, brLsl dec, sl1yo, [brk1, sl1yo] twice; rep from * to last st, k1. Do *not* turn, slide.
Row 9 LS DC: as Row 1 LS DC.

Row 11 LS LC: as Row 9 LS LC.
Row 11 LS DC: as Row 1 LS DC.

Row 13 LS LC: k1, sl1yo, *[brk1, sl1yo] 3 times, brRsl dec, sl1yo, br4st inc, sl1yo, brLsl dec, sl1yo, [brk1, sl1yo] 3 times; rep from * to last st, k1. Do *not* turn, slide.
Row 13 LS DC: as Row 1 LS DC.

Row 15 LS LC: as Row 13 LS LC.
Row 15 LS DC: as Row 1 LS DC.

After working last set of DS rows, rep from Row 1 LS LC. ■

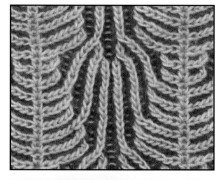

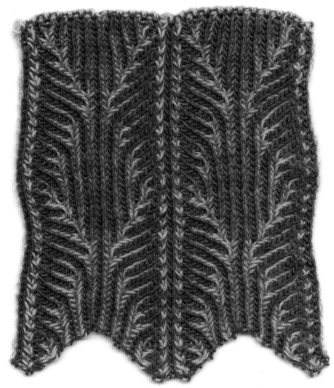

Pier Glass

Pier Glass Brioche Stitch
Using Two-Color Italian Cast-On, begin and end with LC knit st. Cast on a multiple of 24 sts + 3. For the sample shown, I cast on 51 sts.

Set-Up Row DS LC: p1, *sl1yo, p1; rep from * to end. Do *not* turn, slide.
Set-Up Row DS DC: sl1, *brk1, sl1yo; rep from * to last 2 sts, brk1, sl1. Turn.

Row 1 LS LC: k1, sl1yo, *brRsl dec, sl1yo, brkyobrk, sl1yo, [brk1, sl1yo] 6 times, brkyobrk, sl1yo, brLsl dec, sl1yo; rep from * to last st, k1. Do *not* turn, slide.
Row 1 LS DC: sl1, brp1, *sl1yo, brp1, sl1yo, p1, [sl1yo, brp1] 7 times, sl1yo, p1, [sl1yo, brp1] twice; rep from * to last st, sl1. Turn.

Row 2 DS LC and all DS LC rows: p1, *sl1yo, brp1; rep from * to last 2 sts, sl1yo, p1. Do *not* turn, slide.
Row 2 DS DC and all DS DC rows: sl1, *brk1, sl1yo; rep from * to last 2 sts, brk1, sl1. Turn.

Row 3 LS LC: as Row 1 LS LC.
Row 3 LS DC: as Row 1 LS DC.

Row 5 LS LC: k1, sl1yo, *brRsl dec, sl1yo, brk1, sl1yo, brkyobrk, sl1yo, [brk1, sl1yo] 4 times, brkyobrk, sl1yo, brk1, sl1yo, brLsl dec, sl1yo; rep from * to last st, k1. Do *not* turn, slide.
Row 5 LS DC: sl1, brp1, *[sl1yo, brp1] twice, sl1yo, p1, [sl1yo, brp1] 5 times, sl1yo, p1, [sl1yo, brp1] 3 times; rep from * to last st, sl1. Turn.

Row 7 LS LC: as Row 5 LS LC.
Row 7 LS DC: as Row 5 LS DC.

Row 9 LS LC: k1, sl1yo, *brRsl dec, sl1yo, [brk1, sl1yo] twice, brkyobrk, sl1yo, [brk1, sl1yo] twice, brkyobrk, sl1yo, [brk1, sl1yo] twice, brLsl dec, sl1yo; rep from * to last st, k1. Do *not* turn, slide.
Row 9 LS DC: sl1, brp1, *[sl1yo, brp1] 3 times, sl1yo, p1, [sl1yo, brp1] 3 times, sl1yo, p1, [sl1yo, brp1] 4 times; rep from * to last st, sl1. Turn.

Row 11 LS LC: as Row 9 LS LC.
Row 11 LS DC: as Row 9 LS DC.

Pier Glass Chart

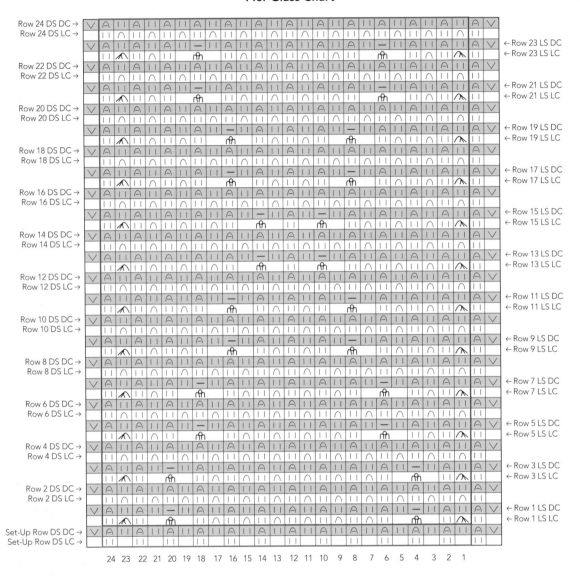

Row 24 DS DC →
Row 24 DS LC →
Row 22 DS DC →
Row 22 DS LC →
Row 20 DS DC →
Row 20 DS LC →
Row 18 DS DC →
Row 18 DS LC →
Row 16 DS DC →
Row 16 DS LC →
Row 14 DS DC →
Row 14 DS LC →
Row 12 DS DC →
Row 12 DS LC →
Row 10 DS DC →
Row 10 DS LC →
Row 8 DS DC →
Row 8 DS LC →
Row 6 DS DC →
Row 6 DS LC →
Row 4 DS DC →
Row 4 DS LC →
Row 2 DS DC →
Row 2 DS LC →
Set-Up Row DS DC →
Set-Up Row DS LC →

← Row 23 LS DC
← Row 23 LS LC
← Row 21 LS DC
← Row 21 LS LC
← Row 19 LS DC
← Row 19 LS LC
← Row 17 LS DC
← Row 17 LS LC
← Row 15 LS DC
← Row 15 LS LC
← Row 13 LS DC
← Row 13 LS LC
← Row 11 LS DC
← Row 11 LS LC
← Row 9 LS DC
← Row 9 LS LC
← Row 7 LS DC
← Row 7 LS LC
← Row 5 LS DC
← Row 5 LS LC
← Row 3 LS DC
← Row 3 LS LC
← Row 1 LS DC
← Row 1 LS LC

24 23 22 21 20 19 18 17 16 15 14 13 12 11 10 9 8 7 6 5 4 3 2 1

Row 13 LS LC: k1, sl1yo, *brRsl dec, sl1yo, [brk1, sl1yo] 3 times, brkyobrk, sl1yo, brkyobrk, sl1yo, [brk1, sl1yo] 3 times, brLsl dec, sl1yo; rep from * to last st, k1. Do *not* turn, slide.
Row 13 LS DC: sl1, brp1, *[sl1yo, brp1] 4 times, sl1yo, p1, sl1yo, brp1, sl1yo, p1, [sl1yo, brp1] 5 times; rep from * to last st, sl1. Turn.

Row 15 LS LC: as Row 13 LS LC.
Row 15 LS DC: as Row 13 LS DC.

Row 17 LS LC: as Row 9 LS LC.
Row 17 LS DC: as Row 9 LS DC.

Row 19 LS LC: as Row 9 LS LC.
Row 19 LS DC: as Row 9 LS DC.

Row 21 LS LC: as Row 5 LS LC.
Row 21 LS DC: as Row 5 LS DC.

Row 23 LS LC: as Row 5 LS LC.
Row 23 LS DC: as Row 5 LS DC.

After working last set of DS rows, rep from Row 1 LS LC. ∎

Sound Waves

Sound Waves Brioche Stitch
Using Two-Color Italian Cast-On, begin and end with LC knit st. Cast on a multiple of 24 sts + 3. For the sample shown, I cast on 51 sts.

Set-Up Row DS LC: p1, *sl1yo, p1; rep from * to end. Do *not* turn, slide.
Set-Up Row DS DC: sl1, *brk1, sl1yo; rep from * to last 2 sts, brk1, sl1. Turn.

Row 1 LS LC: k1, sl1yo, *brRsl dec, sl1yo, [brk1, sl1yo] 3 times, [brkyobrk, sl1yo] twice, [brk1, sl1yo] 3 times, brLsl dec, sl1yo; rep from * to last st, k1. Do *not* turn, slide.
Row 1 LS DC: sl1, brp1, *[sl1yo, brp1] 4 times, sl1yo, p1, sl1yo, brp1, sl1yo, p1, [sl1yo, brp1] 5 times; rep from * to last st, sl1. Turn.

Row 2 DS LC and all DS LC rows: p1, *sl1yo, brp1; rep from * to last 2 sts, sl1yo, p1. Do *not* turn, slide.
Row 2 DS DC and all DS DC rows: sl1, *brk1, sl1yo; rep from * to last 2 sts, brk1, sl1. Turn.

Rows 3, 5, 7 and 9 LS LC: as Row 1 LS LC.
Rows 3, 5, 7 and 9 LS DC: as Row 1 LC DC.

Row 11 LS LC: k1, sl1yo, *brk1, sl1yo; rep from * to last st, k1. Do *not* turn, slide.
Row 11 LS DC: sl1, brp1, *sl1yo, brp1; rep from * to last st, sl1. Turn.

Row 13 LS LC: k1, sl1yo, *brkyobrk, sl1yo, [brk1, sl1yo] 3 times, brLsl dec, sl1yo, brRsl dec, sl1yo, [brk1, sl1yo] 3 times, brkyobrk, sl1yo; rep from * to last st, k1. Do *not* turn, slide.
Row 13 LS DC: sl1, brp1, *sl1yo, p1, [sl1yo, brp1] 9 times, sl1yo, p1, sl1yo, brp1; rep from * to last st, sl1. Turn.

Sound Waves Chart

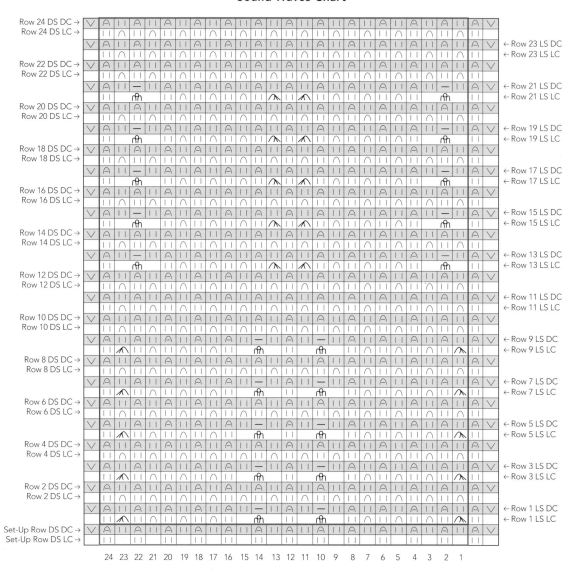

Row 24 DS DC →
Row 24 DS LC →
Row 22 DS DC →
Row 22 DS LC →
Row 20 DS DC →
Row 20 DS LC →
Row 18 DS DC →
Row 18 DS LC →
Row 16 DS DC →
Row 16 DS LC →
Row 14 DS DC →
Row 14 DS LC →
Row 12 DS DC →
Row 12 DS LC →
Row 10 DS DC →
Row 10 DS LC →
Row 8 DS DC →
Row 8 DS LC →
Row 6 DS DC →
Row 6 DS LC →
Row 4 DS DC →
Row 4 DS LC →
Row 2 DS DC →
Row 2 DS LC →
Set-Up Row DS DC →
Set-Up Row DS LC →

← Row 23 LS DC
← Row 23 LS LC
← Row 21 LS DC
← Row 21 LS LC
← Row 19 LS DC
← Row 19 LS LC
← Row 17 LS DC
← Row 17 LS LC
← Row 15 LS DC
← Row 15 LS LC
← Row 13 LS DC
← Row 13 LS LC
← Row 11 LS DC
← Row 11 LS LC
← Row 9 LS DC
← Row 9 LS LC
← Row 7 LS DC
← Row 7 LS LC
← Row 5 LS DC
← Row 5 LS LC
← Row 3 LS DC
← Row 3 LS LC
← Row 1 LS DC
← Row 1 LS LC

24 23 22 21 20 19 18 17 16 15 14 13 12 11 10 9 8 7 6 5 4 3 2 1

Rows 15, 17, 19 and 21 LS LC: as Row 13 LS LC.
Rows 15, 17, 19 and 21 LS DC: as Row 13 LC DC.

Row 23 LS LC: as Row 11 LS LC.
Row 23 LS DC: as Row 11 LC DC.

After working last set of DS rows, rep from Row 1 LS LC. ∎

Exceptions

In the following group of stitch patterns, you'll find exceptions to the standards used in the previous group. For example, for the Reversed Long Leaf Brioche Stitch (page 142), I made the dark color—not the light—the dominant color and side.

The Bart & Francis Compressed Brioche Stitch (page 144) has increases and decreases in *every* light-color row, thus compressing the pattern and giving it a beautifully intricate look.

For several stitch patterns, such as Leafy Lacy III (page 146) and Pine Trees (page 148), I worked the increases in the LS LC row and the decreases, which would be brpRsl or brpLsl decreases, in the LS DC row. This causes the light-color column to stop in its tracks, rather than merging with another column. Of course, on the dark side, the dark-colored columns that were used in the increase do merge.

Another exception is displayed in the Hook, Line and Sinker Brioche Stitch (page 161). Increases and decreases were worked in a LS LC row, then, later on, the increases and decreases were worked in a DS DC row.

A reminder: brioche chart symbols should be viewed as if you're looking at the light side of the work. Please take note that the symbols for decreases made in DS DC rows are slanted in the *opposite* direction from the way the decrease will be made on the dark side. For example, the brLsl dec symbol ⟁ slants to the *right*, which is the way it appears, when finished, on the light side of the work. On the dark side, it is worked as a *left*-slant decrease. Several stitch patterns have an increase worked in a LS LC row with its complementary decrease worked in a DS DC row.

This section ends with the Syncopated Wavy Palm Leaves Brioche Stitch (page 159). Syncopated brioche is one of my favorite techniques, since switching the light and dark columns can create so many new and interesting stitch patterns. I hope you are as inspired by it as I've been.

DS AND LS ARE REVERSED

Reversed Long Leaf

For this little pattern, I switched the dark side and the light side so that each set of rows begins with the dark color, and the dark side is dominant.

Reversed Long Leaf Brioche Stitch
Using Two-Color Italian Cast-On, begin and end with DC knit st. Cast on a multiple of 12 sts + 3. For the sample shown, I cast on 39 sts.

Set-Up Row LS DC: p1, *sl1yo, p1; rep from * to end. Do *not* turn, slide.
Set-Up Row LS LC: sl1, *brk1, sl1yo; rep from * to last 2 sts, brk1, drop LC to back, sl1. Turn.

Row 1 DS DC: k1, sl1yo, *brRsl dec, sl1yo, brk1, sl1yo, brkyobrk, sl1yo, [brk1, sl1yo] twice; rep from * to last st, k1. Do *not* turn, slide.
Row 1 DS LC: sl1, brp1, *[sl1yo, brp1] twice, sl1yo, p1, [sl1yo, brp1] 3 times; rep from * to last st, drop LC to front, sl1. Turn.

Row 2 LS DC and all LS DC rows: p1, *sl1yo, brp1; rep from * to last 2 sts, sl1yo, p1. Do *not* turn, slide.
Row 2 LS LC and all LS LC rows: sl1, *brk1, sl1yo; rep from * to last 2 sts, brk1, sl1. Turn.

Row 3 DS DC: as Row 1 DS DC.
Row 3 DS LC: as Row 1 DS LC.

Row 5 DS DC: as Row 1 DS DC.
Row 5 DS LC: as Row 1 DS LC.

Row 7 DS DC: k1, sl1yo, * [brk1, sl1yo] twice, brkyobrk, sl1yo, brk1, sl1yo, brLsl dec, sl1yo ; rep from * to last st, k1. Do *not* turn, slide.

Row 7 DS LC: sl1, brp1, *[sl1yo, brp1] twice, sl1yo, p1, [sl1yo, brp1] 3 times; rep from * to last st, drop LC to front, sl1. Turn.

Row 9 DS DC: as Row 7 DS DC.
Row 9 DS LC: as Row 7 DS LC.

Row 11 DS DC: as Row 7 DS DC.
Row 11 DS LC: as Row 7 DS LC.

After working last set of DS rows, rep from Row 1 DS DC. ■

Reversed Long Leaf Chart

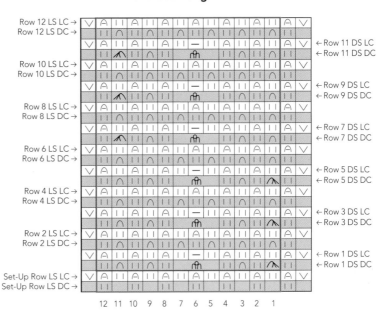

LEGEND for **Reversed Long Leaf Brioche Stitch**

☐ = knit on **DS** rows, purl on **LS** rows

─ = purl on **DS** rows, knit on **LS** rows

∨ = slip stitch purlwise

∩ = brk on **DS** rows, brp on **LS** rows

A = brp on **DS** rows, brk on **LS** rows

‖ = sl1yo

♏ = brkyobrk on **DS DC** rows

⋀ = brRsl dec on **DS DC** rows

⋀ = brLsl dec on **DS DC** rows

INCS WORKED IN LS LC AND DS LC ROWS
DECS WORKED IN LS LC AND DS LC ROWS

Bart & Francis Compressed

This beautiful variation was created by working an increase and a decrease in every LC row, including those on the dark side, compressing the motif. This is one of those stitches that will prompt people to ask: "How did you knit that?" I suggest placing a marker between repeats.

This stitch uses the following unusual manipulations (see Terminology on pages 12–13): brpyobrp, brpLsl dec, and brpRsl dec.

Bart & Francis Compressed Brioche Stitch

Using Two-Color Italian Cast-On, begin and end with LC knit st. Cast on a multiple of 16 sts + 9. For the sample shown, I cast on 57 sts.

Set-Up Row DS LC: p1, *sl1yo, p1; rep from * to end. Do *not* turn, slide.
Set-Up Row DS DC: sl1, *brk1, sl1yo; rep from * to last 2 sts, brk1, sl1. Turn.

Row 1 LS LC: k1, sl1yo, [brk1, sl1yo] 3 times, *brRsl dec, sl1yo, [brk1, sl1yo] 5 times, brkyobrk, sl1yo; rep from * to last st, k1. Do *not* turn, slide.
Row 1 LS DC: sl1, brp1, [sl1yo, brp1] 3 times, *[sl1yo, brp1] 6 times, sl1yo, p1, sl1yo, brp1; rep from * to last st, sl1. Turn.

Row 2 DS LC: p1, *sl1yo, brp1, sl1yo, brpyobrp, sl1yo, [brp1, sl1yo] 4 times, brpLsl dec; rep from * to last 8 sts, [sl1yo, brp1] 3 times, sl1yo, p1. Do *not* turn, slide.

Row 2 DS DC: sl1, *[brk1, sl1yo] twice, k1, sl1yo, [brk1, sl1yo] 5 times; rep from * to last 8 sts, [brk1, sl1yo] 3 times, brk1, sl1. Turn.

Row 3 LS LC: k1, sl1yo, [brk1, sl1yo] 3 times, *brRsl dec, sl1yo, [brk1, sl1yo] 3 times, brkyobrk, sl1yo, [brk1, sl1yo] twice; rep from * to last st, k1. Do *not* turn, slide.
Row 3 LS DC: sl1, brp1, [sl1yo, brp1] 3 times, *[sl1yo, brp1] 4 times, sl1yo, p1, [sl1yo, brp1] 3 times; rep from * to last st, sl1. Turn.

Row 4 DS LC: p1, *sl1yo, [brp1, sl1yo] 3 times, brpyobrp, sl1yo, [brp1, sl1yo] twice, brpLsl dec; rep from * to last 8 sts, [sl1yo, brp1] 3 times, sl1yo, p1. Do *not* turn, slide.
Row 4 DS DC: sl1, *[brk1, sl1yo] 4 times, k1, sl1yo, [brk1, sl1yo] 3 times; rep from * to last 8 sts, [brk1, sl1yo] 3 times, brk1, sl1. Turn.

Row 5 LS LC: k1, sl1yo, [brk1, sl1yo] 3 times, *brRsl dec, sl1yo, brk1, sl1yo, brkyobrk, sl1yo, [brk1, sl1yo] 4 times; rep from * to last st, k1. Do *not* turn, slide.
Row 5 LS DC: sl1, brp1, [sl1yo, brp1] 3 times, *[sl1yo, brp1] twice, sl1yo, p1, [sl1yo, brp1] 5 times; rep from * to last st, sl1. Turn.

Row 6 DS LC: p1, *sl1yo, [brp1, sl1yo] 5 times, brpyobrp, sl1yo, brpLsl dec; rep from * to last 8 sts, [sl1yo, brp1] 3 times, sl1yo, p1. Do *not* turn, slide.
Row 6 DS DC: sl1, *[brk1, sl1yo] 6 times, k1, sl1yo, brk1, sl1yo; rep from * to last 8 sts, [brk1, sl1yo] 3 times, brk1, sl1. Turn.

Row 7 LS LC: k1, sl1yo, *brkyobrk, sl1yo, [brk1, sl1yo] 5 times, brLsl dec, sl1yo; rep from * to last 7 sts, [brk1, sl1yo] 3 times, k1. Do *not* turn, slide.

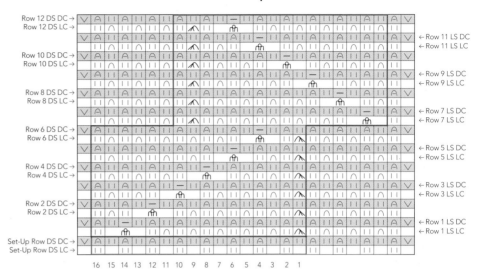

Bart & Francis Compressed Chart

Row 12 DS DC →
Row 12 DS LC →
← Row 11 LS DC
← Row 11 LS LC
Row 10 DS DC →
Row 10 DS LC →
← Row 9 LS DC
← Row 9 LS LC
Row 8 DS DC →
Row 8 DS LC →
← Row 7 LS DC
← Row 7 LS LC
Row 6 DS DC →
Row 6 DS LC →
← Row 5 LS DC
← Row 5 LS LC
← Row 3 LS DC
← Row 3 LS LC
Row 2 DS DC →
Row 2 DS LC →
← Row 1 LS DC
← Row 1 LS LC
Set-Up Row DS DC →
Set-Up Row DS LC →

16 15 14 13 12 11 10 9 8 7 6 5 4 3 2 1

Row 7 LS DC: sl1, brp1, *sl1yo, p1, [sl1yo, brp1] 7 times; rep from * to last 7 sts, [sl1yo, brp1] 3 times, sl1. Turn.

Row 8 DS LC: p1, [sl1yo, brp1] 3 times, *sl1yo, brpRsl dec, sl1yo, [brp1, sl1yo] 4 times, brpyobrp, sl1yo, brp1; rep from * to last 2 sts, sl1yo, p1. Do *not* turn, slide.
Row 8 DS DC: sl1, [brk1, sl1yo] 3 times, *[brk1, sl1yo] 6 times, k1, sl1yo, brk1, sl1yo; rep from * to last 2 sts, brk1, sl1. Turn.

Row 9 LS LC: k1, sl1yo, *[brk1, sl1yo] twice, brkyobrk, sl1yo, [brk1, sl1yo] 3 times, brLsl dec, sl1yo; rep from * to last 7 sts, [brk1, sl1yo] 3 times, k1. Do *not* turn, slide.
Row 9 LS DC: sl1, brp1, *[sl1yo, brp1] twice, sl1yo, p1, [sl1yo, brp1] 5 times; rep from * to last 7 sts, [sl1yo, brp1] 3 times, sl1. Turn.

Row 10 DS LC: p1, [sl1yo, brp1] 3 times, *sl1yo, brpRsl dec, sl1yo, [brp1, sl1yo] twice, brpyobrp, [sl1yo, brp1] 3 times; rep from * to last 2 sts, sl1yo, p1. Do *not* turn, slide.

Row 10 DS DC: sl1, [brk1, sl1yo] 3 times, *[brk1, sl1yo] 4 times, k1, sl1yo, [brk1, sl1yo] 3 times; rep from * to last 2 sts, brk1, sl1. Turn.

Row 11 LS LC: k1, sl1yo, *[brk1, sl1yo] 4 times, brkyobrk, sl1yo, brk1, sl1yo, brLsl dec, sl1yo; rep from * to last 7 sts, [brk1, sl1yo] 3 times, k1. Do *not* turn, slide.
Row 11 LS DC: sl1, brp1, *[sl1yo, brp1] 4 times, sl1yo, p1, [sl1yo, brp1] 3 times; rep from * to last 7 sts, [sl1yo, brp1] 3 times, sl1. Turn.

Row 12 DS LC: p1, [sl1yo, brp1] 3 times, *sl1yo, brpRsl dec, sl1yo, brpyobrp, [sl1yo, brp1] 5 times; rep from * to last 2 sts, sl1yo, p1. Do *not* turn, slide.
Row 12 DS DC: sl1, [brk1, sl1yo] 3 times, *[brk1, sl1yo] twice, k1, sl1yo, [brk1, sl1yo] 5 times; rep from * to last 2 sts, brk1, sl1. Turn.

Rep from Row 1 LS LC. ∎

INCS WORKED IN LS LC ROW
DECS WORKED IN LS DC ROW

Leafy Lacy III

For this variation, the increases were worked in the LS LC rows and the decreases were worked in the LS DC rows. (See pages 76–77 for Leafy Lacy I and Leafy Lacy II.)

Leafy Lacy III Brioche Stitch

Using Two-Color Italian Cast-On, begin and end with LC knit st. Cast on a multiple of 18 sts + 3. For the sample shown, I cast on 57 sts.

Set-Up Row DS LC: p1, *sl1yo, p1; rep from * to end. Do *not* turn, slide.
Set-Up Row DS DC: sl1, *brk1, sl1yo; rep from * to last 2 sts, brk1, sl1. Turn.

Row 1 LS LC: k1, sl1yo, *[brk1, sl1yo] 4 times, br4st inc, sl1yo, [brk1, sl1yo] 4 times; rep from * to last st, k1. Do *not* turn, slide.
Row 1 LS DC: sl1, brp1, *[sl1yo, brp1] twice, sl1yo, brpRsl dec, [sl1yo, p1] twice, sl1yo, brpLsl dec, [sl1yo, brp1] 3 times; rep from * to last st, sl1. Turn.

Row 2 DS LC and all DS LC rows: p1, *sl1yo, brp1; rep from * to last 2 sts, sl1yo, p1. Do *not* turn, slide.
Row 2 DS DC and all DS DC rows: sl1, *brk1, sl1yo; rep from * to last 2 sts, brk1, sl1. Turn.

Row 3 LS LC: k1, sl1yo, *[brk1, sl1yo] 3 times, brkyobrk, sl1yo, brk1, sl1yo, brkyobrk, sl1yo, [brk1, sl1yo] 3 times; rep from * to last st, k1. Do *not* turn, slide.

Row 3 LS DC: sl1, brp1, *sl1yo, brp1, sl1yo, brpRsl dec, sl1yo, p1, [sl1yo, brp1] twice, sl1yo, p1, sl1yo, brpLsl dec, [sl1yo, brp1] twice; rep from * to last st, sl1. Turn.

Row 5 LS LC: k1, sl1yo, *[brk1, sl1yo] twice, brkyobrk, sl1yo, [brk1, sl1yo] 3 times, brkyobrk, sl1yo, [brk1, sl1yo] twice; rep from * to last st, k1. Do *not* turn, slide.
Row 5 LS DC: sl1, brp1, *sl1yo, brpRsl dec, sl1yo, p1, [sl1yo, brp1] 4 times, sl1yo, p1, sl1yo, brpLsl dec, sl1yo, brp1; rep from * to last st, sl1. Turn.

After working last set of DS rows, rep from Row 1 LS LC. ■

Leafy Lacy III Chart

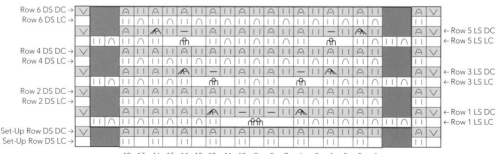

INCS WORKED IN LS LC ROW
DECS WORKED IN DS DC ROW

Fanny and Feathery

Fanny and Feathery Brioche Stitch
Using Two-Color Italian Cast-On, begin and end with LC knit st. Cast on a multiple of 16 sts + 3. For the sample shown, I cast on 35 sts.

Set-Up Row DS LC: p1, *sl1yo, p1; rep from * to end. Do *not* turn, slide.
Set-Up Row DS DC: sl1, *brk1, sl1yo; rep from * to last 2 sts, brk1, sl1. Turn.

Row 1 LS LC: k1, *[sl1yo, brk1] 7 times, sl1yo, br8st inc; rep from * to last 2 sts, sl1yo, k1. Do *not* turn, slide.
Row 1 LS DC: sl1, *[brp1, sl1yo] 8 times, [p1, sl1yo] 4 times; rep from * to last 2 sts, brp1, sl1. Turn.

Row 2 DS LC: p1, sl1yo, *brp1, sl1yo; rep from * to last st, p1. Do *not* turn, slide.
Row 2 DS DC: sl1, brk1, *[sl1yo, brk1] 4 times, [sl1yo, brLsl dec] 4 times; rep from * to last st, sl1. Turn.

Row 3 LS LC: k1, *sl1yo, brk1, sl1yo; rep from * to last 2 sts, sl1yo, k1. Do *not* turn, slide.
Row 3 LS DC: sl1, *brp1, sl1yo; rep from * to last 2 sts, brp1, sl1. Turn.

Row 4 DS LC: as Row 2 DS LC.
Row 4 DS DC: sl1, *brk1, sl1yo; rep from * to last 2 sts, brk1, sl1. Turn.

Rep from Row 1 LS LC. ■

Fanny and Feathery Chart

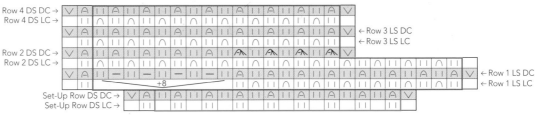

INCS WORKED IN LS LC ROW
DECS WORKED IN LS DC ROW

Pine Trees

This is a variation of Under Dutch Skies Brioche Stitch (page 102). The increases are worked in the LS LC rows, and the decreases are worked in the LS DC rows.

Pine Trees Brioche Stitch

Using Two-Color Italian Cast-On, begin and end with LC knit st. Cast on a multiple of 16 sts + 21. For the sample shown, I cast on 53 sts.

Set-Up Row DS LC: p1, *sl1yo, p1; rep from * to end. Do *not* turn, slide.
Set-Up Row DS DC: sl1, *brk1, sl1yo; rep from * to last 2 sts, brk1, sl1. Turn.

Row 1 LS LC: k1, sl1yo, brkyobrk, *sl1yo, [brk1, sl1yo] 7 times, br4st inc; rep from * to last 18 sts, sl1yo, [brk1, sl1yo] 7 times, brkyobrk, sl1yo, k1. Do *not* turn, slide.
Row 1 LS DC: sl1, brp1, sl1yo, p1, sl1yo, *brpLsl dec, sl1yo, [brp1, sl1yo] 4 times, brpRsl dec, [sl1yo, p1] twice, sl1yo; rep from * to last 20 sts, brpLsl dec, sl1yo, [brp1, sl1yo] 4 times, brpRsl dec, sl1yo, p1, sl1yo, brp1, sl1. Turn.

Row 2 DS LC and all DS LC rows: p1, *sl1yo, brp1; rep from * to last 2 sts, sl1yo, p1. Do *not* turn, slide.
Row 2 DS DC and all DS DC rows: sl1, *brk1, sl1yo; rep from * to last 2 sts, brk1, sl1. Turn.

Row 3 LS LC: as Row 1 LS LC.
Row 3 LS DC: sl1, brp1, sl1yo, p1, sl1yo, *brp1, sl1yo, brpLsl dec, sl1yo, [brp1, sl1yo] twice, brpRsl dec, sl1yo, brp1, [sl1yo, p1] twice, sl1yo; rep from * to last 20 sts, brp1, sl1yo, brpLsl dec, sl1yo, [brp1, sl1yo] twice, brpRsl dec, sl1yo, brp1, sl1yo, p1, sl1yo, brp1, sl1. Turn.

Row 5 LS LC: as Row 1 LS LC.
Row 5 LS DC: sl1, brp1, sl1yo, p1, sl1yo, *[brp1, sl1yo] twice, brpLsl dec, sl1yo, brpRsl dec, [sl1yo, brp1] twice, [sl1yo, p1] twice, sl1yo; rep from * to last 20 sts, [brp1, sl1yo] twice, brpLsl dec, sl1yo, brpRsl dec, [sl1yo, brp1] twice, sl1yo, p1, sl1yo, brp1, sl1. Turn.

Row 7 LS LC: k1, sl1yo, *[brk1, sl1yo] 4 times, br4st inc, sl1yo, [brk1, sl1yo] 3 times; rep from * to last 19 sts, [brk1, sl1yo] 4 times, br4st inc, sl1yo, [brk1, sl1yo] 4 times, k1. Do *not* turn, slide.
Row 7 LS DC: sl1, brp1, *sl1yo, [brp1, sl1yo] twice, brpRsl dec, [sl1yo, p1] twice, sl1yo, brpLsl dec, [sl1yo, brp1] twice; rep from * to last 23 sts, sl1yo, [brp1, sl1yo] twice, brpRsl dec, [sl1yo, p1] twice, sl1yo, brpLsl dec, [sl1yo, brp1] 3 times, sl1. Turn.

Row 9 LS LC: as Row 7 LS LC.
Row 9 LS DC: sl1, brp1, *sl1yo, brp1, sl1yo, brpRsl dec, sl1yo, brp1, [sl1yo, p1] twice, sl1yo, brp1, sl1yo, brpLsl dec, sl1yo, brp1; rep from * to last 23 sts, sl1yo, brp1, sl1yo, brpRsl dec, sl1yo, brp1, [sl1yo, p1] twice, sl1yo, brp1, sl1yo, brpLsl dec, [sl1yo, brp1] twice, sl1. Turn.

Row 11 LS LC: as Row 7 LS LC.
Row 11 LS DC: sl1, brp1, *sl1yo, brpRsl dec, [sl1yo, brp1] twice, [sl1yo, p1] twice, [sl1yo, brp1] twice, sl1yo, brpLsl dec; rep from * to last 23 sts, sl1yo, brpRsl dec, [sl1yo, brp1] twice, [sl1yo, p1] twice, [sl1yo, brp1] twice, sl1yo, brpLsl dec, sl1yo, brp1, sl1. Turn.

After working last set of DS rows, rep from Row 1 LS LC. ■

Pine Trees Chart

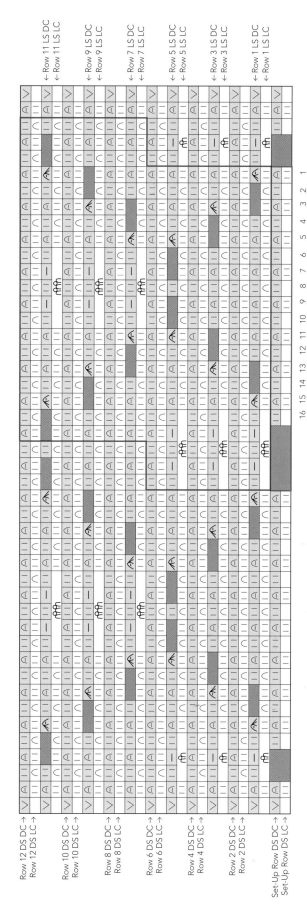

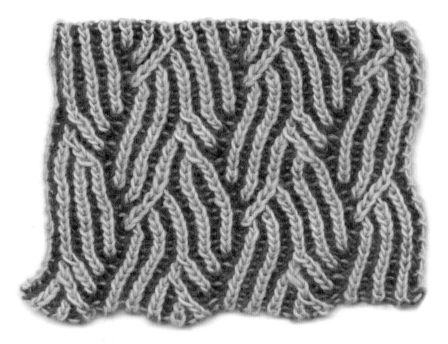

INCS WORKED IN LS DC ROW
DECS WORKED IN LS LC ROW

River Rapids

This variation on Mr. Flood's Brioche Stitch (page 107) places the increase in a LS DC burp row, and follows with its complementary decrease in a LS LC row.

River Rapids Brioche Stitch

Using Two-Color Italian Cast-On, begin and end with LC knit st. Cast on a multiple of 10 sts + 5. For the sample shown, I cast on 35 sts.

Set-Up Row DS LC: p1, *sl1yo, p1; rep from * to end. Do *not* turn, slide.
Set-Up Row DS DC: sl1, *brk1, sl1yo; rep from * to last 2 sts, brk1, sl1. Turn.

Row 1 LS LC: k1, sl1yo, *brk1, sl1yo; rep from * to last st, k1. Do *not* turn, slide.
Row 1 LS DC: sl1, brp1, sl1yo, brp1, *sl1yo, brp1, sl1yo, brpyobrp, [sl1yo, brp1] 3 times; rep from * to last st, sl1. Turn.

Row 2 DS LC: p1, *[sl1yo, brp1] 3 times, sl1yo, p1, [sl1yo, brp1] twice; rep from * to last 4 sts, sl1yo, brp1, sl1yo, p1. Do *not* turn, slide.
Row 2 DS DC: sl1, *brk1, sl1yo; rep from * to last 2 sts, brk1, sl1. Turn.

Row 3 LS LC: k1, sl1yo, brk1, sl1yo, *[brk1, sl1yo] 3 times, brLsl dec, sl1yo, brk1, sl1yo; rep from * to last st, k1. Do *not* turn, slide.
Row 3 LS DC: as Row 1 LS DC.

Row 4 DS LC: as Row 2 DS LC.
Row 4 DS DC: as Row 2 DS DC.

Row 5 LS LC: k1, sl1yo, brk1, sl1yo, *[brk1, sl1yo] 4 times, brLsl dec, sl1yo; rep from * to last st, k1. Do *not* turn, slide.
Row 5 LS DC: as Row 1 LS DC.

Row 6 DS LC: as Row 2 DS LC.
Row 6 DS DC: as Row 2 DS DC.

Row 7 LS LC: k1, sl1yo, brk1, sl1yo, *[brk1, sl1yo] 4 times, brLsl dec, sl1yo; rep from * to last st, k1. Do *not* turn, slide.
Row 7 LS DC: sl1, *brp1, sl1yo; rep from * to last 2 sts, brp1, sl1. Turn.

Row 8 DS LC: p1, *sl1yo, brp1; rep from * to last 2 sts, sl1yo, p1. Do *not* turn, slide.
Row 8 DS DC: as Row 2 DS DC.

Row 9 LS LC: k1, sl1yo, *brk1, sl1yo; rep from * to last st, k1. Do *not* turn, slide.
Row 9 LS DC: sl1, brp1, *[sl1yo, brp1] twice, sl1yo, brpyobrp, [sl1yo, brp1] twice; rep from * to last 3 sts, sl1yo, brp1, sl1. Turn.

Row 10 DS LC: p1, sl1yo, brp1, *[sl1yo, brp1] twice, sl1yo, p1, [sl1yo, brp1] 3 times; rep from * to last 2 sts, sl1yo, p1. Do *not* turn, slide.
Row 10 DS DC: as Row 2 DS DC.

Row 11 LS LC: k1, sl1yo, *[brk1, sl1yo] twice, brRsl dec, sl1yo, [brk1, sl1yo] twice; rep from * to last 3 sts, brk1, sl1yo, k1. Do *not* turn, slide.
Row 11 LS DC: as Row 9 LS DC.

Row 12 DS LC: as Row 10 DS LC.
Row 12 DS DC: as Row 2 DS DC.

River Rapids Chart

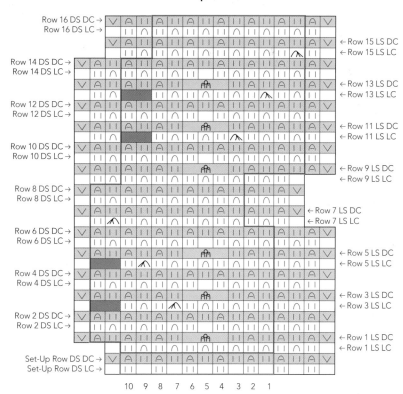

Row 13 LS LC: k1, sl1yo, *brk1, sl1yo, brRsl dec, sl1yo, [brk1, sl1yo] 3 times; rep from * to last 3 sts, brk1, sl1yo, k1. Do *not* turn, slide.
Row 13 LS DC: as Row 9 LS DC.

Row 14 DS LC: as Row 10 DS LC.
Row 14 DS DC: as Row 2 DS DC.

Row 15 LS LC: k1, sl1yo, *brRsl dec, sl1yo, [brk1, sl1yo] 4 times; rep from * to last 3 sts, brk1, sl1yo, k1. Do *not* turn, slide.
Row 15 LS DC: as Row 7 LS DC.

Row 16 DS LC: as Row 8 DS LC.
Row 16 DS DC: as Row 2 DS DC.

Rep from Row 1 LS LC. ∎

INCS WORKED IN LS LC ROW
DECS WORKED IN DS DC ROW

Swaying Fringe

This pattern is similar to Crossing Paths Brioche Stitch (page 69), the difference being that the decreases are worked in a DS DC row, stopping the column on the light side.

Swaying Fringe Brioche Stitch
Using Two-Color Italian Cast-On, begin and end with LC knit st. Cast on a multiple of 4 sts + 3. For the sample shown, I cast on 23 sts.

Set-Up Row DS LC: p1, *sl1yo, p1; rep from * to end. Do *not* turn, slide.
Set-Up Row DS DC: sl1, *brk1, sl1yo; rep from * to last 2 sts, brk1, sl1. Turn.

Row 1 LS LC: k1, sl1yo, *brkyobrk, sl1yo, brk1, sl1yo; rep from * to last st, k1. Do *not* turn, slide.
Row 1 LS DC: sl1, brp1, *sl1yo, p1, [sl1yo, brp1] twice; rep from * to last st, sl1. Turn.

Row 2 DS LC: p1, *sl1yo, brp1; rep from * to last 2 sts, sl1yo, p1. Do *not* turn, slide.
Row 2 DS DC: sl1, *brk1, sl1yo; rep from * to last 2 sts, brk1, sl1. Turn.

Row 3 LS LC: k1, sl1yo, *brk1, sl1yo; rep from * to last st, k1. Do *not* turn, slide.
Row 3 LS DC: sl1, brp1, *sl1yo, brp1; rep from * to last st, sl1. Turn.

Row 4 DS LC: as Row 2 DS LC.
Row 4 DS DC: sl1, *brRsl dec, sl1yo, brk1, sl1yo; rep from * to last 2 sts, brk1, sl1. Turn.

Rep from Row 1 LS LC. ■

Swaying Fringe Chart

Row 4 DS DC →
Row 4 DS LC →
← Row 3 LS DC
← Row 3 LS LC
Row 2 DS DC →
Row 2 DS LC →
← Row 1 LS DC
← Row 1 LS LC
Set-Up Row DS DC →
Set-Up Row DS LC →

4 3 2 1

INCS WORKED IN LS LC ROW
DECS WORKED IN DS DC ROW

Branches

This pattern is similar to Swaying Fringe Brioche Stitch (opposite), but here the increases zigzag up one column. The increases are worked in a LS LC row and the decreases in a DS DC row.

Branches Brioche Stitch
Using Two-Color Italian Cast-On, begin and end with LC knit st. Cast on a multiple of 4 sts + 3. For the sample shown, I cast on 27 sts.

Set-Up Row DS LC: p1, *sl1yo, p1; rep from * to end. Do *not* turn, slide.
Set-Up Row DS DC: sl1, *brk1, sl1yo; rep from * to last 2 sts, brk1, sl1. Turn.

Row 1 LS LC: k1, sl1yo, *brkyobrk, sl1yo, brk1, sl1yo; rep from * to last st, k1. Do *not* turn, slide.
Row 1 LS DC: sl1, brp1, *sl1yo, p1, [sl1yo, brp1] twice; rep from * to last st, sl1. Turn.

Row 2 DS LC: p1, *sl1yo, brp1; rep from * to last 2 sts, sl1yo, p1. Do *not* turn, slide.

Row 2 DS DC: sl1, *brk1, sl1yo; rep from * to last 2 sts, brk1, sl1. Turn.

Row 3 LS LC: k1, sl1yo, *brk1, sl1yo; rep from * to last st, k1. Do *not* turn, slide.
Row 3 LS DC: sl1, brp1, *sl1yo, brp1; rep from * to last st, sl1. Turn.

Row 4 DS LC: as Row 2 DS LC.
Row 4 DS DC: sl1, *brRsl dec, sl1yo, brk1, sl1yo; rep from * to last 2 sts, brk1, sl1. Turn.

Row 5 LS LC: k1, sl1yo, *brk1, sl1yo, brkyobrk, sl1yo; rep from * to last st, k1. Do *not* turn, slide.

Row 5 LS DC: sl1, brp1, *sl1yo, brp1, sl1yo, p1, sl1yo, brp1; rep from * to last st, sl1. Turn.

Row 6 DS LC: as Row 2 DS LC.
Row 6 DS DC: as Row 2 DS DC.

Row 7 LS LC: as Row 3 LS LC.
Row 7 LS DC: as Row 3 LS DC.

Row 8 DS LC: as Row 2 DS LC.
Row 8 DS DC: sl1, brk1, *sl1yo, brk1, sl1yo, brLsl dec; rep from * to last st, sl1. Turn.

Rep from Row 1 LS LC. ■

Branches Chart

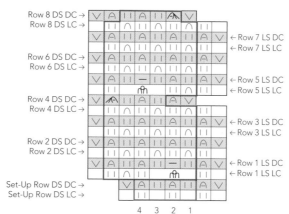

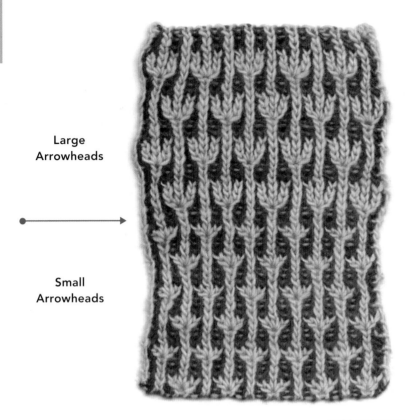

Large Arrowheads

Small Arrowheads

INCS WORKED IN LS LC ROW
DECS WORKED IN DS DC ROW

Small Arrowheads and Large Arrowheads

Small Arrowheads Brioche Stitch
Using Two-Color Italian Cast-On, begin and end with LC knit st. Cast on a multiple of 4 sts + 3. For the sample shown, I cast on 23 sts.

Set-Up Row DS LC: p1, *sl1yo, p1; rep from * to end. Do *not* turn, slide.
Set-Up Row DS DC: sl1, *brk1, sl1yo; rep from * to last 2 sts, brk1, sl1. Turn.

Row 1 LS LC: k1, sl1yo, *br4st inc, sl1yo, brk1, sl1yo; rep from * to last st, k1. Do *not* turn, slide.
Row 1 LS DC: sl1, brp1, *[sl1yo, p1] twice, [sl1yo, brp1] twice; rep from * to last st, sl1. Turn.

Row 2 DS LC: p1, *sl1yo, brp1; rep from * to last 2 sts, sl1yo, p1. Do *not* turn, slide.
Row 2 DS DC: sl1, brk1, *sl1yo, brRsl dec, sl1yo, brLsl dec; rep from * to last st, sl1. Turn.

Row 3 LS LC: k1, sl1yo, *brk1, sl1yo; rep from * to last st, k1. Do *not* turn, slide.
Row 3 LS DC: sl1, brp1, *sl1yo, brp1; rep from * to last st, sl1. Turn.

Row 4 DS LC: as Row 2 DS LC.
Row 4 DS DC: sl1, brk1, *sl1yo, brk1; rep from * to last st, sl1. Turn.

Row 5 LS LC: k1, sl1yo, *brk1, sl1yo, br4st inc, sl1yo; rep from * to last st, k1. Do *not* turn, slide.

Row 5 LS DC: sl1, brp1, *sl1yo, brp1, [sl1yo, p1] twice, sl1yo, brp1; rep from * to last st, sl1. Turn.

Row 6 DS LC: as Row 2 DS LC.
Row 6 DS DC: sl1, *brRsl dec, sl1yo, brLsl dec. sl1yo; rep from * to last 2 sts, brk1, sl1. Turn.

Row 7 LS LC: as Row 3 LS LC.
Row 7 LS DC: as Row 3 LS DC.

Row 8 DS LC: as Row 2 DS LC.
Row 8 DS DC: as Row 4 DS DC.

Rep from Row 1 LS LC. ■

This pattern is similar to Small Arrowheads Brioche Stitch, but the arrowheads here have been lengthened by 2 rows.

Large Arrowheads Brioche Stitch

Using Two-Color Italian Cast-On, begin and end with LC knit st. Cast on a multiple of 4 sts + 3. For the sample shown, I cast on 23 sts.

Set-Up Row DS LC: p1, *sl1yo, p1; rep from * to end. Do *not* turn, slide.
Set-Up Row DS DC: sl1, *brk1, sl1yo; rep from * to last 2 sts, brk1, sl1. Turn.

Row 1 LS LC: k1, sl1yo, *br4st inc, sl1yo, brk1, sl1yo; rep from * to last st, k1. Do *not* turn, slide.
Row 1 LS DC: sl1, brp1, *[sl1yo, p1] twice, [sl1yo, brp1] twice; rep from * to last st, sl1. Turn.

Row 2 DS LC: p1, *sl1yo, brp1; rep from * to last 2 sts, sl1yo, p1. Do *not* turn, slide.
Row 2 DS DC: sl1, *brk1, sl1yo; rep from * to last 2 sts, brk1, sl1. Turn.

Row 3 LS LC: k1, sl1yo, *brk1, sl1yo; rep from * to last st, k1. Do *not* turn, slide.
Row 3 LS DC: sl1, brp1, *sl1yo, brp1; rep from * to last st, sl1. Turn.

Row 4 DS LC: as Row 2 DS LC.
Row 4 DS DC: sl1, brk1, *sl1yo, brRsl dec, sl1yo, brLsl dec; rep from * to last st, sl1. Turn.

Row 5 LS LC: as Row 3 LS LC.
Row 5 LS DC: as Row 3 LS DC.

Row 6 DS LC: as Row 2 DS LC.
Row 6 DS DC: as Row 2 DS DC.

Row 7 LS LC: k1, sl1yo, *brk1, sl1yo, br4st inc, sl1yo; rep from * to last st, k1. Do *not* turn, slide.
Row 7 LS DC: sl1, brp1, *sl1yo, brp1, [sl1yo, p1] twice, sl1yo, brp1; rep from * to last st, sl1. Turn.

Row 8 DS LC: as Row 2 DS LC.
Row 8 DS DC: as Row 2 DS DC.

Row 9 LS LC: as Row 3 LS LC.
Row 9 LS DC: as Row 3 LS DC.

Row 10 DS LC: as Row 2 DS LC.
Row 10 DS DC: sl1, *brRsl dec, sl1yo, brLsl dec. sl1yo; rep from * to last 2 sts, brk1, sl1. Turn.

Row 11 LS LC: as Row 3 LS LC.
Row 11 LS DC: as Row 3 LS DC.

Row 12 DS LC: as Row 2 DS LC.
Row 12 DS DC: as Row 2 DS DC.

Rep from Row 1 LS LC. ■

Large Arrowheads Chart

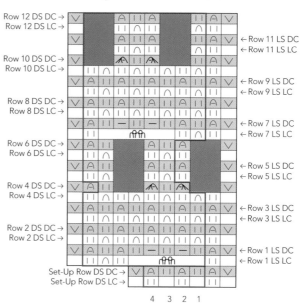

Small Arrowheads Chart

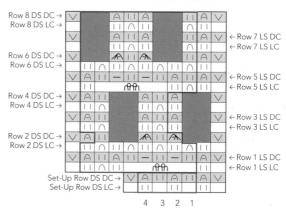

INCS WORKED IN LS LC ROW
DECS WORKED IN DS DC ROW

Fern and Fans

Fern and Fans Brioche Stitch
Using Two-Color Italian Cast-On, begin and end with LC knit st. Cast on a multiple of 32 sts + 33. For the sample shown, I cast on 65 sts.

Set-Up Row DS LC: p1, *sl1yo, p1; rep from * to end. Do *not* turn, slide.
Set-Up Row DS DC: sl1, *brk1, sl1yo; rep from * to last 2 sts, brk1, sl1. Turn.

Row 1 LS LC: k1, sl1yo, *[brk1, sl1yo] 5 times, br4st inc, sl1yo, [brk1, sl1yo] 3 times, br4st inc, sl1yo, [brk1, sl1yo] 6 times; rep from * to last 31 sts, [brk1, sl1yo] 5 times, br4st inc, sl1yo, [brk1, sl1yo] 3 times, br4st inc, sl1yo, [brk1, sl1yo] 5 times, k1. Do *not* turn, slide.
Row 1 LS DC: sl1, brp1, *[sl1yo, brp1] 5 times, [sl1yo, p1] twice, [sl1yo, brp1] 4 times, [sl1yo, p1] twice, [sl1yo, brp1] 7 times; rep from * to last 39 sts, [sl1yo, brp1] 5 times, [sl1yo, p1] twice, [sl1yo, brp1] 4 times, [sl1yo, p1] twice, [sl1yo, brp1] 6 times, sl1. Turn.

Row 2 DS LC: p1, *sl1yo, brp1; rep from * to last 2 sts, sl1yo, p1. Do *not* turn, slide.
Row 2 DS DC: sl1, brRsl dec, sl1yo, [brk1, sl1yo] 6 times, brLsl dec, *sl1yo, brRsl dec, sl1yo, [brk1, sl1yo] 6 times, brLsl dec; rep from * to last st, sl1. Turn.

Row 3 LS LC: k1, sl1yo, *[brk1, sl1yo] 4 times, br4st inc, sl1yo, [brk1, sl1yo] 5 times, br4st inc, sl1yo, [brk1, sl1yo] 5 times; rep from * to last 31 sts, [brk1, sl1yo] 4 times, br4st inc, sl1yo, [brk1, sl1yo] 5 times, br4st inc, sl1yo, [brk1, sl1yo] 4 times, k1. Do *not* turn, slide.
Row 3 LS DC: sl1, brp1, *[sl1yo, brp1] 4 times, [sl1yo, p1] twice, [sl1yo, brp1] 6 times, [sl1yo, p1] twice, [sl1yo, brp1] 6 times; rep from * to last 39 sts, [sl1yo, brp1] 4 times, [sl1yo, p1] twice, [sl1yo, brp1] 6 times, [sl1yo, p1] twice, [sl1yo, brp1] 5 times, sl1. Turn.

Row 4 DS LC: as Row 2 DS LC.
Row 4 DS DC: as Row 2 DS DC.

Row 5 LS LC: k1, sl1yo, *[brk1, sl1yo] 3 times, br4st inc, sl1yo, [brk1, sl1yo] 7 times, br4st inc, sl1yo, [brk1, sl1yo] 4 times; rep from * to last 31 sts, [brk1, sl1yo] 3 times, br4st inc, sl1yo, [brk1, sl1yo] 7 times, br4st inc, sl1yo, [brk1, sl1yo] 3 times, k1. Do *not* turn, slide.
Row 5 LS DC: sl1, brp1, *[sl1yo, brp1] 3 times, [sl1yo, p1] twice, [sl1yo, brp1] 8 times, [sl1yo, p1] twice, [sl1yo, brp1] 5 times; rep from * to last 39 sts, [sl1yo, brp1] 3 times, [sl1yo, p1] twice, [sl1yo, brp1] 8 times, [sl1yo, p1] twice, [sl1yo, brp1] 4 times, sl1. Turn.

Row 6 DS LC: as Row 2 DS LC.
Row 6 DS DC: as Row 2 DS DC.

Row 7 LS LC: k1, sl1yo, *[brk1, sl1yo] twice, br4st inc, sl1yo, [brk1, sl1yo] 9 times, br4st inc, sl1yo, [brk1, sl1yo] 3 times; rep from * to last 31 sts, [brk1, sl1yo] twice, br4st inc, sl1yo, [brk1, sl1yo] 9 times, br4st inc, sl1yo, [brk1, sl1yo] twice, k1. Do *not* turn, slide.
Row 7 LS DC: sl1, brp1, *[sl1yo, brp1] twice, [sl1yo, p1] twice, [sl1yo, brp1] 10 times, [sl1yo, p1] twice, [sl1yo, brp1] 4 times; rep from * to last 39 sts, [sl1yo, brp1] twice, [sl1yo, p1] twice, [sl1yo, brp1] 10 times, [sl1yo, p1] twice, [sl1yo, brp1] 3 times, sl1. Turn.

Row 8 DS LC: as Row 2 DS LC.
Row 8 DS DC: as Row 2 DS DC.

Row 9 LS LC: k1, sl1yo, *brk1, sl1yo, br4st inc, sl1yo, [brk1, sl1yo] 11 times, br4st inc, sl1yo, [brk1, sl1yo] twice; rep from * to last 31 sts, brk1, sl1yo, br4st inc, sl1yo, [brk1, sl1yo] 11 times, br4st inc, sl1yo, brk1, sl1yo, k1. Do *not* turn, slide.
Row 9 LS DC: sl1, brp1, *sl1yo, brp1, [sl1yo, p1] twice, [sl1yo, brp1] 12 times, [sl1yo, p1] twice, [sl1yo, brp1] 3 times; rep from * to last 39 sts, sl1yo, brp1, [sl1yo, p1] twice, [sl1yo, brp1] 12 times, [sl1yo, p1] twice, [sl1yo, brp1] twice, sl1. Turn.

Row 10 DS LC: as Row 2 DS LC.
Row 10 DS DC: as Row 2 DS DC.

Rep from Row 1 LS LC. ■

Fern and Fans Chart: Left Side

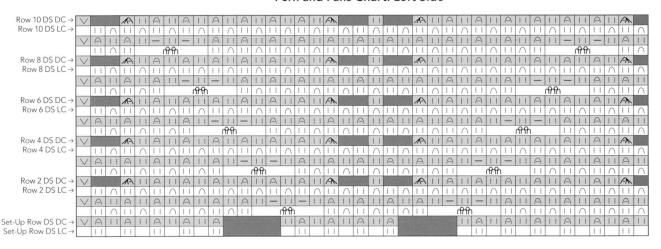

Row 10 DS DC →
Row 10 DS LC →

Row 8 DS DC →
Row 8 DS LC →

Row 6 DS DC →
Row 6 DS LC →

Row 4 DS DC →
Row 4 DS LC →

Row 2 DS DC →
Row 2 DS LC →

Set-Up Row DS DC →
Set-Up Row DS LC →

Fern and Fans Chart: Right Side

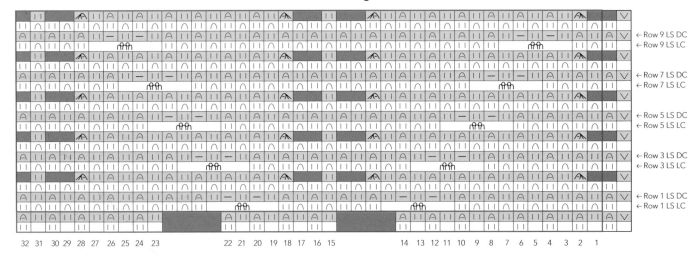

← Row 9 LS DC
← Row 9 LS LC

← Row 7 LS DC
← Row 7 LS LC

← Row 5 LS DC
← Row 5 LS LC

← Row 3 LS DC
← Row 3 LS LC

← Row 1 LS DC
← Row 1 LS LC

32 31 30 29 28 27 26 25 24 23   22 21 20 19 18 17 16 15   14 13 12 11 10 9 8 7 6 5 4 3 2 1

■ To more easily follow this chart, make a copy of both left and right sides.
Cut them out and tape them together to make a complete chart.

Syncopated Wavy Palm Leaves

This stitch pattern is a variation of Wavy Palm Leaves Brioche Stitch. The pattern is syncopated so that it is prominent in both the light and the dark colors. Please note that the legend in the chart has changed for this syncopated version.

Syncopated Wavy Palm Leaves Brioche Stitch

Using Two-Color Italian Cast-On, begin and end with LC knit st. Cast on a multiple of 30 sts + 3. For the sample shown, I cast on 63 sts.

Set-Up Row DS LC: p1, *[sl1yo, k1] 7 times, sl1yo, [p1, sl1yo] 7 times, p1; rep from * to last 2 sts, sl1yo, p1. Do *not* turn, slide.
Set-Up Row DS DC: sl1, *[brp1, sl1yo] 8 times, [brk1, sl1yo] 7 times; rep from * to last 2 sts, brk1, sl1. Turn.

Row 1 LS LC: k1, sl1yo, *brLsl dec, sl1yo, [brk1, sl1yo] 3 times, br4st inc, sl1yo, brRsl dec, sl1yo, [brp1, sl1yo] 7 times; rep from * to last st, k1. Do *not* turn, slide.
Row 1 LS DC: sl1, brp1, *[sl1yo, brp1] 4 times, [sl1yo, p1] twice, sl1yo, brp1, sl1yo, brLsl dec, sl1yo, [brk1, sl1yo] 3 times, br4st inc, sl1yo, brRsl dec; rep from * to last st, sl1. Turn.

Row 2 DS LC: p1, *sl1yo, brk1, sl1yo, [k1, sl1yo] twice, [brk1, sl1yo] 4 times, [brp1, sl1yo] 7 times, brp1; rep from * to last 2 sts, sl1yo, p1. Do *not* turn, slide.
Row 2 DS DC: sl1, *[brp1, sl1yo] 8 times, [brk1, sl1yo] 7 times; rep from * to last 2 sts, brk1, sl1. Turn.

Syncopated Wavy Palm Leaves Chart

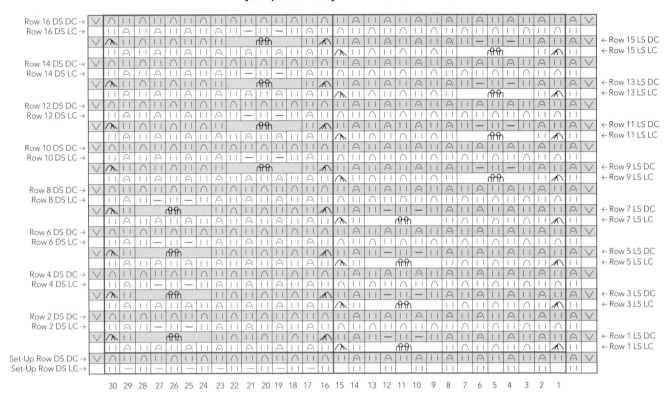

Row 16 DS DC →
Row 16 DS LC →
← Row 15 LS DC
← Row 15 LS LC
Row 14 DS DC →
Row 14 DS LC →
← Row 13 LS DC
← Row 13 LS LC
Row 12 DS DC →
Row 12 DS LC →
← Row 11 LS DC
← Row 11 LS LC
Row 10 DS DC →
Row 10 DS LC →
← Row 9 LS DC
← Row 9 LS LC
Row 8 DS DC →
Row 8 DS LC →
← Row 7 LS DC
← Row 7 LS LC
Row 6 DS DC →
Row 6 DS LC →
← Row 5 LS DC
← Row 5 LS LC
Row 4 DS DC →
Row 4 DS LC →
← Row 3 LS DC
← Row 3 LS LC
Row 2 DS DC →
Row 2 DS LC →
← Row 1 LS DC
← Row 1 LS LC
Set-Up Row DS DC →
Set-Up Row DS LC →

30 29 28 27 26 25 24 23 22 21 20 19 18 17 16 15 14 13 12 11 10 9 8 7 6 5 4 3 2 1

Rows 3, 5 and 7 LS LC: as Row 1 LS LC.
Rows 3, 5 and 7 LS DC: as Row 1 LC DC.

Rows 4, 6 and 8 DS LC: as Row 2 DS LC.
Rows 4, 6 and 8 DS DC: as Row 2 DS DC.

Row 9 LS LC: k1, sl1yo, *brLsl dec, sl1yo, br4st inc, sl1yo, [brk1, sl1yo] 3 times, brRsl dec, sl1yo, [brp1, sl1yo] 7 times; rep from * to last st, k1. Do *not* turn, slide.
Row 9 LS DC: sl1, brp1, *sl1yo, brp1, sl1yo, [p1, sl1yo] twice, [brp1, sl1yo] 4 times, brLsl dec, sl1yo, br4st inc, sl1yo, [brk1, sl1yo] 3 times, brRsl dec; rep from * to last st, sl1. Turn.

LEGEND for Syncopated Wavy Palm Leaves

☐ = knit on **LS** rows, purl on **DS** rows

⊟ = purl on **LS** rows, knit on **DS** rows

∨ = slip stitch purlwise

∩ = brk on **LS** rows, brp on **DS** rows

Ａ = brp on **LS** rows, brk on **DS** rows

‖ = sl1yo

[⋔⋔⋔] = br4st inc | = this line is used to indicate the division of the leaf and body

⋀ = brRsl dec

⋀ = brLsl dec

Row 10 DS LC: p1, *[sl1yo, brk1] 4 times, sl1yo, [k1, sl1yo] twice, brk1, sl1yo, [brp1, sl1yo] 7 times, brp1; rep from * to last 2 sts, sl1yo, p1. Do *not* turn, slide.
Row 10 DS DC: sl1, *[brp1, sl1yo] 8 times, [brk1, sl1yo] 7 times; rep from * to last 2 sts, brk1, sl1. Turn.

Rows 11, 13 and 15 LS LC: as Row 9 LS LC.

Rows 11, 13 and 15 LS DC: as Row 9 LC DC.

Rows 12, 14 and 16 DS LC: as Row 10 DS LC.
Rows 12, 14 and 16 DS DC: as Row 10 DS DC.

Rep from Row 1 LS LC. ∎

160

INCS AND DECS WORKED ONCE IN LS LC ROW, THEN
INCS AND DECS WORKED IN DS DC ROW

Hook, Line and Sinker

For this delicate pattern, the first set of increases and decreases is worked in a LS LC row. Then the second set is worked in a DS DC row. This creates the little dot that appears on the light side.

**Hook, Line and Sinker
Brioche Stitch**
Using Two-Color Italian Cast-On, begin and end with LC knit st. Cast on a multiple of 6 sts + 3. For the sample shown, I cast on 27 sts.

Set-Up Row DS LC: p1, *sl1yo, p1; rep from * to end. Do *not* turn, slide.
Set-Up Row DS DC: sl1, *brk1, sl1yo; rep from * to last 2 sts, brk1, sl1. Turn.

Row 1 LS LC: k1, sl1yo, *brkyobrk, sl1yo, brLsl dec, sl1yo; rep from * to last st, k1. Do *not* turn, slide.

Row 1 LS DC: sl1, brp1, *sl1yo, p1, [sl1yo, brp1] twice; rep from * to last st, sl1. Turn.

Row 2 DS LC: p1, *sl1yo, brp1; rep from * to last 2 sts, sl1yo, p1. Do *not* turn, slide.
Row 2 DS DC: sl1, *brk1, sl1yo; rep from * to last 2 sts, brk1, sl1. Turn.

Row 3 LS LC: k1, sl1yo, *brk1, sl1yo; rep from * to last st, k1. Do *not* turn, slide.
Row 3 LS DC: sl1, brp1, *sl1yo, brp1; rep from * to last st, sl1. Turn.

Row 4 DS LC: as Row 2 DS LC.
Row 4 DS DC: sl1, *brkyobrk, sl1yo, brLsl dec, sl1yo; rep from * to last 2 sts, brk1, sl1. Turn.

Row 5 LS LC: k1, sl1yo, *[brk1, sl1yo] twice, k1, sl1yo; rep from * to last st, k1. Do *not* turn, slide.
Row 5 LS DC: as Row 3 LS DC.

Row 6 DS LC: as Row 2 DS LC.
Row 6 DS DC: as Row 2 DS DC.

Rep from Row 1 LS LC. ■

Hook, Line and Sinker Chart

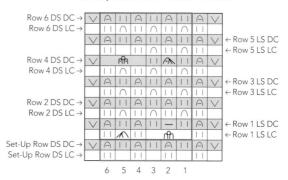

INCS WORKED IN LS LC ROW
DECS WORKED IN DS DC ROW

Thumbs Up

Thumbs Up Brioche Stitch
Using Two-Color Italian Cast-On, begin and end with LC knit st. Cast on a multiple of 4 sts + 3. For the sample shown, I cast on 23 sts.

Set-Up Row DS LC: p1, *sl1yo, p1; rep from * to end. Do *not* turn, slide.
Set-Up Row DS DC: sl1, *brk1, sl1yo; rep from * to last 2 sts, brk1, sl1. Turn.

Row 1 LS LC: k1, sl1yo, *brkyobrk, sl1yo, brk1, sl1yo; rep from * to last st, k1. Do *not* turn, slide.
Row 1 LS DC: sl1, brp1, *sl1yo, p1, [sl1yo, brp1] twice; rep from * to last st, sl1. Turn.

Row 2 DS LC: p1, *sl1yo, brp1; rep from * to last 2 sts, sl1yo, p1. Do *not* turn, slide.
Row 2 DS DC: sl1, *brk1, sl1yo; rep from * to last 2 sts, brk1, sl1. Turn.

Row 3 LS LC: k1, sl1yo, *brk1, sl1yo; rep from * to last st, k1. Do *not* turn, slide.

Row 3 LS DC: sl1, brp1, *sl1yo, brp1; rep from * to last st, sl1. Turn.

Row 4 DS LC: as Row 2 DS LC.
Row 4 DS DC: sl1, *brk1, sl1yo, brRsl dec, sl1yo; rep from * to last 2 sts, brk1, sl1. Turn.

Row 5 LS LC: k1, sl1yo, *brk1, sl1yo, brkyobrk, sl1yo; rep from * to last st, k1. Do *not* turn, slide.
Row 5 LS DC: sl1, brp1, *sl1yo, brp1, sl1yo, p1, sl1yo, brp1; rep from * to last st, sl1. Turn.

Row 6 DS LC: as Row 2 DS LC.
Row 6 DS DC: as Row 2 DS DC.

Row 7 LS LC: as Row 3 LS LC.
Row 7 LS DC: as Row 3 LS DC.

Row 8 DS LC: as Row 2 DS LC.
Row 8 DS DC: sl1, *brLsl dec, sl1yo, brk1, sl1yo; rep from * to last 2 sts, brk1, sl1. Turn.

Rep from Row 1 LS LC. ■

Thumbs Up Chart

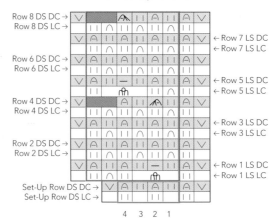

Stegosaurus *page 184*

The Projects

I've designed these shawls and scarves as examples of the kinds of beautiful projects you can create using the original stitch patterns in this book.

With all the wonderful yarns to choose from these days, you should not limit yourself to the ones I have used. Since the projects are all neck accessories, gauge is not that important. The same stitch pattern knit in lace, DK, worsted, or bulky yarn will give you versions ranging from small to large. If you want to tighten up the stitch pattern, go down in needle size; go up to make it looser and lacier. Different fibers will also affect the final product: if you work with mohair and silk, your scarf will look much different from one knitted in Lopi wool on the same size needles.

The colors you choose will also evoke a particular feeling. High-contrast colors will add drama to your projects, whereas tones close to each other on the color wheel will look subtler.

As explained in the introduction, I generally work with yarns that have a "bite." Slippery yarns such as alpaca, silk, or superwash wool tend to grow lengthwise in brioche: the yarn overs allow the stitch to elongate, and the weight of a scarf can stretch it down. But many beautiful yarns are made from these slippery materials, and you can reduce stretching by distributing the weight of the scarf loosely around your neck. Fiber combinations such as mohair and silk work beautifully, because the mohair, or other non-slippery yarn, keeps the stitches in place.

I suggest placing markers between each pattern repeat. When using color-changing yarns, place a marker on the light color as it comes out of the skein and on the light side of the work. This will reduce confusion when the yarn transitions to a darker color.

Ring of Fire

I traveled to Denver to record my Explorations in Brioche Knitting class for Craftsy.com. What a wonderful experience! Stefanie Japel took me to the Fancy Tiger Crafts store, and I found this red-hot Handmaiden *Maiden Hair*: luxury, pure and simple.

Finished Measurements
16¼" (41cm) high × 34" (86cm)
in circumference

Yarn
Handmaiden Fine Yarn *Maiden Hair*
(67% silk, 23% kid mohair, 10% nylon) **②**

■ 1 skein = 3½oz/100g (328yd/300m);
cowl shown weighs 5½oz/150g

■ Colors: 1 skein each in amethyst (DC)
and sangria (LC)

Needles
Size 4 (3.5mm) circular needle, 24"/60cm
long

Gauge
Two pattern repeats: 24 sts = 6" (15cm)
and 12 LC and DC rounds = 4½" (11.5cm)

PATTERN NOTES
1) This cowl is worked in the round. Please see the instructions on page 16 for casting on a large number of stitches using the Two-Color Italian Cast-On with a lifeline, and see page 228 for a guide to working brioche in the round.

2) With such a large project, I suggest running a lifeline every several rounds.

3) This stitch pattern is a multiple of 12 stitches.

4) Place a marker at the beginning of the round and on the first stitch of the pattern (Round 1 DC), so you can count rounds. I also suggest that you place markers between each pattern repeat.

5) For this cowl, the main color is the dark color (DC), so you begin with a DC round followed by a LC round.

COWL
Cast on 156 sts using Two-Color Italian Cast-On, beginning with DC knit st and ending with LC purl st.
Join to begin working in the rnd, being careful not to twist sts. Remember to drop first "knot" at beginning of cast-on.

Set-Up Round 1 DC: *k1, sl1yo; rep from * to end of round. Drop DC in front.
Set-Up Round 1 LC: *sl1yo, brp1; rep from * to end of round. Drop LC in front.

Rounds 1, 3 and 5 DC: *brRsl dec, sl1yo, brk1, sl1yo, brkyobrk, sl1yo, [brk1, sl1yo] twice; rep from * to end of round. Drop DC in front.
Rounds 1, 3 and 5 LC: *[sl1yo, brp1] twice, sl1yo, p1, [sl1yo, brp1] 3 times; rep from * to end of round. Drop LC in front.

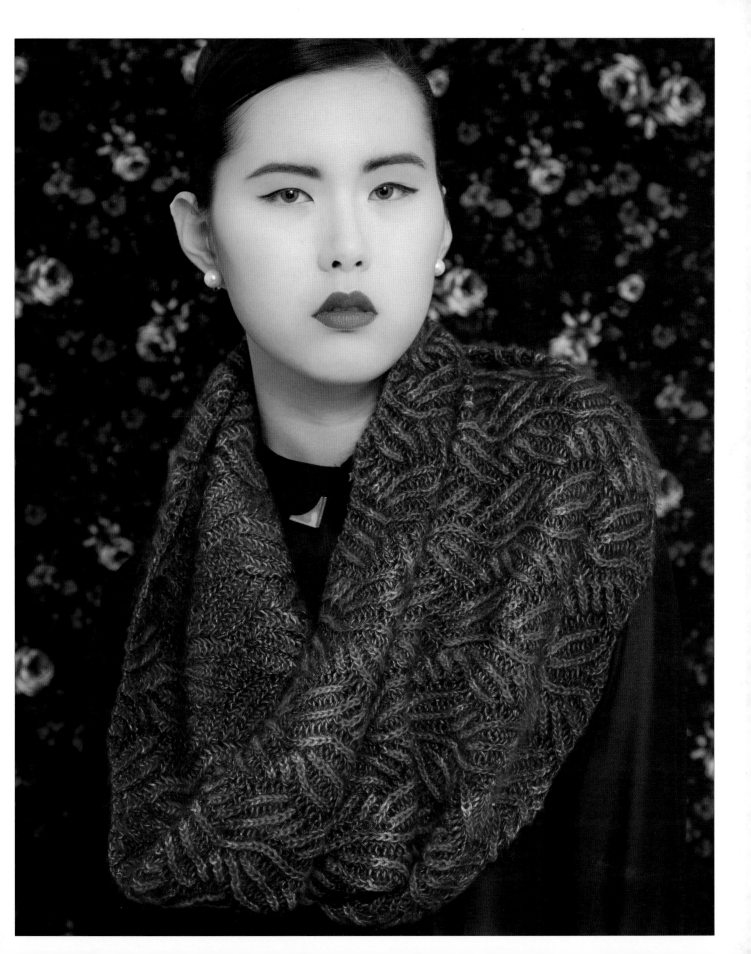

Ring of Fire

Rounds 2, 4, 6, 8, 10 and 12 DC: *brk1, sl1yo; rep from * to end of round. Drop DC in front.
Rounds 2, 4, 6, 8, 10 and 12 LC: *sl1yo, brp1; rep from * to end of round. Drop LC in front.

Rounds 7, 9 and 11 DC: *[brk1, sl1yo] twice, brkyobrk, sl1yo, brk1, sl1yo, brLsl dec, sl1yo ; rep from *. Drop DC in front.
Rounds 7, 9 and 11 LC: *[sl1yo, brp1] twice, sl1yo, p1, [sl1yo, brp1] 3 times; rep from *. Drop LC in front.

After working last set of DS rows, rep from Round 1 DC.

When desired length has been worked, ending with a Round 6 LC or Round 12 LC, bind off loosely, preferably with Italian Bind-Off. Work in ends and block as desired. I steam blocked the cowl shown. ■

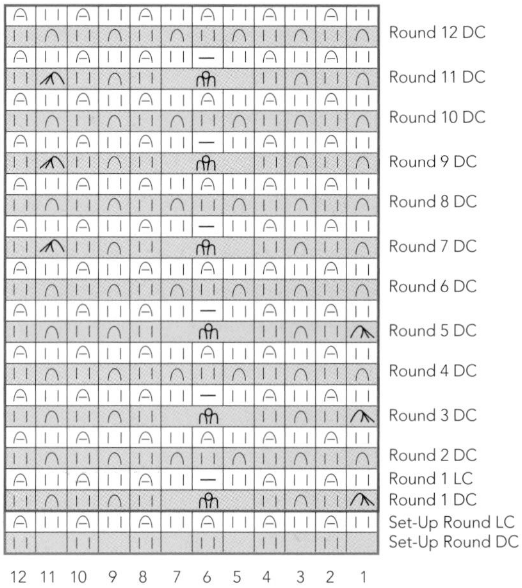
Round 12 DC
Round 11 DC
Round 10 DC
Round 9 DC
Round 8 DC
Round 7 DC
Round 6 DC
Round 5 DC
Round 4 DC
Round 3 DC
Round 2 DC
Round 1 LC
Round 1 DC
Set-Up Round LC
Set-Up Round DC
12 11 10 9 8 7 6 5 4 3 2 1

LEGEND for **Ring of Fire**

- [ ] = knit
- [—] = purl
- [∩] = brk
- [| |] = sl1yo
- [brp symbol] = brp
- [brLsl dec symbol] = brLsl dec
- [brRsl dec symbol] = brRsl dec
- [brkyobrk symbol] = brkyobrk

Willow

I just love a good mohair and silk blend. I get teased all the time about making "yet another mohair scarf." The staff at de Afstap yarn store in Amsterdam know where I am headed when I walk in the door: right to Rowan's *Kidsilk Haze*.

Finished Measurements
14½" (37cm) wide × 71" (180cm) long

Yarn
Rowan *Kidsilk Haze* (70% super kid mohair, 30% silk) (1)

■ 1 ball = .88oz/25g (210yd/229m); scarf shown weighs 3oz/85g

■ Colors: 2 balls each in #581 meadow (LC) and #629 fern (DC)

Needles
Size 7 (4.5mm) circular needle

Gauge
One pattern repeat: 32 sts = 6¾" (17cm) and 24 rows = 6" (15cm)

SCARF
Cast on 69 sts using Two-Color Italian Cast-On, beginning and ending with LC knit st.

Set-Up Row 1 DS LC: p1, *sl1yo, p1; rep from * to end. Do *not* turn, slide.
Set-Up Row 1 DS DC: sl1, *brk1, sl1yo; rep from * to last 2 sts, brk1, sl1. Turn.

Row 1 LS LC: k1, sl1yo, brkyobrk, sl1yo, *[brk1, sl1yo] twice, brLsl dec, sl1yo, [brk1, sl1yo] 7 times, brRsl dec, sl1yo, [brk1, sl1yo] twice, br4st inc, sl1yo; rep from * to last 33 sts, [brk1, sl1yo] twice, brLsl dec, sl1yo, [brk1, sl1yo] 7 times, brRsl dec, sl1yo, [brk1, sl1yo] twice, brkyobrk, sl1yo, k1. Do *not* turn, slide.
Row 1 LS DC: sl1, brp1, sl1yo, p1, sl1yo, brp1, *[sl1yo, brp1]13 times, [sl1yo, p1] twice, brp1; rep from * to last 31 sts, [sl1yo, brp1] 13 times, sl1yo, p1, sl1yo, brp1, sl1. Turn.

Row 2 DS LC and all DS LC rows: p1, *sl1yo, brp1; rep from * to last 2 sts, sl1yo, p1. Do *not* turn, slide.
Row 2 DS DC and all DS DC rows: sl1, *brk1, sl1yo; rep from * to last 2 sts, brk1, sl1. Turn.

Row 3 LS LC: k1, sl1yo, brkyobrk, sl1yo, *[brk1, sl1yo] 3 times, brLsl dec, sl1yo, [brk1, sl1yo] 5 times, brRsl dec, sl1yo, [brk1, sl1yo] 3 times, br4st inc, sl1yo; rep from * to last 33 sts, [brk1, sl1yo] 3 times, brLsl dec, sl1yo, [brk1, sl1yo] 5 times, brRsl dec, sl1yo, [brk1, sl1yo] 3 times, brkyobrk, sl1yo, k1. Do *not* turn, slide.
Row 3 LS DC: as Row 1 LS DC.

Willow

Row 5 LS LC: k1, sl1yo, brkyobrk, sl1yo, *[brk1, sl1yo] 4 times, brLsl dec, sl1yo, [brk1, sl1yo] 3 times, brRsl dec, sl1yo, [brk1, sl1yo] 4 times, br4st inc, sl1yo; rep from * to last 33 sts, [brk1, sl1yo] 4 times, brLsl dec, sl1yo, [brk1, sl1yo] 3 times, brRsl dec, sl1yo, [brk1, sl1yo] 4 times, brkyobrk, sl1yo, k1. Do *not* turn, slide.
Row 5 LS DC: as Row 1 LS DC.

Row 7 LS LC: k1, sl1yo, brkyobrk, sl1yo, *[brk1, sl1yo] 5 times, brLsl dec, sl1yo, brk1, sl1yo, brRsl dec, sl1yo, [brk1, sl1yo] 5 times, br4st inc, sl1yo; rep from * to last 33 sts, [brk1, sl1yo] 5 times, brLsl dec, sl1yo, brk1, sl1yo, brRsl dec, sl1yo, [brk1, sl1yo] 5 times, brkyobrk, sl1yo, k1. Do *not* turn, slide.
Row 7 LS DC: as Row 1 LS DC.

Row 9 LS LC: k1, sl1yo, brkyobrk, sl1yo, *[brk1, sl1yo] 6 times, br4st dec, sl1yo, [brk1, sl1yo] 6 times, br4st inc, sl1yo; rep from * to last 33 sts, [brk1, sl1yo] 6 times, br4st dec, sl1yo, [brk1, sl1yo] 6 times, brkyobrk, sl1yo, k1. Do *not* turn, slide.
Row 9 LS DC: as Row 1 LS DC.

Row 11 LS LC: k1, sl1yo, *brk1, sl1yo; rep from *, end with k1. Do *not* turn, slide.
Row 11 LS DC: sl1, brp1, *sl1yo, brp1; rep from * to last st, sl1. Turn.

Row 13 LS LC: k1, sl1yo, [brk1, sl1yo] 4 times, brRsl dec, sl1yo, [brk1, sl1yo] twice, br4st inc, sl1yo, *[brk1, sl1yo] twice, brLsl dec, sl1yo, [brk1, sl1yo] 7 times, brRsl dec, sl1yo, [brk1, sl1yo] twice, br4st inc, sl1yo; rep from * to last 17 sts, [brk1, sl1yo] twice, brLsl dec, sl1yo, [brk1, sl1yo] 4 times, k1. Do *not* turn, slide.
Row 13 LS DC: sl1, [brp1, sl1yo] 8 times, [p1, sl1yo] twice, brp1 *[sl1yo, brp1] 13 times, [sl1yo, p1] twice, sl1yo, brp1; rep from * to last 15 sts, [sl1yo, brp1] 7 times, sl1. Turn.

Row 15 LS LC: k1, sl1yo, [brk1, sl1yo] 3 times, brRsl dec, sl1yo, [brk1, sl1yo] 3 times, br4st inc, sl1yo, *[brk1, sl1yo] 3 times, brLsl dec, sl1yo, [brk1, sl1yo] 5 times, brRsl dec, sl1yo, [brk1, sl1yo] 3 times, br4st inc, sl1yo; rep from * to last 17 sts, [brk1, sl1yo] 3 times, brLsl dec, sl1yo, [brk1, sl1yo] 3 times, k1. Do *not* turn, slide.
Row 15 LS DC: as Row 13 LS DC.

Row 17 LS LC: k1, sl1yo, [brk1, sl1yo] twice, brRsl dec, sl1yo, [brk1, sl1yo] 4 times, br4st inc, sl1yo, *[brk1, sl1yo] 4 times, brLsl dec, sl1yo, [brk1, sl1yo] 3 times, brRsl dec, sl1yo, [brk1, sl1yo] 4 times, br4st inc, sl1yo; rep from * to last 17 sts, [brk1, sl1yo] 4 times, brLsl dec, sl1yo, [brk1, sl1yo] twice, k1. Do *not* turn, slide.
Row 17 LS DC: as Row 13 LS DC.

Row 19 LS LC: k1, sl1yo, brk1, sl1yo, brRsl dec, sl1yo, [brk1, sl1yo] 5 times, br4st inc, sl1yo, *[brk1, sl1yo] 5 times, brLsl dec, sl1yo, brk1, sl1yo, brRsl dec, sl1yo, [brk1, sl1yo] 5 times, br4st inc, sl1yo; rep from * to last 17 sts, [brk1, sl1yo] 5 times, brLsl dec, sl1yo, brk1, sl1yo, k1. Do *not* turn, slide.
Row 19 LS DC: as Row 13 LS DC.

Row 21 LS LC: k1, sl1yo, brRsl dec, sl1yo, [brk1, sl1yo] 6 times, br4st inc, sl1yo, *[brk1, sl1yo] 6 times, br4st dec, sl1yo, [brk1, sl1yo] 6 times, br4st inc, sl1yo; rep from * to last 17 sts, [brk1, sl1yo] 6 times, brLsl dec, sl1yo, k1. Do *not* turn, slide.
Row 21 LS DC: as Row 13 LS DC.

Row 23 LS LC: as Row 11 LS LC.
Row 23 LS DC: as Row 11 LS DC.

After working last set of DS rows, rep from Row 1 LS LC.

When desired length has been worked, ending with a Row 12 DS DC or Row 24 DS DC, bind off loosely, preferably with Italian Bind-Off. Work in ends and block as desired. I wet blocked the scarf shown. ■

Willow

Reptilian Cowl

I first met Tina of Knitwhits at a knitting event in California. Her Freia Fine Handpaint Yarns were wonderful—such a dramatic display. Everyone wanted her yarns. Since then I've seen Tina at a lot of knitting events, and each time she comes with a truckload of slow-changing colors.

Finished Measurements
6" (15cm) wide × 41" (104cm) around

Yarn
Freia Fine Handpaints *Ombrè Worsted* (100% wool) (**4**)

■ 1 ball = 2.64oz/75g (127yd/115m); cowl shown weighs 5½oz/150g

■ Color: 2 balls of same color, lichen (LC and DC), but where color begins in different places

Needles
Size 9 (5.5mm) circular needle

Gauge
Cowl is two pattern repeats:
20 sts = 6" (15cm) and
28 rows = 6¾" (17cm)

PATTERN NOTES

1) This cowl is worked flat and sewn together at the ends.

2) If you use the suggested yarn, begin the LC and DC at different places in the color change of the ball; for example, I began one ball from the outside (purple gray) and one ball from the inside (olive green). The colors kept shifting as I worked, and at one point they were almost the same. I happen to like that effect: the pattern or contrast disappearing for a stretch, and then reappearing as the colors continue to change.

3) If you begin with the Italian Cast-On and end with the Italian Bind-Off, you will have an almost invisible seam when you sew the cowl into a circle using a running stitch.

4) The stitch pattern is a multiple of 10 stitches. The pattern will increase up to 16 stitches (Row 1 LS DC) and then down to 8 stitches (Row 7 LS DC). Take note that the decreases for the second part of the pattern begin in a DC row (Row 7 LS DC).

5) This pattern uses syncopation, which means that the barks and burps switch back and forth within each row.

6) This flat cowl does not use selvedge edges, so you will end some rows with a sl1yo. Be sure to maintain this yarn over when you work the brioche stitch in the following row.

7) Place markers between stitches 9 and 10 and between stitches 10 and 1, to indicate when syncopation occurs. Also place a marker on Row 1 LS LC, so you can count rows. This will also indicate the LS, whose color will change throughout the knitting if you are using the Freia yarn. I also place a marker on the working LC yarn as it comes out of the ball, to avoid confusion as the colors change.

Reptilian Cowl

COWL

Cast on 20 sts using Two-Color Italian Cast-On, beginning with LC knit st and ending with DC purl st.

Set-Up Row 1 DS LC: *sl1yo, p1; rep from * to end of row. Do *not* turn, slide.
Set-Up Row 1 DS DC: *brp1, sl1yo, [brk1, sl1yo] 4 times; rep from * to end of row. Turn.

Row 1 LS LC: *[brk1, sl1yo] 3 times, brRsl dec, pm, sl1yo, pm; rep from * to end of row. Do *not* turn, slide.
Row 1 LS DC: *[sl1yo, brp1] 3 times, sl1yo, sm, br8st inc, sm; rep from * to end of row. Turn.

Row 2 DS LC: *[sl1yo, k1] 4 times, sl1yo, sm, [brp1, sl1yo] 3 times, brp1, sm; rep from * to end of row. Do *not* turn, slide.
Row 2 DS DC: *[brp1, sl1yo] 4 times, brp1, sm, [sl1yo, brk1] 3 times, sl1yo, sm; rep from * to end of row. Turn.

Row 3 LS LC: *[brk1, sl1yo] twice, brRsl dec, sm, [sl1yo, brp1] 4 times, sl1yo, sm; rep from * to end of row.
Do *not* turn, slide.
Row 3 LS DC: *[sl1yo, brp1] twice, sl1yo, sm, [brk1, sl1yo] 4 times, brk1, sm; rep from * to end of row. Turn.

Row 4 DS LC: *[sl1yo, brk1] 4 times, sl1yo, sm, [brp1, sl1yo] twice, brp1, sm; rep from * to end of row. Do *not* turn, slide.
Row 4 DS DC: *[brp1, sl1yo] 4 times, brp1, sm, [sl1yo, brk1] twice, sl1yo, sm; rep from * to end of row. Turn.

Row 5 LS LC: *brk1, sl1yo, brRsl dec, sm, [sl1yo, brp1] 4 times, sl1yo, sm; rep from * to end of row. Do *not* turn, slide.
Row 5 LS DC: *sl1yo, brp1, sl1yo, sm, [brk1, sl1yo] 4 times, brk1, sm; rep from * to end of row. Turn.

Row 6 DS LC: *[sl1yo, brk1] 4 times, sl1yo, sm, brp1, sl1yo, brp1, sm; rep from * to end of row. Do *not* turn, slide.
Row 6 DS DC: *[brp1, sl1yo] 4 times, brp1, sm, sl1yo, brk1, sl1yo, sm; rep from * to end of row. Turn.

Row 7 LS LC: *brRsl dec, sm, [sl1yo, brp1] 4 times, sl1yo, sm; rep from * to end of row. Do *not* turn, slide.
Row 7 LS DC: *sl1yo, sm, brLsl dec, [sl1yo, brk1] 3 times, sm; rep from * to end of row. Turn.

Row 8 DS LC: *[sl1yo, brk1] 3 times, sl1yo, sm, brp1, sm; rep from * to end of row. Do *not* turn, slide.
Row 8 DS DC: *[brp1, sl1yo] 3 times, brp1, sm, sl1yo, sm; rep from * to end of row. Turn.

Row 9 LS LC: *br8st inc, sm, [sl1yo, brp1] 3 times, sl1yo, sm; rep from * to end of row. Do *not* turn, slide.
Row 9 LS DC: *[sl1yo, p1] 4 times, sl1yo, sm, brLsl dec, [sl1yo, brk1] twice, sm; rep from * to end of row. Turn.

Row 10 DS LC: *[sl1yo, brk1] twice, sl1yo, sm, [brp1, sl1yo] 4 times, brp1, sm; rep from * to end of row. Do *not* turn, slide.
Row 10 DS DC: *[brp1, sl1yo] twice, brp1, sm, [sl1yo, brk1] 4 times, sl1yo, sm; rep from * to end of row. Turn.

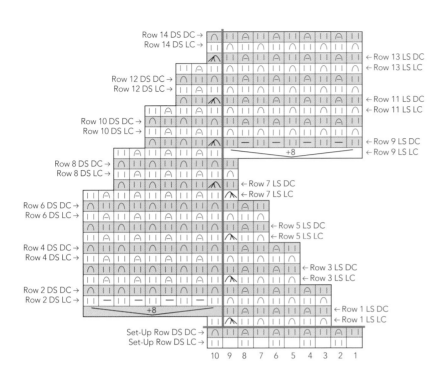

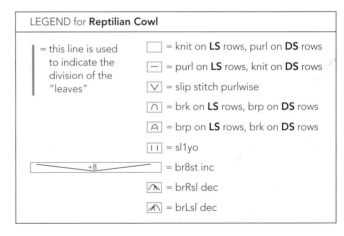

Row 11 LS LC: *[brk1, sl1yo] 4 times, brk1, sm, [sl1yo, brp1] twice, sl1yo, sm; rep from * to end of row. Do *not* turn, slide.
Row 11 LS DC: *[sl1yo, brp1] 4 times, sl1yo, sm, brLsl dec, sl1yo, brk1, sm; rep from * to end of row. Turn.

Row 12 DS LC: *sl1yo, brk1, sl1yo, sm, [brp1, sl1yo] 4 times, brp1, sm; rep from * to end of row. Do *not* turn, slide.
Row 12 DS DC: *brp1, sl1yo, brp1, sm, [sl1yo, brk1] 4 times, sl1yo, sm; rep from * to end of row. Turn.

Row 13 LS LC: *[brk1, sl1yo] 4 times, brk1, sm, sl1yo, brp1, sl1yo, sm; rep from * to end of row. Do *not* turn, slide.
Row 13 LS DC: *[sl1yo, brp1] 4 times, sl1yo, sm, brLsl dec, sm; rep from * to end of row. Turn.

Row 14 DS LC: *sl1yo, sm, [brp1, sl1yo] 4 times, brp1, sm; rep from * to end of row. Do *not* turn, slide.
Row 14 DS DC: *brp1, sm, [sl1yo, brk1] 4 times, sl1yo, sm; rep from * to end of row. Turn.

Rep from Row 1 LS LC.

When desired length has been worked, ending with Row 14 DS DC, bind off loosely, preferably with Italian Bind-Off. Using a running stitch, sew cast-on and bound-off edges together. Work in ends and block as desired. I steam blocked the cowl shown. ∎

LEGEND for **Reptilian Cowl**

	= this line is used to indicate the division of the "leaves"

☐ = knit on **LS** rows, purl on **DS** rows

⊟ = purl on **LS** rows, knit on **DS** rows

ⓥ = slip stitch purlwise

∩ = brk on **LS** rows, brp on **DS** rows

Ⓐ = brp on **LS** rows, brk on **DS** rows

⊓ = sl1yo

+8 = br8st inc

⋏ = brRsl dec

⋏ = brLsl dec

Icicle

Penelope Craft Store in Amsterdam is owned by Malia Mather. She showed me Madelinetosh's *Tosh Merino Light* one day when I went into her shop (swearing that I was not going to buy any yarn!), and I grabbed the Graphite and Silver Fox colors as quickly as I could.

Finished Measurements
7½" (19cm) wide × 71" (180cm) long

Yarn
Madelinetosh *Tosh Merino Light*
(100% superwash merino wool) ①

■ 1 hank = approx 3½oz/100g
(420yd/384m); scarf shown weighs
7 ½oz/205g

■ Colors: 1 hank each in silver fox (LC)
and graphite (DC)

Needles
Size 5 (3.75mm) circular needle

Gauge
One pattern repeat: 14 sts = 2 ¼" (5.5cm)
and 20 rows = 3½" (9cm)

PATTERN NOTES
1) To avoid confusion, place a marker on the LS LC Row 1. Then you can count up from that row. I also suggest placing markers between each pattern repeat.

2) This stitch pattern uses a multiple of 14 sts + 7.

SCARF
Cast on 49 sts using Two-Color Italian Cast-On, beginning and ending with LC knit st.

Set-Up Row 1 DS LC: p1, *sl1yo, p1; rep from * to end.
Do *not* turn, slide.
Set-Up Row 1 DS DC: sl1, *brk1, sl1yo; rep from * to last 2 sts, brk1, sl1. Turn.

Row 1 LS LC: k1, sl1yo, [brk1, sl1yo] twice, *[brk1, sl1yo] 4 times, brRsl dec, sl1yo, brkyobrk, sl1yo; rep from * to last st, k1. Do *not* turn, slide.
Row 1 LS DC: sl1, brp1, [sl1yo, brp1] twice, *[sl1yo, brp1] 5 times, sl1yo, p1, sl1yo, brp1; rep from * to last st, sl1. Turn.

Row 2 DS LC and all DS LC rows: p1, *sl1yo, brp1; rep from * to last 2 sts, sl1yo, p1. Do *not* turn, slide.
Row 2 DS DC and all DS DC rows: sl1, *brk1, sl1yo; rep from * to last 2 sts, brk1, sl1. Turn.

Row 3 LS LC: k1, sl1yo, [brk1, sl1yo] twice, *[brk1, sl1yo] 3 times, brRsl dec, sl1yo, brkyobrk, sl1yo, brk1, sl1yo; rep from * to last st, k1. Do *not* turn, slide.
Row 3 LS DC: sl1, brp1, [sl1yo, brp1] twice, *[sl1yo, brp1] 4 sl1yo, p1, [sl1yo, brp1] twice; rep from * to last st, sl1. Turn.

Row 5 LS LC: k1, sl1yo, [brk1, sl1yo] twice, *[brk1, sl1yo] twice, brRsl dec, sl1yo, brkyobrk, sl1yo, [brk1, sl1yo] twice; rep from * to last st, k1. Do *not* turn, slide.
Row 5 LS DC: sl1, brp1, [sl1yo, brp1] twice, *[sl1yo, brp1] 3 times, sl1yo, p1, [sl1yo, brp1] 3 times; rep from * to last st, sl1. Turn.

Icicle

Row 7 LS LC: k1, sl1yo, [brk1, sl1yo] twice, *brk1, sl1yo, brRsl dec, sl1yo, brkyobrk, sl1yo, [brk1, sl1yo] 3 times; rep from * to last st, k1. Do *not* turn, slide.
Row 7 LS DC: sl1, brp1, [sl1yo, brp1] twice, *[sl1yo, brp1] twice, sl1yo, p1, [sl1yo, brp1] 4 times; rep from * to last st, sl1. Turn.

Row 9 LS LC: k1, sl1yo, [brk1, sl1yo] twice, *brRsl dec, sl1yo, brkyobrk, sl1yo, [brk1, sl1yo] 4 times; rep from * to last st, k1. Do *not* turn, slide.
Row 9 LS DC: sl1, brp1, [sl1yo, brp1] twice, *sl1yo, brp1, sl1yo, p1, [sl1yo, brp1] 5 times; rep from * to last st, sl1. Turn.

Row 11 LS LC: k1, sl1yo, *brkyobrk, sl1yo, brLsl dec, sl1yo, [brk1, sl1yo] 4 times; rep from * to last 5 sts, [brk1, sl1yo] twice, k1. Do *not* turn, slide.
Row 11 LS DC: sl1, brp1, *sl1yo, p1, [sl1yo, brp1] 6 times; rep from * to last 5 sts, [sl1yo, brp1] twice, sl1. Turn.

Row 13 LS LC: k1, sl1yo, *brk1, sl1yo, brkyobrk, sl1yo, brLsl dec, sl1yo, [brk1, sl1yo] 3 times; rep from * to last 5 sts, [brk1, sl1yo] twice, k1. Do *not* turn, slide.
Row 13 LS DC: sl1, brp1, *sl1yo, brp1, sl1yo, p1, [sl1yo, brp1] 5 times; rep from * to last 5 sts, [sl1yo, brp1] twice, sl1. Turn.

Row 15 LS LC: k1, sl1yo, *[brk1, sl1yo] twice, brkyobrk, sl1yo, brLsl dec, sl1yo, [brk1, sl1yo] twice; rep from * to last 5 sts, [brk1, sl1yo] twice, k1. Do *not* turn, slide.
Row 15 LS DC: sl1, brp1, *[sl1yo, brp1] twice, sl1yo, p1, [sl1yo, brp1] 4 times; rep from * to last 5 sts, [sl1yo, brp1] twice, sl1. Turn.

Row 17 LS LC: k1, sl1yo, *[brk1, sl1yo] 3 times, brkyobrk, sl1yo, brLsl dec, sl1yo, brk1, sl1yo; rep from * to last 5 sts, [brk1, sl1yo] twice, k1. Do *not* turn, slide.
Row 17 LS DC: sl1, brp1, *[sl1yo, brp1] 3 times, sl1yo, p1, [sl1yo, brp1] 3 times; rep from * to last 5 sts, [sl1yo, brp1] twice, sl1. Turn.

Row 19 LS LC: k1, sl1yo, *[brk1, sl1yo] 4 times, brkyobrk, sl1yo, brLsl dec, sl1yo; rep from * to last 5 sts, [brk1, sl1yo] twice, k1. Do *not* turn, slide.
Row 19 LS DC: sl1, brp1, *[sl1yo, brp1] 4 times, sl1yo, p1, [sl1yo, brp1] twice; rep from * to last 5 sts, [sl1yo, brp1] twice, sl1. Turn.

Rep from Row 1 LS LC.

When desired length has been worked, ending with a Row 10 DS DC or Row 20 DS DC, bind off loosely, preferably with Italian Bind-Off. Work in ends and block as desired. I steam blocked the scarf shown. ∎

Row 20 DS DC →
Row 20 DS LC →
← Row 19 LS DC
← Row 19 LS LC
Row 18 DS DC →
Row 18 DS LC →
← Row 17 LS DC
← Row 17 LS LC
Row 16 DS DC →
Row 16 DS LC →
← Row 15 LS DC
← Row 15 LS LC
Row 14 DS DC →
Row 14 DS LC →
← Row 13 LS DC
← Row 13 LS LC
Row 12 DS DC →
Row 12 DS LC →
← Row 11 LS DC
← Row 11 LS LC
Row 10 DS DC →
Row 10 DS LC →
← Row 9 LS DC
← Row 9 LS LC
Row 8 DS DC →
Row 8 DS LC →
← Row 7 LS DC
← Row 7 LS LC
Row 6 DS DC →
Row 6 DS LC →
← Row 5 LS DC
← Row 5 LS LC
Row 4 DS DC →
Row 4 DS LC →
← Row 3 LS DC
← Row 3 LS LC
Row 2 DS DC →
Row 2 DS LC →
← Row 1 LS DC
← Row 1 LS LC
Set-Up Row DS DC →
Set-Up Row DS LC →

14 13 12 11 10 9 8 7 6 5 4 3 2 1

183

Stegosaurus

One of my daughters came home with several friends while I was working on this shawl. One of them exclaimed, "Are you knitting a dinosaur?" Thereupon, Stegosaurus.

Finished Measurements
Off-centered triangular shawl is 40" (102cm) wide x 25" (69cm) deep.

Yarn
Manos del Uruguay *Silk Blend* (70% extrafine merino wool, 30% silk) **3**

■ 1 hank = 1¾oz/50g (300yd/270m); shawl shown weighs 5½oz/160g

■ Colors: 1 hank each in #4635 rust-orange (DC) and #9695 green (LC)

Needles
Size 6 (4mm) circular needle

Gauge
15 sts and 24 rows = 4" (10cm) in 2-color brioche stitch

● PATTERN NOTES

1) This shawl is constructed by first building up a "leaf" on the left edge. The right edge gradually increases to an elongated triangle. Syncopated brioche is used, so the colors shift on one side from the dark-colored triangular shape to the light-colored leaf on the left edge.

2) Note that the Dark Side (DS) is the public side of this shawl, and that you work with the Dark Color (DC) first in each set of rows. The legend for the chart has been changed to reflect this.

3) I made my scarf 6½ "leaves" high, then I bound off all the stitches except the leaf, using a two-color bind-off. I finished working the single leaf until only 2 stitches remained, which I then bound off.

4) Place a marker between the leaf and the body of the shawl, so you have an indication of when syncopation occurs. Then slip the marker as you work.

TWO-COLOR BIND-OFF
Work this bind-off when both threads are hanging from the same end. Work each stitch with its opposite color, so the bound-off stitches that lie across the top of each column will match the column color. Remember to bind off loosely.

For example: work a dark-color column stitch with the light color, then work following stitch with dark color, bind off one stitch loosely, work following stitch with light color, bind off one stitch loosely, work following stitch with dark color, bind off one stitch, etc.

SHAWL
Using LC and backward-loop cast-on, cast on 3 sts. Turn work and attach DC.

Set-Up Row LS DC: p1, sl1yo, p1. Do *not* turn, slide stitches to the other end of the needle.

Stegosaurus

Set-Up Row LS LC: sl1, brk1, place marker (pm), sl1yo. Turn.
Note: Last st of each LS LC row ends with sl1yo. Maintain this yo when working first st of foll row.

Row 1 DS DC: brkyobrk, sm, sl1yo, k1. Do *not* turn, slide.
Row 1 DS LC: sl1, p1, sl1yo, sm, br4st inc, sl1. Turn.

Row 2 LS DC: p1, [sl1yo, k1] twice, sl1yo, sm, brp1, sl1yo, p1. Do *not* turn, slide.
Row 2 LS LC: sl1, [brp1, sl1yo] twice, brp1, sm, sl1yo, brk1, sl1yo. Turn.

Row 3 DS DC: brkyobrk, sl1yo, brk1, sm, [sl1yo, brp1] twice, sl1yo, k1. Do *not* turn, slide.
Row 3 DS LC: sl1, p1, sl1yo, brp1, sl1yo, sm, brk1, sl1yo, br4st inc, sl1yo, brk1, sl1. Turn.

Row 4 LS DC: p1, sl1yo, brk1, [sl1yo, k1] twice, sl1yo, brk1, sl1yo, sm, [brp1, sl1yo] twice, p1. Do *not* turn, slide.
Row 4 LS LC: sl1, [brp1, sl1yo] 4 times, brp1, sm, [sl1yo, brk1] twice, sl1yo. Turn. 15 sts.

Row 5 DS DC: brkyobrk, *sl1yo, brk1; rep from * to marker, sm, [sl1yo, brp1] 4 times, sl1yo, k1. Do *not* turn, slide.
Row 5 DS LC: sl1, p1, sl1yo, *brp1, sl1yo; rep from * to marker, sm, [brk1, sl1yo] twice, br4st inc, [sl1yo, brk1] twice, sl1. Turn.

Row 6 LS DC: p1, [sl1yo, brk1] twice, [sl1yo, k1] twice, [sl1yo, brk1] twice, sl1yo, sm, *brp1, sl1yo; rep from * to last st, p1. Do *not* turn, slide.
Row 6 LS LC: sl1, [brp1, sl1yo] 6 times, brp1, sm, *sl1yo, brk1; rep from * to last st, sl1yo. Turn.

Row 7 DS DC: brkyobrk, *sl1yo, brk1; rep from * to marker, sm, [sl1yo, brp1] 6 times, sl1yo, k1. Do *not* turn, slide.
Row 7 DS LC: sl1, p1, sl1yo, *brp1, sl1yo; rep from * to marker, sm, [brk1, sl1yo] 6 times, brk1, sl1. Turn.

Row 8 LS DC: p1, [sl1yo, brk1], 6 times, sl1yo, sm, *brp1, sl1yo; rep from * to last st, p1. Do *not* turn, slide.
Row 8 LS LC: sl1, [brp1, sl1yo] 6 times, brp1, sm, *sl1yo, brk1; rep from * to last st, sl1yo. Turn.

Row 9 DS DC: brkyobrk, *sl1yo, brk1; rep from * to marker, sm, [sl1yo, brp1] 6 times, sl1yo, k1. Do *not* turn, slide.
Row 9 DS LC: sl1, p1, sl1yo, *brp1, sl1yo; rep from * to marker, sm, [brk1, sl1yo] 5 times, brRsl dec, sl1. Turn.

Row 10 LS DC: p1, [sl1yo, brk1], 5 times, sl1yo, sm, *brp1, sl1yo; rep from * to last st, p1. Do *not* turn, slide.
Row 10 LS LC: sl1, [brp1, sl1yo] 5 times, brp1, sm, *sl1yo, brk1; rep from * to last st, sl1yo. Turn.

Row 11 DS DC: brkyobrk, *sl1yo, brk1; rep from * to marker, sm, [sl1yo, brp1] 5 times, sl1yo, k1. Do *not* turn, slide.
Row 11 DS LC: sl1, p1, sl1yo, *brp1, sl1yo; rep from * to marker, sm, [brk1, sl1yo] 4 times, brRsl dec, sl1. Turn.

Row 12 LS DC: p1, [sl1yo, brk1], 4 times, sl1yo, sm, *brp1, sl1yo; rep from * to last st, p1. Do *not* turn, slide.
Row 12 LS LC: sl1, [brp1, sl1yo] 4 times, brp1, sm, *sl1yo, brk1; rep from * to last st, sl1yo. Turn.

Row 13 DS DC: brkyobrk, *sl1yo, brk1; rep from * to marker, sm, [sl1yo, brp1] 4 times, sl1yo, k1. Do *not* turn, slide.
Row 13 DS LC: sl1, p1, sl1yo, *brp1, sl1yo; rep from * to marker, sm, [brk1, sl1yo] 3 times, brRsl dec, sl1. Turn.

Row 14 LS DC: p1, [sl1yo, brk1], 3 times, sl1yo, sm, *brp1, sl1yo; rep from * to last st, p1. Do *not* turn, slide.
Row 14 LS LC: sl1, [brp1, sl1yo] 3 times, brp1, sm, *sl1yo, brk1; rep from * to last st, sl1yo. Turn.

Row 15 DS DC: brkyobrk, *sl1yo, brk1; rep from * to marker, sm, [sl1yo, brp1] 3 times, sl1yo, k1. Do *not* turn, slide.
Row 15 DS LC: sl1, p1, sl1yo, *brp1, sl1yo; rep from * to marker, sm, [brk1, sl1yo] twice, brRsl dec, sl1. Turn.

Row 16 LS DC: p1, [sl1yo, brk1] twice, sl1yo, sm, *brp1, sl1yo; rep from * to last st, p1. Do *not* turn, slide.
Row 16 LS LC: sl1, [brp1, sl1yo] twice, brp1, sm, *sl1yo, brk1; rep from * to last st, sl1yo. Turn.

Row 17 DS DC: brkyobrk, *sl1yo, brk1; rep from * to marker, sm, [sl1yo, brp1] twice, sl1yo, k1. Do *not* turn, slide.
Row 17 DS LC: sl1, p1, sl1yo, *brp1, sl1yo; rep from * to marker, sm, brk1, sl1yo, brRsl dec, sl1. Turn.

Stegosaurus

Row 18 LS DC: p1, sl1yo, brk1, sl1yo, sm, *brp1, sl1yo; rep from * to last st, p1. Do *not* turn, slide.
Row 18 LS LC: sl1, brp1, sl1yo, brp1, sm, *sl1yo, brk1; rep from * to last st, sl1yo. Turn.

Row 19 DS DC: brkyobrk, *sl1yo, brk1; rep from * to marker, sm, sl1yo, brp1, sl1yo, k1. Do *not* turn, slide.
Row 19 DS LC: sl1, p1, sl1yo, *brp1, sl1yo; rep from * to marker, sm, brRsl dec, sl1. Turn.

Row 20 LS DC: p1, sl1yo, sm, *brp1, sl1yo; rep from * to last st, p1. Do *not* turn, slide.
Row 20 LS LC: sl1, brp1, sm, *sl1yo, brk1; rep from * to last st, sl1yo. Turn.

Row 21 DS DC: brkyobrk, *sl1yo, brk1; rep from * to marker, sm, sl1yo, k1. Do *not* turn, slide.
Row 21 DS LC: sl1, p1, sl1yo, *brp1, sl1yo; rep from * to marker, sm, brk1, sl1. Turn.

Row 22 LS DC: p1, sl1yo, sm, *brp1, sl1yo; rep from * to last st, p1. Do *not* turn, slide.
Row 22 LS LC: sl1, brp1, sm, *sl1yo, brk1; rep from * to last st, sl1yo. Turn.

Row 23 DS DC: brkyobrk, *sl1yo, brk1; rep from * to marker, sm, sl1yo, k1. Do *not* turn, slide.
Row 23 DS LC: sl1, p1, sl1yo, *brp1, sl1yo; rep from * to marker, sm, br4st inc, sl1. Turn.

Row 24 LS DC: p1, [sl1yo, k1] twice, sl1yo, sm, *brp1, sl1yo; rep from * to last st, p1. Do *not* turn, slide.
Row 24 LS LC: sl1, [brp1, sl1yo] twice, brp1, sm, *sl1yo, brk1; rep from * to last st, sl1yo. Turn.

Row 25 DS DC: brkyobrk, *sl1yo, brk1; rep from * to marker, sm, [sl1yo, brp1] twice, sl1yo, k1. Do *not* turn, slide.
Row 25 DS LC: sl1, p1, sl1yo, *brp1, sl1yo; rep from * to marker, sm, brk1, sl1yo, br4st inc, sl1yo, brk1, sl1. Turn.

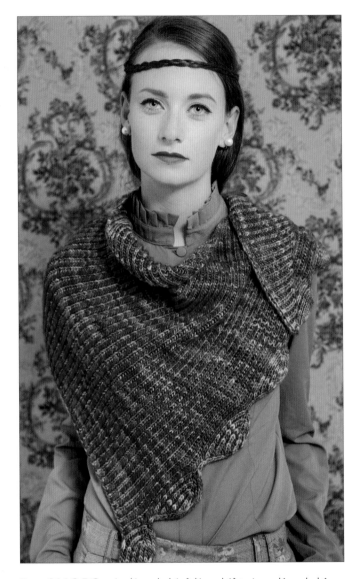

Row 26 LS DC: p1, sl1yo, brk1, [sl1yo, k1] twice, sl1yo, brk1, sl1yo, sm, *brp1, sl1yo; rep from * to last st, p1.
Do *not* turn, slide.
Row 26 LS LC: sl1, [brp1, sl1yo] 4 times, brp1, sm, *sl1yo, brk1; rep from * to last st, sl1yo. Turn.

Repeat from Row 5 DS DC.

Make the shawl 6½ "leaves" high, ending with a Row 8 LS LC. Then bind off all stitches except the leaf, using a two-color bind-off so both threads will be at the leaf end of the shawl to work the rest of the leaf. Work Rows 9–22 of the leaf only, bind off. Block lightly and weave in ends. I steam blocked the shawl shown. ∎

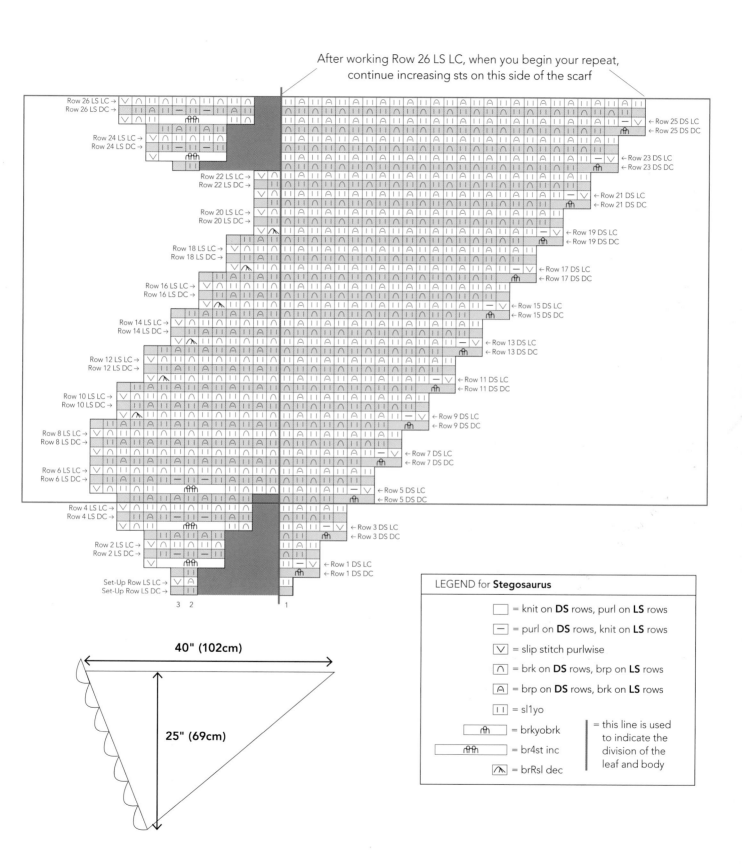

After working Row 26 LS LC, when you begin your repeat, continue increasing sts on this side of the scarf

Row 26 LS LC →
Row 26 LS DC →
← Row 25 DS LC
← Row 25 DS DC
Row 24 LS LC →
Row 24 LS DC →
← Row 23 DS LC
← Row 23 DS DC
Row 22 LS LC →
Row 22 LS DC →
← Row 21 DS LC
← Row 21 DS DC
Row 20 LS LC →
Row 20 LS DC →
← Row 19 DS LC
← Row 19 DS DC
Row 18 LS LC →
Row 18 LS DC →
← Row 17 DS LC
← Row 17 DS DC
Row 16 LS LC →
Row 16 LS DC →
← Row 15 DS LC
← Row 15 DS DC
Row 14 LS LC →
Row 14 LS DC →
← Row 13 DS LC
← Row 13 DS DC
Row 12 LS LC →
Row 12 LS DC →
← Row 11 DS LC
← Row 11 DS DC
Row 10 LS LC →
Row 10 LS DC →
← Row 9 DS LC
← Row 9 DS DC
Row 8 LS LC →
Row 8 LS DC →
← Row 7 DS LC
← Row 7 DS DC
Row 6 LS LC →
Row 6 LS DC →
← Row 5 DS LC
← Row 5 DS DC
Row 4 LS LC →
Row 4 LS DC →
← Row 3 DS LC
← Row 3 DS DC
Row 2 LS LC →
Row 2 LS DC →
← Row 1 DS LC
← Row 1 DS DC
Set-Up Row LS LC →
Set-Up Row LS DC →

3 2   1

40" (102cm)

25" (69cm)

LEGEND for **Stegosaurus**		
□	= knit on **DS** rows, purl on **LS** rows	
−	= purl on **DS** rows, knit on **LS** rows	
V	= slip stitch purlwise	
∩	= brk on **DS** rows, brp on **LS** rows	
A	= brp on **DS** rows, brk on **LS** rows	
‖	= sl1yo	
ᵐ	= brkyobrk	
ᵐᵐ	= br4st inc	= this line is used to indicate the division of the leaf and body
⋀	= brRsl dec	

Veda's Peacock

Veda is my best friend. She is the New Yorker and I am the country bumpkin standing next to her. She exudes class—just like this elegant scarf.

Finished Measurements
9½" (24cm) wide × 68" (172cm) long

Yarn
Madelinetosh *Tosh Merino Light* (100% superwash merino wool)

- 1 hank = approx 3½oz/100g (420yd/384m); scarf shown weighs 6oz/170g

- Colors: 1 hank each in winterwheat (LC) and cedar (DC)

Needles
Size 5 (3.75mm) circular needle

Gauge
One pattern repeat: 45 sts = 9½" (24cm) and 48 rows = 9½" (44cm)

PATTERN NOTES

1) This stitch pattern is a multiple of 20 sts + 25.

2) Rows 1–8 (Chart A) are repeated 3 times (24 counted rows), then Rows 9–16 (Chart B) are repeated 3 times (24 counted rows). Then you begin again with Row 1.

3) In the LS LC rows, the number of stitches increase because you are only working increases. Then, in the following DS DC row, you work decreases and get back to the original number of stitches.

4) To more easily follow Veda's Peacock Charts A and B, make a copy of both left and right sides. Cut them out and tape them together to make a complete chart.

SCARF
Cast on 45 sts using Two-Color Italian Cast-On, begin and end with LC knit st.
Note: Also see Chart A.

Set-Up Row 1 DS LC: p1, *sl1yo, p1; rep from * to end. Do *not* turn, slide.
Set-Up Row 1 DS DC: sl1, *brk1, sl1yo; rep from * to last 2 sts, brk1, sl1. Turn.

Row 1 LS LC: k1, sl1yo, brkyobrk, sl1yo, [brk1, sl1yo] 4 times, brk1, *sl1yo, [brk1, sl1yo] 4 times, br4st inc, sl1yo, [brk1, sl1yo] 4 times, brk1; rep from * to last 12 sts, sl1yo, [brk1, sl1yo] 4 times, brkyobrk, sl1yo, k1. Do *not* turn, slide.
Row 1 LS DC: sl1, brp1, sl1yo, p1, sl1yo, [brp1, sl1yo] 5 times, *[brp1, sl1yo] 5 times, [p1, sl1yo] twice, [brp1, sl1yo] 5 times; rep from * to last 14 sts, [brp1, sl1yo] 5 times, p1, sl1yo, brp1, sl1. Turn.

Row 2 DS LC: p1, *sl1yo, brp1; rep from * to last 2 sts, sl1yo, p1. Do *not* turn, slide.
Row 2 DS DC: sl1, [brk1, sl1yo] 5 times, brLsl dec, *sl1yo, brRsl dec, sl1yo, [brk1, sl1yo] 8 times, brLsl dec; rep from * to last 15 sts, sl1yo, brRsl dec, [sl1yo, brk1] 5 times, sl1. Turn.

190

Veda's Peacock

Row 3 LS LC: as Row 1 LS LC.
Row 3 LS DC: as Row 1 LS DC.

Row 4 DS LC: Row 2 DS LC.
Row 4 DS DC: sl1, [brk1, sl1yo] 4 times, brLsl dec, sl1yo, brk1, *sl1yo, brk1, sl1yo, brRsl dec, sl1yo, [brk1, sl1yo] 6 times, brLsl dec, sl1yo, brk1; rep from * to last 15 sts, sl1yo, brk1, sl1yo, brRsl dec, [sl1yo, brk1] 4 times, sl1. Turn.

Row 5 LS LC: as Row 1 LS LC.
Row 5 LS DC: as Row 1 LS DC.

Row 6 DS LC: as Row 2 DS LC.
Row 6 DS DC: sl1, [brk1, sl1yo] 3 times, brLsl dec, [sl1yo, brk1] twice, *sl1yo, [brk1, sl1yo] twice, brRsl dec, sl1yo, [brk1, sl1yo] 4 times, brLsl dec, [sl1yo, brk1] twice; rep from * to last 15 sts, sl1yo, [brk1, sl1yo] twice, brRsl dec, [sl1yo, brk1] 3 times, sl1. Turn.

Row 7 LS LC: as Row 1 LS LC.
Row 7 LS DC: as Row 1 LS DC.

Row 8 DS LC: as Row 2 DS LC.
Row 8 DS DC: sl1, [brk1, sl1yo] twice, brLsl dec, [sl1yo, brk1] 3 times, *sl1yo, [brk1, sl1yo] 3 times, brRsl dec, sl1yo, [brk1, sl1yo] twice, brLsl dec, [sl1yo, brk1] 3 times; rep from * to last 15 sts, sl1yo, [brk1, sl1yo] 3 times, brRsl dec, [sl1yo, brk1] twice, sl1. Turn.

Rep Rows 1–8 (Chart A) two more times.

Note: Also see Chart B.
Row 9 LS LC: k1, sl1yo, [brk1, sl1yo] 5 times, *br4st inc, sl1yo, [brk1, sl1yo] 9 times; rep from * to last 13 sts, br4st inc, sl1yo, [brk1, sl1yo] 5 times, k1. Do *not* turn, slide.
Row 9 LS DC: sl1, [brp1, sl1yo] 5 times, brp1, *sl1yo, [p1, sl1yo] twice, [brp1, sl1yo] 9 times, brp1; rep from * to last 17 sts, sl1yo, [p1, sl1yo] twice, [brp1, sl1yo] 5 times, brp1, sl1. Turn.

Row 10 DS LC: as Row 2 DS LC.
Row 10 DS DC: sl1, brk1, sl1yo, brRsl dec, sl1yo, [brk1, sl1yo] 5 times, *[brk1, sl1yo] 3 times, brLsl dec, sl1yo, brRsl dec, sl1yo, [brk1, sl1yo] 5 times; rep from * to last 12 sts, [brk1, sl1yo] 3 times, brLsl dec, sl1yo, brk1, sl1. Turn.

Row 11 LS LC: as Row 9 LS LC.
Row 11 LS DC: as Row 9 LS DC.

Row 12 DS LC: as Row 2 DS LC.
Row 12 DS DC: sl1, [brk1, sl1yo] twice, brRsl dec, sl1yo, [brk1, sl1yo] 4 times, *[brk1, sl1yo] twice, brRsl dec, sl1yo, [brk1, sl1yo] twice, brRsl dec, sl1yo, [brk1, sl1yo] 4 times; rep from * to last 12 sts, [brk1, sl1yo] twice, brLsl dec, [sl1yo, brk1] twice, sl1. Turn.

Row 13 LS LC: as Row 9 LS LC.
Row 13 LS DC: as Row 9 LS DC.

Row 14 DS LC: as Row 2 DS LC.
Row 14 DS DC: sl1, [brk1, sl1yo] 3 times, brRsl dec, sl1yo, [brk1, sl1yo] 3 times, *brk1, sl1yo, brLsl dec, sl1yo, [brk1, sl1yo] 4 times, brRsl dec, sl1yo, [brk1, sl1yo] 3 times; rep from * to last 12 sts, brk1, sl1yo, brLsl dec, [sl1yo, brk1] 3 times, sl1. Turn.

Row 15 LS LC: as Row 9 LS LC.
Row 15 LS DC: as Row 9 LS DC.

Row 16 DS LC: as Row 2 DS LC.
Row 16 DS DC: sl1, [brk1, sl1yo] 4 times, brRsl dec, sl1yo, [brk1, sl1yo] twice, *brLsl dec, sl1yo, [brk1, sl1yo] 6 times, brRsl dec, sl1yo, [brk1, sl1yo] twice; rep from * to last 12 sts, brLsl dec, [sl1yo, brk1] 4 times, sl1. Turn.

Rep Rows 9–16 (Chart B) two more times.

Rep from Row 1 LS LC.

When desired length has been worked, ending with a Row 8 DS DC or Row 16 DS DC, bind off loosely, preferably with Italian Bind-Off. Work in ends and block as desired. I wet blocked the scarf shown. ∎

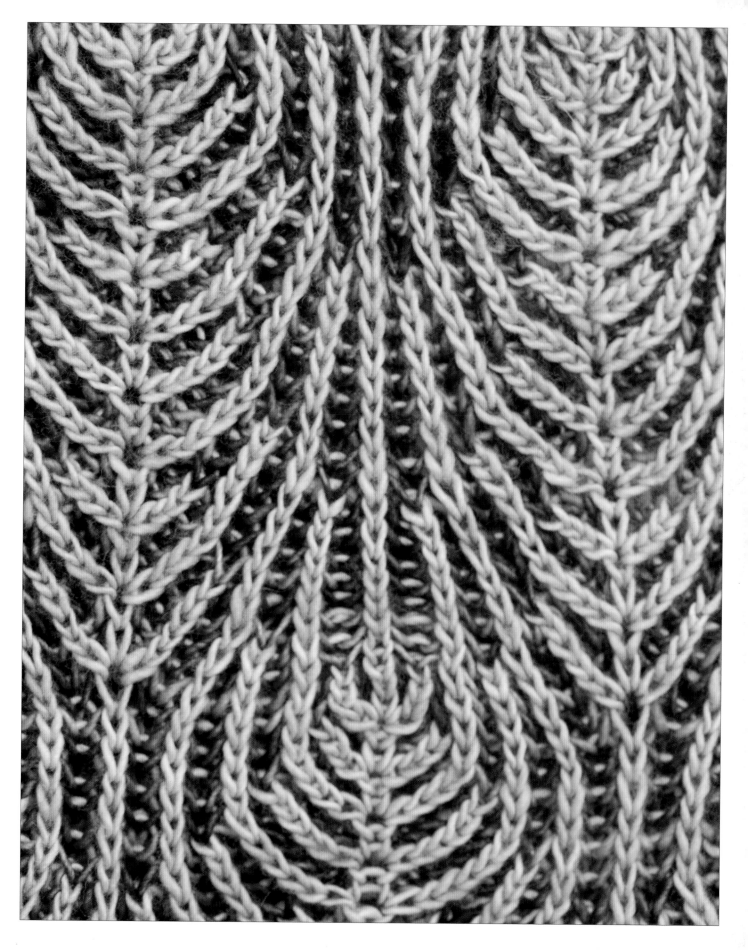

Veda's Peacock

LEGEND for Veda's Peacock

□	= knit on **LS** rows, purl on **DS** rows
−	= purl on **LS** rows, knit on **DS** rows
∨	= slip stitch purlwise
∩	= brk on **LS** rows, brp on **DS** rows
A	= brp on **LS** rows, brk on **DS** rows
‖	= sl1yo
⋔	= brkyobrk
⋔⋔	= br4st inc
⟋	= brLsl dec on **DS DC** Row
⟍	= brRsl dec on **DS DC** Row

Brioche symbols are made to have the appearance as if looking at them on the LS of the work.

Please take note that the symbols for these decreases made in the DS DC rows are slanted in the opposite direction from how the decrease will be made on the DS. For example, the brLsl dec symbol ⟋ (a left slant dec) heads to the right, which is the way it appears, when finished, on the LS of the work.

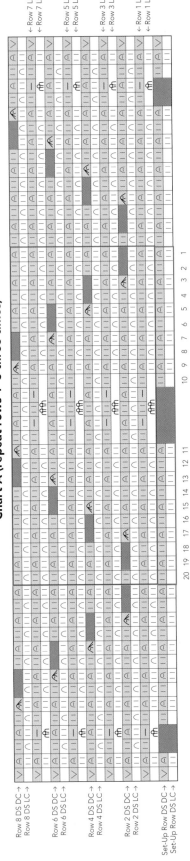

Sister Janie

My knitting buddy Alex first showed me this gorgeous yarn, and I immediately put in an order. Combining a mottled-colored yarn with a more solid one heightens the effect of both yarns.

Finished Measurements
6¼" (16cm) wide × 66" (167cm) long

Yarn
Pigeonroof Studios *Siren Two Sock Yarn* (80% superwash merino, 10% cashmere, 10% nylon) **①**

■ 1 skein = 3½oz/100g (380yd/416m); scarf shown weighs 7oz/205g

■ Colors: 1 skein each in roison (LC) and aubergine (DC)
Note The yarn I used for this scarf has since been discontinued. As an alternative, I suggest Madelinetosh *Tosh Sock*, which comes in a multitude of colorways.

Needles
Size 4 (3.5mm) circular needle

Gauge
One pattern repeat: 14 sts = 2½" (6cm) and 20 rows = 3⅓" (8.5cm)

PATTERN NOTES
1) To avoid confusion, place a marker on the LS LC Row 1. Then you can count up from that row.

2) This stitch pattern uses a multiple of 14 sts + 13.

3) This scarf uses increases and decreases at the very edge of the scarf. See below for special instructions for working them.

EDGE INCREASE
kyok: k1, leaving st on LH needle, yo, then k1 into same st.

EDGE DECREASE
edge brRsl dec: slip first st knitwise, take DC thread to back, then with LC k next st, pass slipped st over, place st on LH needle and pass following st over. Place st on RH needle.
Foll LS DC row: sl1, bring DC to front to cont in pattern.
edge brLsl dec: slip first st knitwise, k the following 2 sts tog, pass slipped st over.

SCARF
Cast on 41 sts using Two-Color Italian Cast-On, beginning and ending with LC knit st.

Set-Up Row 1 DS LC: p1, *sl1yo, p1; rep from * to end.
Do *not* turn, slide.
Set-Up Row 1 DS DC: sl1, *brk1, sl1yo; rep from * to last 2 sts, brk1, sl1. Turn.

Row 1 LS LC: k1, sl1yo, [brk1, sl1yo] twice, *brRsl dec, sl1yo, brk1, sl1yo, brkyobrk, sl1yo, [brk1, sl1yo] 3 times; rep from * to last 7 sts, brRsl dec, sl1yo, brk1, sl1yo, kyok.
Do *not* turn, slide.
Row 1 LS DC: sl1, brp1, [sl1yo, brp1] twice, *[sl1yo, brp1] twice, sl1yo, p1, [sl1yo, brp1] 4 times; rep from * to last 7 sts, [sl1yo, brp1] twice, sl1yo, p1, sl1. Turn.

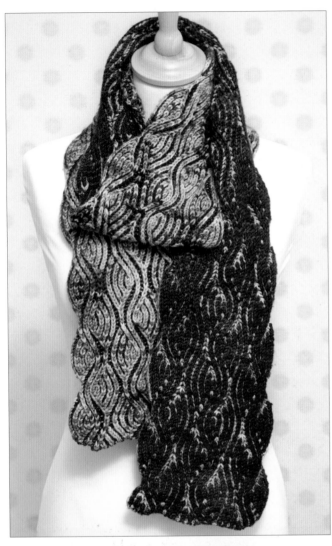

Sister Janie

Row 2 DS LC and all DS LC rows: p1, *sl1yo, brp1; rep from * to last 2 sts, sl1yo, p1. Do *not* turn, slide.

Row 2 DS DC and all DS DC rows: sl1, *brk1, sl1yo; rep from * to last 2 sts, brk1, sl1. Turn.

Row 3 LS LC: k1, sl1yo, brk1, sl1yo, brRsl dec, sl1yo, *brk1, sl1yo, brkyobrk, sl1yo, [brk1, sl1yo] 3 times, brRsl dec, sl1yo; rep from * to last 5 sts, brk1, sl1yo, brkyobrk, sl1yo, k1. Do *not* turn, slide.

Row 3 LS DC: sl1, brp1, [sl1yo, brp1] twice, *sl1yo, brp1, sl1yo, p1, [sl1yo, brp1] 5 times; rep from * to last 7 sts, sl1yo, brp1, sl1yo, p1, sl1yo, brp1, sl1. Turn.

Row 5 LS LC: k1, sl1yo, brRsl dec, sl1yo, brk1, sl1yo, *brkyobrk, sl1yo, [brk1, sl1yo] 3 times, brRsl dec, sl1yo, brk1, sl1yo; rep from * to last 5 sts, brkyobrk, sl1yo, brk1, sl1yo, k1. Do *not* turn, slide.

Row 5 LS DC: sl1, brp1, [sl1yo, brp1] twice, *sl1yo, p1, [sl1yo, brp1] 6 times; rep from * to last 7 sts, sl1yo, p1, [sl1yo, brp1] twice, sl1. Turn.

Row 7 LS LC: edge brRsl dec, sl1yo, brk1, sl1yo, brkyobrk, sl1yo, *[brk1, sl1yo] 3 times, brRsl dec, sl1yo, brk1, sl1yo, brkyobrk, sl1yo; rep from * to last 5 sts, [brk1, sl1yo] twice, k1. Do *not* turn, slide.

Row 7 LS DC: sl1, [brp1, sl1yo] twice, p1, sl1yo, brp1, *[sl1yo, brp1] 5 times, sl1yo, p1, sl1yo, brp1; rep from * to last 5 sts, [sl1yo, brp1] twice, sl1. Turn.

Row 9 LS LC: k1, sl1yo, *brk1, sl1yo; rep from * to last st, k1. Do *not* turn, slide.

Row 9 LS DC: sl1, *brp1, sl1yo; rep from * to last 2 sts, brp1, sl1. Turn.

Row 11 LS LC: kyok, sl1yo, brk1, sl1yo, *brLsl dec, sl1yo, [brk1, sl1yo] 3 times, brkyobrk, sl1yo, brk1, sl1yo; rep from * to last 9 sts, brLsl dec, sl1yo, [brk1, sl1yo] twice, k1. Do *not* turn, slide.

Row 11 LS DC: sl1, p1, [sl1yo, brp1] twice, *[sl1yo, brp1] 4 times, sl1yo, p1, [sl1yo, brp1] twice; rep from * to last 7 sts, [sl1yo, brp1] 3 times, sl1. Turn.

Row 20 DS DC →
Row 20 DS LC →
← Row 19 LS DC
← Row 19 LS LC
Row 18 DS DC →
Row 18 DS LC →
← Row 17 LS DC
← Row 17 LS LC
Row 16 DS DC →
Row 16 DS LC →
← Row 15 LS DC
← Row 15 LS LC
Row 14 DS DC →
Row 14 DS LC →
← Row 13 LS DC
← Row 13 LS LC
Row 12 DS DC →
Row 12 DS LC →
← Row 11 LS DC
← Row 11 LS LC
Row 10 DS DC →
Row 10 DS LC →
← Row 9 LS DC
← Row 9 LS LC
Row 8 DS DC →
Row 8 DS LC →
← Row 7 LS DC
← Row 7 LS LC
Row 6 DS DC →
Row 6 DS LC →
← Row 5 LS DC
← Row 5 LS LC
Row 4 DS DC →
Row 4 DS LC →
← Row 3 LS DC
← Row 3 LS LC
Row 2 DS DC →
Row 2 DS LC →
← Row 1 LS DC
← Row 1 LS LC
Set-Up Row DS DC →
Set-Up Row DS LC →

14 13 12 11 10 9 8 7 6 5 4 3 2 1

Row 13 LS LC: k1, sl1yo, brkyobrk, sl1yo, *brk1, sl1yo, brLsl dec, sl1yo, [brk1, sl1yo] 3 times, brkyobrk, sl1yo; rep from * to last 9 sts, brk1, sl1yo, brLsl dec, sl1yo, brk1, sl1yo, k1. Do *not* turn, slide.

Row 13 LS DC: sl1, brp1, sl1yo, p1, sl1yo, brp1, *[sl1yo, brp1] 5 times, sl1yo, p1, sl1yo, brp1; rep from * to last 7 sts, [sl1yo, brp1] 3 times, sl1. Turn.

Row 15 LS LC: k1, sl1yo, brk1, sl1yo, brkyobrk, sl1yo, *brk1, sl1yo, brLsl dec, sl1yo, [brk1, sl1yo] 3 times, brkyobrk, sl1yo; rep from * to last 7 sts, brk1, sl1yo, brLsl dec, sl1yo, k1. Do *not* turn, slide.

Row 15 LS DC: sl1, [brp1, sl1yo] twice, p1, sl1yo, brp1, *[sl1yo, brp1] 5 times, sl1yo, p1, sl1yo, brp1; rep from * to last 5 sts, [sl1yo, brp1] twice, sl1. Turn.

Row 17 LS LC: k1, sl1yo, [brk1, sl1yo] twice, *brkyobrk, sl1yo, brk1, sl1yo, brLsl dec, sl1yo, [brk1, sl1yo] 3 times; rep from * to last 7 sts, brkyobrk, sl1yo, brk1, sl1yo, edge brLsl dec. Do *not* turn, slide.

Row 17 LS DC: sl1, brp1, [sl1yo, brp1] twice, *sl1yo, p1, [sl1yo, brp1] 6 times; rep from * to last 7 sts, sl1yo, p1, [sl1yo, brp1] twice, sl1. Turn.

Row 19 LS LC: as Row 9 LS LC.
Row 19 LS DC: as Row 9 LS DC.

After working last set of DS rows, rep from Row 1 LS LC.

When desired length has been worked, ending with a Row 10 DS DC or Row 20 DS DC, bind off loosely, preferably with Italian Bind-Off. Work in ends and block as desired. I steam blocked the scarf shown. ∎

Cathedral

When I was in graduate school at Fiberworks in Berkeley, California (a long, long time ago), I worked at Straw Into Gold for Susan Druding. This was a textile student/artist's dream store. Every form of fiber, dye, and book was available. Susan no longer owns a store, but she does own Crystal Palace Yarns. I love the long color change that you get with their *Mini Mochi.*

Finished Measurements
6½" (16cm) wide × 67" (170cm) long

Yarn
Crystal Palace *Mini Mochi*
(80% merino wool, 20% nylon) ①

■ 1 ball = 1¾oz/50g (195yd/180m);
scarf shown weighs 5oz/145g

■ Colors: 2 skeins each in #305 (LC)
and #116 (DC)

Needles
Size 4 (3.5mm) circular needle

Gauge
One pattern repeat: 49 sts = 6½" (16cm)
and 24 rows = 5½" (14cm)

PATTERN NOTES

1) Note that the Dark Side (DS) is the public side of this scarf, and that you work with the Dark Color (DC) first in each set of rows. The legend for the chart has been changed to reflect this.

2) While working the pattern, also note that Row 1 and Row 3 are the same, as are Rows 5 and 7, Rows 9 and 11, and Rows 13 and 15. These rows are then worked backward: Rows 17 and 19 are the same as Rows 9 and 11; Rows 21 and 23 are the same as Rows 5 and 7. The pattern is then repeated again from Row 1.

3) To avoid confusion, place a marker on the DS Row 1 on the right fork of the first increase. Then you can count up from that row.

4) This stitch pattern uses a multiple of 22 sts + 27.

SCARF

Cast on 49 sts using Two-Color Italian Cast-On, beginning and ending with a DC knit st.

Set-Up Row 1 LS DC: p1, *sl1yo, p1; rep from * to end.
Do *not* turn, slide.
Set-Up Row 1 LS LC: sl1, *brk1, sl1yo; rep from * to last 2 sts, brk1, sl1. Turn.

Rows 1 and 3 DS DC: k1, sl1yo, brRsl dec, sl1yo, *brkyobrk, sl1yo, [brk1, sl1yo] 6 times, brkyobrk, sl1yo, br4st dec, sl1yo; rep from * to last 21 sts, brkyobrk, sl1yo, [brk1, sl1yo] 6 times, brkyobrk, sl1yo, brLsl dec, sl1yo, k1. Do *not* turn, slide.
Rows 1 and 3 DS LC: sl1, brp1, sl1yo, brp1, *sl1yo, p1, [sl1yo, brp1] 7 times, sl1yo, p1, [sl1yo, brp1] twice; rep from * to last st, sl1. Turn.

Row 2 LS DC and all LS DC rows: p1, *sl1yo, brp1; rep from * to last 2 sts, sl1yo, p1. Do *not* turn, slide.
Row 2 LS LC and all LS LC rows: sl1, *brk1, sl1yo; rep from * to last 2 sts, brk1, sl1. Turn.

Cathedral

Rows 5 and 7 DS DC: k1, sl1yo, brRsl dec, sl1yo, *brk1, sl1yo, brkyobrk, sl1yo, [brk1, sl1yo] 4 times, brkyobrk, sl1yo, brk1, sl1yo, br4st dec, sl1yo; rep from * to last 21 sts, brk1, sl1yo, brkyobrk, sl1yo, [brk1, sl1yo] 4 times, brkyobrk, sl1yo, brk1, sl1yo, brLsl dec, sl1yo, k1. Do *not* turn, slide.
Rows 5 and 7 DS LC: sl1, brp1, sl1yo, brp1, *sl1yo, brp1, sl1yo, p1, [sl1yo, brp1] 5 times, sl1yo, p1, [sl1yo, brp1] 3 times; rep from * to last st, sl1. Turn.

Rows 9 and 11 DS DC: k1, sl1yo, brRsl dec, sl1yo, *[brk1, sl1yo] twice, brkyobrk, sl1yo, [brk1, sl1yo] twice, brkyobrk, sl1yo, [brk1, sl1yo] twice, br4st dec, sl1yo; rep from * to last 21 sts, [brk1, sl1yo] twice, brkyobrk, sl1yo, [brk1, sl1yo] twice, brkyobrk, sl1yo, [brk1, sl1yo] twice, brLsl dec, sl1yo, k1. Do *not* turn, slide.
Rows 9 and 11 DS LC: sl1, brp1, sl1yo, brp1, *[sl1yo, brp1] twice, sl1yo, p1, [sl1yo, brp1] 3 times, sl1yo, p1, [sl1yo, brp1] 4 times; rep from * to last st, sl1. Turn.

Rows 13 and 15 DS DC: k1, sl1yo, brRsl dec, sl1yo, *[brk1, sl1yo] 3 times, [brkyobrk, sl1yo] twice, [brk1, sl1yo] 3 times, br4st dec, sl1yo; rep from * to last 21 sts, [brk1, sl1yo] 3 times, [brkyobrk, sl1yo] twice, [brk1, sl1yo] 3 times, brLsl dec, sl1yo, k1. Do *not* turn, slide.
Rows 13 and 15 DS LC: sl1, brp1, sl1yo, brp1, *[sl1yo, brp1] 3 times, [sl1yo, p1, sl1yo, brp1] twice, [sl1yo, brp1] 4 times; rep from * to last st, sl1. Turn.

Rows 17 and 19 DS DC: as Row 9 DS DC.
Rows 17 and 19 DS LC: as Row 9 DS LC.

Rows 21 and 23 DS DC: as Row 5 DS DC.
Rows 21 and 23 DS LC: as Row 5 DS LC.

After working last set of DS rows, rep from Row 1 DS DC.

When desired length has been worked, ending with a Row 4 LS LC or Row 16 LS LC, bind off loosely, preferably with Italian Bind-Off. Work in ends and block as desired. I steam blocked the scarf shown. ■

LEGEND for **Cathedral**	
☐	= knit on **DS** rows, purl on **LS** rows
⊟	= purl on **DS** rows, knit on **LS** rows
▽	= slip stitch purlwise
∩	= brk on **DS** rows, brp on **LS** rows
⌂	= brp on **DS** rows, brk on **LS** rows
⊔	= sl1yo
⋔	= brkyobrk on **DS DC** rows
⋏	= brRsl dec on **DS DC** rows
⋏	= brLsl dec on **DS DC** rows
⋏	= br4st dec on **DS DC** rows

Row 23 DS LC ↓ / Row 23 DS DC ↓
Row 21 DS LC ↓ / Row 21 DS DC ↓
Row 19 DS LC ↓ / Row 19 DS DC ↓
Row 17 DS LC ↓ / Row 17 DS DC ↓
Row 15 DS LC ↓ / Row 15 DS DC ↓
Row 13 DS LC ↓ / Row 13 DS DC ↓
Row 11 DS LC ↓ / Row 11 DS DC ↓
Row 9 DS LC ↓ / Row 9 DS DC ↓
Row 7 DS LC ↓ / Row 7 DS DC ↓
Row 5 DS LC ↓ / Row 5 DS DC ↓
Row 3 DS LC ↓ / Row 3 DS DC ↓
Row 1 DS LC ↓ / Row 1 DS DC ↓

Column numbers: 22 21 20 19 18 17 16 15 14 13 12 11 10 9 8 7 6 5 4 3 2 1

Row 24 LS LC → / Row 24 LS DC →
Row 22 LS LC → / Row 22 LS DC →
Row 20 LS LC → / Row 20 LS DC →
Row 18 LS LC → / Row 18 LS DC →
Row 16 LS LC → / Row 16 LS DC →
Row 14 LS LC → / Row 14 LS DC →
Row 12 LS LC → / Row 12 LS DC →
Row 10 LS LC → / Row 10 LS DC →
Row 8 LS LC → / Row 8 LS DC →
Row 6 LS LC → / Row 6 LS DC →
Row 4 LS LC → / Row 4 LS DC →
Row 2 LS LC → / Row 2 LS DC →
Set-Up Row LS LC → / Set-Up Row LS DC →

Miss B

Miss B is my buddy Nancy Bush. We like to travel together, mainly to Estonia. We have a lot of things in common, one of them being that we both studied Japanese textiles. The stitch pattern in Miss B, a triangular shawl, is very evocative of Japan.

Finished Measurements
63" (160cm) wide x 24 ½" (62cm) deep, after blocking.

Yarn
KnitWitches Yarns *Seriously Gorgeous Laceweight Kid/Silk* (60% kid mohair, 40% silk) (**1**)

■ 1¾oz/50g (656yd/600m); shawl shown weighs 1½oz/37g

■ Colors: 20g each in Anne's silver (LC) and winter sea (DC)

Needles
Size 7 (4.5mm) circular needle

Gauge
One pattern repeat: 16 sts = 4" (10cm) and 12 rows = 3" (7.5cm)

PATTERN NOTES

1) This shawl starts at the upper middle of the shawl with a wrap cast-on.

2) I advise using bamboo needles when working with slippery yarns such as alpaca or silk.

3) Place a marker on the LS middle stitch (this will be a purl column), and place markers between each pattern repeat to keep track of stitches.

4) With such a large project, I suggest running a lifeline every several rows.

5) This shawl does not have a selvedge stitch. You will "brioche" the edge stitches to keep it firm. Be aware that when you come to the end of a LC row, you need to either brk1 or brp1. These stitches at the very end of the row often look like 2 separate stitches, so be sure to work them together.

6) To more easily follow the Miss B Repeat Chart, make a copy of both left and right edges. Cut them out, making sure you cut away one of the middle stitches on the chart, so that only one middle stitch remains. Tape them together to make a complete chart.

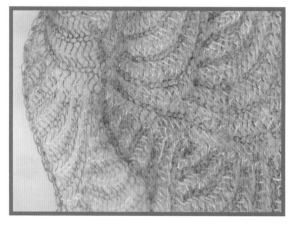

WRAP CAST-ON
If you are an English style knitter, make a circle by wrapping both yarns clockwise around your left index finger once. If you are a Continental style knitter, wrap both yarns clockwise around a large knitting needle once. With LC, go into the middle of the circle knitwise (English style: use your finger as LH needle), and k1, yo, k1, yo, k1, yo, k1; creating 7 stitches in the wrap. Tighten up the wrapped circle.

SHAWL
Work Wrap Cast-On. Do *not* turn; slide sts back to opposite end of needle.

Miss B

Set-Up Row 1 LS DC: [sl1yo, p1] 3 times, sl1yo. Turn. 7 sts.

Set-Up Row 2 DS LC: brp1, *sl1yo, brp1; rep from *.
Do *not* turn; slide.
Set-Up Row 2 DS DC: sl1yo, *brk1, sl1yo; rep from *. Turn.

BEGINNING MISS B
Row 1 LS LC: brk1, sl1yo, [br4st inc, sl1yo] twice, brk1.
Do *not* turn; slide.
Row 1 LS DC: sl1yo , brp1, [sl1yo, p1] twice, sl1yo, brp1,
[sl1yo, p1] twice, sl1yo, brp1, sl1yo. Turn. 15 sts.

Row 2 and all DS LC rows: brp1, *sl1yo, brp1; rep from *.
Do *not* turn; slide.
Row 2 and all DS LC rows: sl1yo, *brk1, sl1yo; rep from *.
Turn.

Row 3 LS LC: [brk1, sl1yo] 3 times, brkyobrk, sl1yo, brkyobrk,
[sl1yo, brk1] 3 times. Do *not* turn; slide.
Row 3 LS DC: [sl1yo, brp1] 3 times, sl1yo, p1, sl1yo, brp1,
sl1yo, p1, [sl1yo, brp1] 3 times, sl1yo. Turn. 19 sts.

Row 5 LS LC: [brk1, sl1yo] 4 times, brkyobrk, sl1yo, brkyobrk,
[sl1yo, brk1] 4 times. Do *not* turn; slide.
Row 5 LS DC: [sl1yo, brp1] 4 times, sl1yo, p1, sl1yo, brp1,
sl1yo, p1, [sl1yo, brp1] 4 times, sl1yo. Turn. 23 sts.

Row 7 LS LC: [brk1, sl1yo] 5 times, brkyobrk, sl1yo, brkyobrk,
[sl1yo, brk1] 5 times. Do *not* turn; slide.
Row 7 LS DC: [sl1yo, brp1] 5 times, sl1yo, p1, sl1yo, brp1,
sl1yo, p1, [sl1yo, brp1] 5 times, sl1yo. Turn. 27 sts.

Row 9 LS LC: [brk1, sl1yo] 6 times, brkyobrk, sl1yo, brkyobrk,
[sl1yo, brk1] 6 times. Do *not* turn; slide.
Row 9 LS DC: [sl1yo, brp1] 6 times, sl1yo, p1, sl1yo, brp1,
sl1yo, p1, [sl1yo, brp1] 6 times, sl1yo. Turn. 31 sts.

Row 11 LS LC: brk1, sl1yo, brkyobrk, sl1yo, [brk1, sl1yo] 5
times, brkyobrk, sl1yo, brkyobrk, [sl1yo, brk1] 5 times, sl1yo,
brkyobrk, sl1yo, brk1. Do *not* turn; slide.
Row 11 LS DC: sl1yo , brp1, sl1yo, p1, [sl1yo, brp1] 6 times,
sl1yo, p1, sl1yo, brp1, sl1yo, p1, [sl1yo, brp1] 6 times, sl1yo, p1,
sl1yo, brp1, sl1yo. Turn. 39 sts.

MISS B REPEAT
Note: See both Left Side and Right Side charts.
Mark the middle stitch, a DC purl column on the LS.

Row 13 LS LC: brk1, sl1yo, br4st inc, *[sl1yo, brk1] 5 times,
sl1yo, brRsl dec, sl1yo, brkyobrk*, rep from * to * to middle
st, sl1yo (this is the middle st), ^brkyobrk, sl1yo, brLsl dec,
[sl1yo, brk1] 5 times, sl1yo^, rep from ^ to ^ to last 3 sts,
br4st inc, sl1yo, brk1. Do *not* turn; slide.
Row 13 LS DC: sl1yo , brp1, sl1yo, [p1, sl1yo] twice, *[brp1,
sl1yo] 7 times, p1, sl1yo*, rep from * to * to middle st, brp1
(this is the middle st), ^sl1yo, p1, [sl1yo, brp1] 7 times^, rep
from ^ to ^ to last 7 sts, [sl1yo, p1] twice, sl1yo, brp1, sl1yo.
Turn.

Row 15 LS LC: [brk1, sl1yo] 3 times, brkyobrk, *[sl1yo, brk1] 4
times, sl1yo, brRsl dec, sl1yo, brk1, sl1yo, brkyobrk*, rep from
* to * to middle st, sl1yo, ^brkyobrk, sl1yo, brk1, sl1yo, brLsl
dec, [sl1yo, brk1] 4 times, sl1yo^, rep from ^ to ^ to last 7 sts,
brkyobrk, [sl1yo, brk1] 3 times. Do *not* turn; slide.
Row 15 LS DC: [sl1yo, brp1] 3 times, sl1yo, p1, sl1yo,*[brp1,
sl1yo] 7 times, p1, sl1yo*, rep from * to * to middle st, brp1,
^sl1yo, p1, [sl1yo, brp1] 7 times^, rep from ^ to ^ to last 9
sts, sl1yo, p1, [sl1yo, brp1] 3 times, sl1yo. Turn.

Row 17 LS LC: [brk1, sl1yo] 4 times, brkyobrk, *[sl1yo, brk1]
3 times, sl1yo, brRsl dec, [sl1yo, brk1] twice, sl1yo, brkyobrk*,
rep from * to * to middle st, sl1yo, ^brkyobrk, sl1yo, [brk1,
sl1yo] twice, brLsl dec, [sl1yo, brk1] 3 times, sl1yo^, rep from
^ to ^ to last 9 sts, brkyobrk, [sl1yo, brk1] 4 times.
Do *not* turn; slide.
Row 17 LS DC: [sl1yo, brp1] 4 times, sl1yo, p1, sl1yo,*[brp1,
sl1yo] 7 times, p1, sl1yo*, rep from * to * to middle st, brp1,
^sl1yo, p1, [sl1yo, brp1] 7 times^, rep from ^ to ^ to last 11
sts, sl1yo, p1, [sl1yo, brp1] 4 times, sl1yo. Turn.

Row 19 LS LC: [brk1, sl1yo] 5 times, brkyobrk, *[sl1yo, brk1]
twice, sl1yo, brRsl dec, [sl1yo, brk1] 3 times, sl1yo, brkyobrk*,
rep from * to * to middle st, sl1yo, ^brkyobrk, sl1yo, [brk1,
sl1yo] 3 times, brLsl dec, [sl1yo, brk1] twice, sl1yo^, rep from
^ to ^ to last 11 sts, brkyobrk, [sl1yo, brk1] 5 times.
Do *not* turn; slide.
Row 19 LS DC: [sl1yo, brp1] 5 times, sl1yo, p1, sl1yo,*[brp1,
sl1yo] 7 times, p1, sl1yo*, rep from * to * to middle st, brp1,
^sl1yo, p1, [sl1yo, brp1] 7 times^, rep from ^ to ^ to last
13 sts, sl1yo, p1, [sl1yo, brp1] 5 times, sl1yo. Turn.

Miss B

Row 21 LS LC: [brk1, sl1yo] 6 times, brkyobrk, *sl1yo, brk1, sl1yo, brRsl dec, [sl1yo, brk1] 4 times, sl1yo, brkyobrk*, rep from * to * to middle st, sl1yo, ^brkyobrk, sl1yo, [brk1, sl1yo] 4 times, brLsl dec, sl1yo, brk1, sl1yo^, rep from ^ to ^ to last 13 sts, brkyobrk, [sl1yo, brk1] 6 times. Do *not* turn; slide.

Row 21 LS DC: [sl1yo, brp1] 6 times, sl1yo, p1, sl1yo,*[brp1, sl1yo] 7 times, p1, sl1yo*, rep from * to * to middle st, brp1, ^sl1yo, p1, [sl1yo, brp1] 7 times^, rep from ^ to ^ to last 15 sts, sl1yo, p1, [sl1yo, brp1] 6 times, sl1yo. Turn.

Row 23 LS LC: brk1, sl1yo, brkyobrk, sl1yo, [brk1, sl1yo] 5 times, brkyobrk, *sl1yo, brRsl dec, [sl1yo, brk1] 5 times, sl1yo, brkyobrk*, rep from * to * to middle st, sl1yo, ^brkyobrk, sl1yo, [brk1, sl1yo] 5 times, brLsl dec, sl1yo^, rep from ^ to ^ to last 15 sts, brkyobrk, [sl1yo, brk1] 5 times, sl1yo, brkyobrk, sl1yo, brk1. Do *not* turn; slide.

Row 23 LS DC: sl1yo, brp1, sl1yo, p1, [sl1yo, brp1] 6 times, sl1yo, p1, sl1yo, *[brp1, sl1yo] 7 times, p1, sl1yo*, rep from * to * to middle st, brp1, ^sl1yo, p1, [sl1yo, brp1] 7 times^, rep from ^ to ^ to last 19 sts, sl1yo, p1, [sl1yo, brp1] 6 times, sl1yo, p1, sl1yo, brp1, sl1yo. Turn.
After working last set of DS rows, rep from Row 13 LS LC.

Work Rows 13–24 seven times and then bind off as follows: k1, k1, *insert LH needle into these two stitches on RH needle and knit them together, k1; rep from * to end.

Work in ends and wet block the shawl. ■

Miss B Beginning Chart - work once

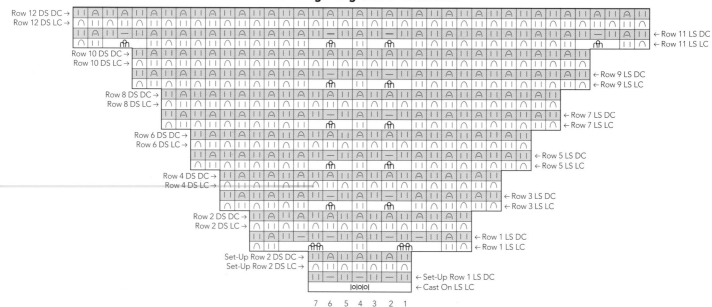

Miss B Repeat Chart: Left Side

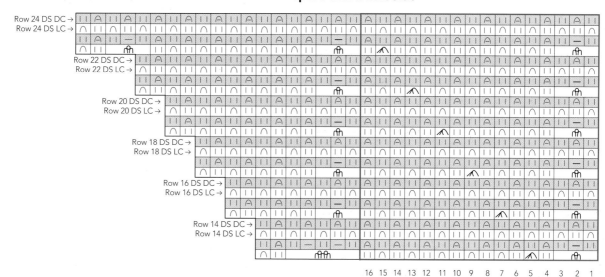

Row 24 DS DC →
Row 24 DS LC →
Row 22 DS DC →
Row 22 DS LC →
Row 20 DS DC →
Row 20 DS LC →
Row 18 DS DC →
Row 18 DS LC →
Row 16 DS DC →
Row 16 DS LC →
Row 14 DS DC →
Row 14 DS LC →

16 15 14 13 12 11 10 9 8 7 6 5 4 3 2 1

middle stitch
↓

Miss B Repeat Chart: Right Side

← Row 23 LS DC
← Row 23 LS LC
← Row 21 LS DC
← Row 21 LS LC
← Row 19 LS DC
← Row 19 LS LC
← Row 17 LS DC
← Row 17 LS LC
← Row 15 LS DC
← Row 15 LS LC
← Row 13 LS DC
← Row 13 LS LC

16 15 14 13 12 11 10 9 8 7 6 5 4 3 2 1

■ The Miss B Repeat Chart has been split to fit onto the page. To more easily follow this chart, make a copy of both left and right sides. Cut them out and tape them together to make a complete chart.

Nan's Other Cowl

Jacki is one of my knitting buddies, and Nan is one of her oldest and dearest friends. We have spent time together at several knitting events, and Nan once admired a cowl I was wearing and asked for the pattern. The cowl shown here is a variation on the original Nan's Cowl.

Finished Measurements
67" (170cm) long × 34" (86cm) in circumference

Yarn
Bart & Francis *Shantung Yaspee* (100% shantung silk) **1**

■ 1 cone = 1¾oz/50g (273yd/250m); cowl shown weighs 2½oz/70g

■ Colors: 1 cone each in #980 rust (LC) and #875 dark brown-black (DC)

Needles
Size 3 (3mm) circular needle, 24"/60cm long

Gauge
Two pattern repeats: 20 sts = 4½" (11.5cm); and 15 LC and DC rounds = 4½" (11.5cm)

● PATTERN NOTES
1) This cowl is worked in the round. Please see the instructions on page 16 for casting on a large number of stitches using the Two-Color Italian Cast-On with a lifeline, and see page 228 for a guide to working brioche in the round.

2) The stitch pattern is a multiple of 10 sts. The pattern will increase up to 16 stitches (Round 1 DC) and then down to 8 stitches (Round 8 DC). Take note that the decreases for the second part of the pattern begin in a DC round (Round 8 DC).

3) This pattern uses syncopation, which means the barks and burps switch back and forth with each color. This also means you will end a round with a sl1yo, so be sure to maintain this yarn over when working the stitch in the following round.

4) Place a marker at the beginning of the round and on the first stitch of the pattern (Round 1 LC), so that you can count rounds. Also, placing a marker between stitches 9 and 10 and between stitches 10 and 1 will help indicate when syncopation occurs.

COWL
Cast on 150 sts using Two-Color Italian Cast-On, beginning with LC knit st and ending with DC purl st.

Join to begin working in the rnd, being careful not to twist sts. Remember to drop first "knot" at beginning of cast-on. Place marker to indicate beginning of rnd.

Set-Up Round 1 LC: *k1, sl1yo; rep from * around, leaving yarn to front at end of rnd.
Set-Up Round 1 DC: *sl1yo, brp1; rep from * around, leaving yarn to front at end of rnd.

Set-Up Round 2 LC: *brk1, sl1yo; rep from * around, leaving yarn to front at end of rnd.
Set-Up Round 2 DC: *sl1yo, brp1; rep from * around, leaving yarn to front at end of rnd.

Nan's Other Cowl

Round 1 LC: take LC to back, *[brk1, sl1yo] 3 times, brRsl dec, pm, sl1yo, pm; rep from * around, leaving yarn to front at end of rnd.
Round 1 DC: *[sl1yo, brp1] 3 times, sl1yo, sm, br8st inc, sm; rep from * around, leaving yarn to front at end of rnd.

Round 2 LC: take LC to back, *[brk1, sl1yo] 3 times, brk1, sm, sl1yo, [p1, sl1yo] 4 times, sm; rep from * around, leaving yarn to front at end of rnd.
Round 2 DC: *[sl1yo, brp1] 3 times, sl1yo, sm, [brk1, sl1yo] 4 times, brk1, sm; rep from * around, leaving yarn to front at end of rnd.

Round 3 LC: take LC to back, *[brk1, sl1yo] twice, brRsl dec, sm, sl1yo, [brp1, sl1yo] 4 times, sm; rep from * around, leaving yarn to front at end of rnd.
Round 3 DC: *[sl1yo, brp1] twice, sl1yo, sm, [brk1, sl1yo] 4 times, brk1, sm; rep from * around, leaving yarn to front at end of rnd.

Round 4 LC: take LC to back, *[brk1, sl1yo] twice, brk1, sm, [sl1yo, brp1] 4 times, sl1yo, sm; rep from * around, leaving yarn to front at end of rnd.
Round 4 DC: *[sl1yo, brp1] twice, sl1yo, sm, [brk1, sl1yo] 4 times, brk1, sm; rep from * around, leaving yarn to front at end of rnd.

Round 5 LC: take LC to back, *brk1, sl1yo, brRsl dec, sm, sl1yo, [brp1, sl1yo] 4 times, sm; rep from * around, leaving yarn to front at end of rnd.
Round 5 DC: *sl1yo, brp1, sl1yo, sm, [brk1, sl1yo] 4 times, brk1, sm; rep from * around, leaving yarn to front at end of rnd.

Round 6 LC: take LC to back, *brk1, sl1yo, brk1, sm, [sl1yo, brp1] 4 times, sl1yo, sm; rep from * around, leaving yarn to front at end of rnd.
Round 6 DC: *sl1yo, brp1, sl1yo, sm, [brk1, sl1yo] 4 times, brk1, sm; rep from * around, leaving yarn to front at end of rnd.

Round 7 LC: take LC to back, *brRsl dec, sm, sl1yo, [brp1, sl1yo] 4 times, sm; rep from * around, leaving yarn to front at end of rnd.
Round 7 DC: *sl1yo, sm, [brk1, sl1yo] 4 times, brk1, sm; rep from * around, leaving yarn to front at end of rnd.

Round 8 LC: take LC to back, *brk1, sm, sl1yo, [brp1, sl1yo] 4 times, sm; rep from * around, leaving yarn to front at end of rnd.
Round 8 DC: *sl1yo, sm, brLsl dec, [sl1yo, brk1] 3 times, sm; rep from * around, leaving yarn to front at end of rnd.

Round 9 LC: take LC to back, *br8st inc, sm, sl1yo, [brp1, sl1yo] 3 times, sm; rep from * around, leaving yarn to front at end of rnd.
Round 9 DC: *[sl1yo, p1] 4 times, sl1yo, sm, [brk1, sl1yo] 3 times, brk1, sm; rep from * around, leaving yarn to front at end of rnd.

Round 10 LC: take LC to back, *[brk1, sl1yo] 4 times, brk1, sm, sl1yo, [brp1, sl1yo] 3 times, sm; rep from * around, leaving yarn to front at end of rnd.
Round 10 DC: *[sl1yo, brp1] 4 times, sl1yo, sm, brLsl dec, [sl1yo, brk1] twice, sm; rep from * around, leaving yarn to front at end of rnd.

Round 11 LC: take LC to back, *[brk1, sl1yo] 4 times, brk1, sm, sl1yo, [brp1, sl1yo] twice, sm; rep from * around, leaving yarn to front at end of rnd.
Round 11 DC: *[sl1yo, brp1] 4 times, sl1yo, sm, [brk1, sl1yo] twice, brk1, sm; rep from * around, leaving yarn to front at end of rnd.

Round 12 LC: take LC to back, *[brk1, sl1yo] 4 times, brk1, sm, sl1yo, [brp1, sl1yo] twice, sm; rep from * around, leaving yarn to front at end of rnd.
Round 12 DC: *[sl1yo, brp1] 4 times, sl1yo, sm, brLsl dec, sl1yo, brk1, sm; rep from * around, leaving yarn to front at end of rnd.

Round 13 LC: take LC to back, *[brk1, sl1yo] 4 times, brk1, sm, sl1yo, brp1, sl1yo, sm; rep from * around, leaving yarn to front at end of rnd.
Round 13 DC: *[sl1yo, brp1] 4 times, sl1yo, sm, brk1, sl1yo, brk1, sm; rep from * around, leaving yarn to front at end of rnd.

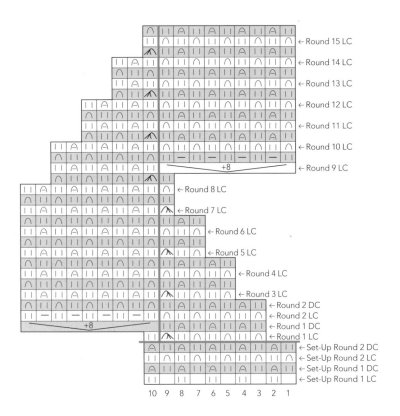

← Round 15 LC
← Round 14 LC
← Round 13 LC
← Round 12 LC
← Round 11 LC
← Round 10 LC
+8 ← Round 9 LC
← Round 8 LC
← Round 7 LC
← Round 6 LC
← Round 5 LC
← Round 4 LC
← Round 3 LC
← Round 2 DC
← Round 2 LC
← Round 1 DC
← Round 1 LC
+8
← Set-Up Round 2 DC
← Set-Up Round 2 LC
← Set-Up Round 1 DC
← Set-Up Round 1 LC

10 9 8 7 6 5 4 3 2 1

LEGEND for **Nan's Other Cowl**	
| = this line is used to indicate the division of the "leaves"	☐ = knit
	− = purl
	∩ = brk
	|| = sl1yo
	⌐ = brp
	⋏ = brLsl dec
	⋏ = brRsl dec
+8	= br8st inc

Nan's Other Cowl

Round 14 LC: take LC to back, *[brk1, sl1yo] 4 times, brk1, sm, sl1yo, brp1, sl1yo, sm; rep from * around, leaving yarn to front at end of rnd.
Round 14 DC: *[sl1yo, brp1] 4 times, sl1yo, sm, brLsl dec, sm; rep from * around, leaving yarn to front at end of rnd.

Round 15 LC: take LC to back, *[brk1, sl1yo] 4 times, brk1, sm, sl1yo, sm; rep from * around, leaving yarn to front at end of rnd.
Round 15 DC: *[sl1yo, brp1] 4 times, sl1yo, sm, brk1, sm; rep from * around, leaving yarn to front at end of rnd.

Repeat from Round 1 LC.

When desired length has been worked, ending with a Round 8 DC or Round 15 DC, bind off loosely, preferably with Italian Bind-Off. Work in ends and block as desired.
I steam blocked the cowl shown. ■

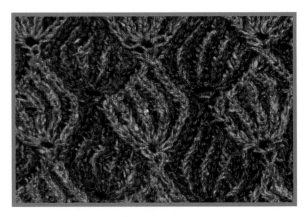

Gretchen's Zigzag

I purchased this yarn at the Vogue Knitting LIVE event in New York City. Gretchen was working in the Solitude Wool booth that day and was so excited about her dyed yarns. I originally had bought the varigated yarn along with a very dark brown contrasting yarn. When I showed them to my knitting buddy Nancy Bush, she suggested that I exchange the dark yarn for a light one—I did just that and love the result.

Finished Measurements
6¾" (17cm) wide × 75" (190cm) long

Yarn
Solitude Wool *Corriedale* (100% wool) 🔵4🔵

- 1 skein = 5oz/141g (240yd/219m); scarf shown weighs 7oz/205g

- Colors: 1 large skein each in natural 2 (LC) and handpainted geology (DC)

Needles
Size 6 (4mm) circular needle

Gauge
One zigzag pattern repeat:
33 sts = 6¾" (17cm) and
20 rows = 4½" (11.5cm)

PATTERN NOTES
1) This scarf starts with a single stitch. Increases are made until you have 33 stitches on the needle, then the zigzag pattern is worked over these 33 stitches, until you are ready to begin decreasing back down to a single stitch at the end.

2) To avoid confusion, place a marker on the LS LC Row 33. Then you can count up from that row.

3) At times, this pattern uses decreases at the very edge of the scarf. See below for instructions for working them.

EDGE DECREASES
⌃ **edge brRsl dec:** slip first st knitwise, take DC thread to back; with LC, k next st, pass slipped st over, place st on LH needle and pass following st over. Place st on RH needle.
Foll LS DC row: sl1, bring DC to front to cont in pattern.
⌃ **edge brLsl dec:** slip first st knitwise, k following 2 stitches tog, pass slipped st over.

SCARF
BEGINNING (CHART A)
Make a slip knot, holding both strands together. Begin by working Row 1 LS LC into the slip knot.

Row 1 LS LC: brkyobrk. Do *not* turn, slide.
Row 1 LS DC: sl1, p1, sl1. Turn.

Row 2 DS LC: p1, sl1yo, p1. Do *not* turn, slide.
Row 2 DS DC: sl1yo, brk1, s1. Turn.

Row 3 LS LC: k1, sl1yo, brkyobrk. Do *not* turn, slide.
Row 3 LS DC: sl1, brp1, sl1yo, p1, sl1. Turn.

Gretchen's Zigzag

Rows 4, 6, 8, 10 and 12 DS LC: p1, *sl1yo, brp1; rep from * to last 2 sts, sl1yo, p1. Do *not* turn, slide.

Rows 4, 6, 8, 10 and 12 DS DC: sl1yo, *brk1, sl1yo; rep from * to last 2 sts, brk1, sl1. Turn.

Rows 5, 7, 9 and 11 LS LC: k1, sl1yo, *brk1, sl1yo; rep from * to last st, brkyobrk. Do *not* turn, slide.

Rows 5, 7, 9 and 11 LS DC: sl1, brp1, *sl1yo, brp1; rep from * to last 3 sts, which are inc sts from previous row, sl1yo, p1, sl1. Turn.

At the end of Row 12 DS DC you should have 13 sts.

Row 13 LS LC: k1, sl1yo, [brk1, sl1yo] 4 times, brkyobrk, sl1yo, k1. Do *not* turn, slide.

Row 13 LS DC: sl1, brp1, [sl1yo, brp1] 4 times, sl1yo, p1, sl1yo, brp1, sl1. Turn.

Row 14 DS LC and all other beginning DS LC rows: p1, *sl1yo, brp1; rep from * to last 2 sts, sl1yo, p1. Do *not* turn, slide.

Row 14 DS DC and all other beginning DS DC rows: sl1, *brk1, sl1yo; rep from * to last 2 sts, brk1, sl1. Turn.

Row 15 LS LC: k1, sl1yo, [brk1, sl1yo] 4 times, brkyobrk, sl1yo, brk1, sl1yo, k1. Do *not* turn, slide.

Row 15 LS DC: sl1, brp1, [sl1yo, brp1] 4 times, sl1yo, p1, [sl1yo, brp1] twice, sl1. Turn.

Row 17 LS LC: k1, sl1yo, [brk1, sl1yo] 4 times, brkyobrk, sl1yo, [brk1, sl1yo] twice, k1. Do *not* turn, slide.

Row 17 LS DC: sl1, brp1, [sl1yo, brp1] 4 times, sl1yo, p1, [sl1yo, brp1] 3 times, sl1. Turn.

Row 19 LS LC: k1, sl1yo, [brk1, sl1yo] 4 times, brkyobrk, sl1yo, [brk1, sl1yo] 3 times, k1. Do *not* turn, slide.

Row 19 LS DC: sl1, brp1, [sl1yo, brp1] 4 times, sl1yo, p1, [sl1yo, brp1] 4 times, sl1. Turn.

Row 21 LS LC: k1, sl1yo, [brk1, sl1yo] 4 times, brkyobrk, sl1yo, [brk1, sl1yo] 4 times, k1. Do *not* turn, slide.

Row 21 LS DC: sl1, brp1, [sl1yo, brp1] 4 times, sl1yo, p1, [sl1yo, brp1] 5 times, sl1. Turn.

At the end of Row 22 DS DC you should have 23 sts.

Row 23 LS LC: k1, sl1yo, [brk1, sl1yo] 5 times, brkyobrk, sl1yo, [brk1, sl1yo] 4 times, k1. Do *not* turn, slide.

Row 23 LS DC: sl1, brp1, [sl1yo, brp1] 5 times, sl1yo, p1, [sl1yo, brp1] 5 times, sl1. Turn.

Row 25 LS LC: k1, sl1yo, [brk1, sl1yo] 6 times, brkyobrk, sl1yo, [brk1, sl1yo] 4 times, k1. Do *not* turn, slide.

Row 25 LS DC: sl1, brp1, [sl1yo, brp1] 6 times, sl1yo, p1, [sl1yo, brp1] 5 times, sl1. Turn.

Row 27 LS LC: k1, sl1yo, [brk1, sl1yo] 7 times, brkyobrk, sl1yo, [brk1, sl1yo] 4 times, k1. Do *not* turn, slide.

Row 27 LS DC: sl1, brp1, [sl1yo, brp1] 7 times, sl1yo, p1, [sl1yo, brp1] 5 times, sl1. Turn.

Row 29 LS LC: k1, sl1yo, [brk1, sl1yo] 8 times, brkyobrk, sl1yo, [brk1, sl1yo] 4 times, k1. Do *not* turn, slide.

Row 29 LS DC: sl1, brp1, [sl1yo, brp1] 8 times, sl1yo, p1, [sl1yo, brp1] 5 times, sl1. Turn.

Row 31 LS LC: k1, sl1yo, [brk1, sl1yo] 9 times, brkyobrk, sl1yo, [brk1, sl1yo] 4 times, k1. Do *not* turn, slide.

Row 31 LS DC: sl1, brp1, [sl1yo, brp1] 9 times, sl1yo, p1, [sl1yo, brp1] 5 times, sl1. Turn.

At the end of Row 32 DS DC you should have 33 sts.

ZIGZAG PATTERN REPEAT (CHART B)

Row 33 LS LC: edge brRsl dec, sl1yo, [brk1, sl1yo] 8 times, brkyobrk, sl1yo, [brk1, sl1yo] 5 times, k1. Do *not* turn, slide.

Row 33 LS DC: sl1, brp1, [sl1yo, brp1] 8 times, sl1yo, p1, [sl1yo, brp1] 6 times, sl1. Turn.

Row 34 DS LC and all zigzag pattern DS LC rows: p1, *sl1yo, brp1; rep from * to last 2 sts, sl1yo, p1. Do *not* turn, slide.

Row 34 DS DC and all zigzag pattern DS DC rows: sl1, *brk1, sl1yo; rep from * to last 2 sts, brk1, sl1. Turn.

Row 35 LS LC: edge brRsl dec, sl1yo, [brk1, sl1yo] 7 times, brkyobrk, sl1yo, [brk1, sl1yo] 6 times, k1. Do *not* turn, slide.

Row 35 LS DC: sl1, brp1, [sl1yo, brp1] 7 times, sl1yo, p1, [sl1yo, brp1] 7 times, sl1. Turn.

Beginning Chart A

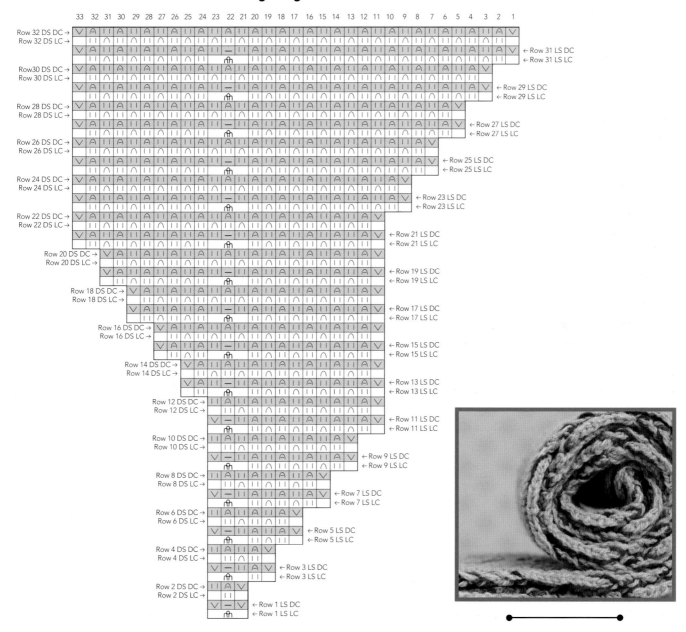

Row 37 LS LC: edge brRsl dec, sl1yo, [brk1, sl1yo] 6 times, brkyobrk, sl1yo, [brk1, sl1yo] 7 times, k1. Do *not* turn, slide.
Row 37 LS DC: sl1, brp1, [sl1yo, brp1] 6 times, sl1yo, p1, [sl1yo, brp1] 8 times, sl1. Turn.

Row 39 LS LC: edge brRsl dec, sl1yo, [brk1, sl1yo] 5 times, brkyobrk, sl1yo, [brk1, sl1yo] 8 times, k1. Do *not* turn, slide.
Row 39 LS DC: sl1, brp1, [sl1yo, brp1] 5 times, sl1yo, p1, [sl1yo, brp1] 9 times, sl1. Turn.

Row 41 LS LC: edge brRsl dec, sl1yo, [brk1, sl1yo] 4 times, brkyobrk, sl1yo, [brk1, sl1yo] 9 times, k1. Do *not* turn, slide.
Row 41 LS DC: sl1, brp1, *[sl1yo, brp1] 4 times, sl1yo, p1, [sl1yo, brp1] 10 times, sl1. Turn.

Row 43 LS LC: k1, sl1yo, [brk1, sl1yo] 5 times, brkyobrk, sl1yo, [brk1, sl1yo] 8 times, edge brLsl dec. Do *not* turn, slide.
Row 43 LS DC: sl1, brp1, [sl1yo, brp1] 5 times, sl1yo, p1, [sl1yo, brp1] 9 times, sl1. Turn.

Gretchen's Zigzag

Pattern Repeat Chart B

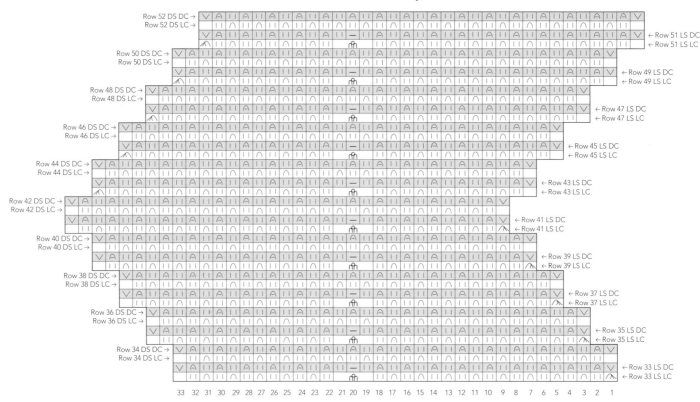

Row 45 LS LC: k1, sl1yo, [brk1, sl1yo] 6 times, brkyobrk, sl1yo, [brk1, sl1yo] 7 times, edge brLsl dec. Do *not* turn, slide.
Row 45 LS DC: sl1, brp1, [sl1yo, brp1] 6 times, sl1yo, p1, [sl1yo, brp1] 8 times, sl1. Turn.

Row 47 LS LC: k1, sl1yo, [brk1, sl1yo] 7 times, brkyobrk, sl1yo, [brk1, sl1yo] 6 times, edge brLsl dec. Do *not* turn, slide.
Row 47 LS DC: sl1, brp1, [sl1yo, brp1] 7 times, sl1yo, p1, [sl1yo, brp1] 7 times, sl1. Turn.

Row 49 LS LC: k1, sl1yo, [brk1, sl1yo] 8 times, brkyobrk, sl1yo, [brk1, sl1yo] 5 times, edge brLsl dec. Do *not* turn, slide.
Row 49 LS DC: sl1, brp1, [sl1yo, brp1] 8 times, sl1yo, p1, [sl1yo, brp1] 6 times, sl1. Turn.

Row 51 LS LC: k1, sl1yo, [brk1, sl1yo] 9 times, brkyobrk, sl1yo, [brk1, sl1yo] 4 times, edge brLsl dec. Do *not* turn, slide.
Row 51 LS DC: sl1, brp1, [sl1yo, brp1] 9 times, sl1yo, p1, [sl1yo, brp1] 5 times, sl1. Turn.

After working last set of DS rows, rep from Row 33 LS LC until ready to work the last zag. End with a Row 52 DS DC.

END (CHART C)
Rows 53, 55, 57, 59 and 61 LS LC: edge brRsl dec, sl1yo, *brk1, sl1yo; rep from * to last st, k1. Do *not* turn, slide.
Rows 53, 55, 57, 59 and 61 LS DC: sl1, brp1, *sl1yo, brp1; rep from * to last st, sl1. Turn.

Row 54 DS LC and all end DS LC rows: p1, *sl1yo, brp1; rep from * to last 2 sts, sl1yo, p1. Do *not* turn, slide.
Row 54 DS DC and all end DS DC rows: sl1, *brk1, sl1yo; rep from * to last 2 sts, brk1, sl1. Turn.

Rows 63, 65, 67, 69 and 71 LS LC: k1, sl1yo, *brk1, sl1yo; rep from * to last 3 sts, edge brLsl dec. Do *not* turn, slide.
Rows 63, 65, 67, 69 and 71 LS DC: sl1, brp1, *sl1yo, brp1; rep from * to last st, sl1. Turn.

End Chart C

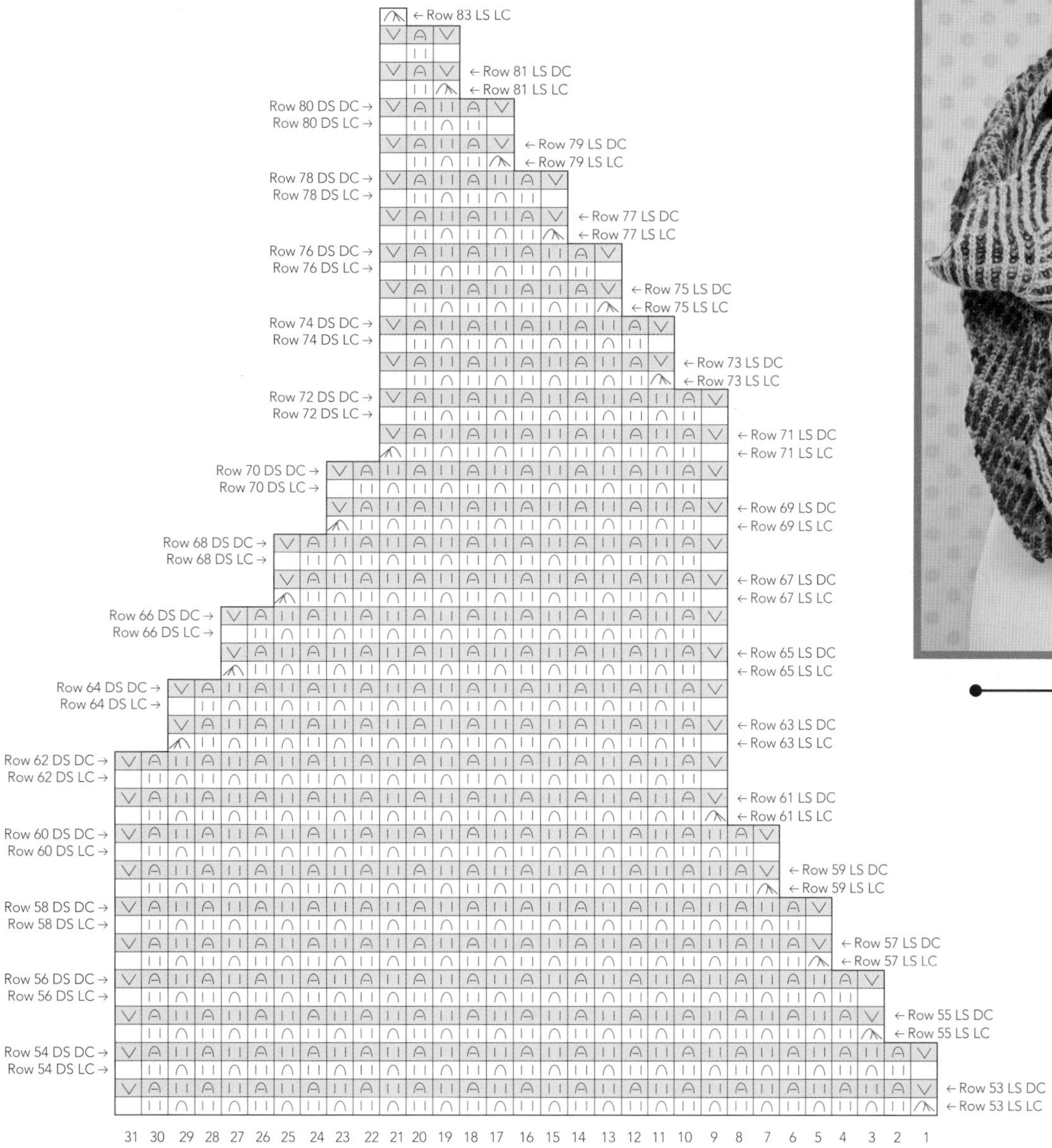

← Row 83 LS LC

← Row 81 LS DC
← Row 81 LS LC

Row 80 DS DC →
Row 80 DS LC →

← Row 79 LS DC
← Row 79 LS LC

Row 78 DS DC →
Row 78 DS LC →

← Row 77 LS DC
← Row 77 LS LC

Row 76 DS DC →
Row 76 DS LC →

← Row 75 LS DC
← Row 75 LS LC

Row 74 DS DC →
Row 74 DS LC →

← Row 73 LS DC
← Row 73 LS LC

Row 72 DS DC →
Row 72 DS LC →

← Row 71 LS DC
← Row 71 LS LC

Row 70 DS DC →
Row 70 DS LC →

← Row 69 LS DC
← Row 69 LS LC

Row 68 DS DC →
Row 68 DS LC →

← Row 67 LS DC
← Row 67 LS LC

Row 66 DS DC →
Row 66 DS LC →

← Row 65 LS DC
← Row 65 LS LC

Row 64 DS DC →
Row 64 DS LC →

← Row 63 LS DC
← Row 63 LS LC

Row 62 DS DC →
Row 62 DS LC →

← Row 61 LS DC
← Row 61 LS LC

Row 60 DS DC →
Row 60 DS LC →

← Row 59 LS DC
← Row 59 LS LC

Row 58 DS DC →
Row 58 DS LC →

← Row 57 LS DC
← Row 57 LS LC

Row 56 DS DC →
Row 56 DS LC →

← Row 55 LS DC
← Row 55 LS LC

Row 54 DS DC →
Row 54 DS LC →

← Row 53 LS DC
← Row 53 LS LC

31 30 29 28 27 26 25 24 23 22 21 20 19 18 17 16 15 14 13 12 11 10 9 8 7 6 5 4 3 2 1

Rows 73, 75, 77 and 79 LS LC: edge brRsl dec, sl1yo, *brk1, sl1yo; rep from * to last st, k1. Do *not* turn, slide.

Rows 73, 75, 77 and 79 LS DC: sl1, brp1, *sl1yo, brp1; rep from * to last st, sl1. Turn.

Row 81 LS LC: edge brRsl dec, sl1yo, k1. Do *not* turn, slide.
Row 81 LS DC: sl1, brp1, sl1. Turn.

Row 83 LS LC: edge brRsl dec.

Work in ends and block as desired. I steam blocked the scarf shown. ∎

Bart & Francis

Bart & Francis are two Belgian men who design yarns. They bring boxes and boxes of their product to yarn events in the Netherlands. Their creations are always interesting, using beautiful colors and unusual combinations of fibers. This lovely *Silk's and Wool's* comes in many colors and makes a very elegant scarf.

Finished Measurements
6½" (16cm) wide × 55" (140cm) long

Yarn
Bart & Francis *Silk's & Wool's*
(45% bombyx Morus silk,
35% Australian wool, 15% shantung silk,
and 5% merino wool) 🔢

■ 1 cone = 1¾oz/50g (383yd/350m); scarf shown weighs 2½oz/65g

■ Colors: 1 cone each in #11 light green (LC) and #12 medium green (DC)

Needles
Size 2 or 3 (2.75 or 3mm) circular needle

Gauge
One pattern repeat:
16 sts = 2½" (6cm) and 24 rows = 4" (10cm)

SCARF
Cast on 41 sts using Two-Color Italian Cast-On, beginning and ending with LC knit st.

Set-Up Row 1 DS LC: p1, *sl1yo, p1; rep from * to end. Do *not* turn, slide.
Set-Up Row 1 DS DC: sl1, *brk1, sl1yo; rep from * to last 2 sts, brk1, sl1. Turn.

Row 1 LS LC: k1, sl1yo, [brk1, sl1yo] 3 times, *brRsl dec, sl1yo, [brk1, sl1yo] 5 times, brkyobrk, sl1yo; rep from * to last st, k1. Do *not* turn, slide.
Row 1 LS DC: sl1, brp1, [sl1yo, brp1] 3 times, *[sl1yo, brp1] 6 times, sl1yo, p1, sl1yo, brp1; rep from * to last st, sl1. Turn.

Row 2 DS LC and all DS LC rows: p1, *sl1yo, brp1; rep from * to last 2 sts, sl1yo, p1. Do *not* turn, slide.
Row 2 DS DC and all DS DC rows: sl1, *brk1, sl1yo; rep from * to last 2 sts, brk1, sl1. Turn.

Row 3 LS LC: k1, sl1yo, [brk1, sl1yo] 3 times, *brRsl dec, sl1yo, [brk1, sl1yo] 4 times, brkyobrk, sl1yo, brk1, sl1yo; rep from * to last st, k1. Do *not* turn, slide.
Row 3 LS DC: sl1, brp1, [sl1yo, brp1] 3 times, *[sl1yo, brp1] 5 times, sl1yo, p1, [sl1yo, brp1] twice; rep from * to last st, sl1. Turn.

Row 5 LS LC: k1, sl1yo, [brk1, sl1yo] 3 times, *brRsl dec, sl1yo, [brk1, sl1yo] 3 times, brkyobrk, sl1yo, [brk1, sl1yo] twice; rep from * to last st, k1. Do *not* turn, slide.
Row 5 LS DC: sl1, brp1, [sl1yo, brp1] 3 times, *[sl1yo, brp1] 4 times, sl1yo, p1, [sl1yo, brp1] 3 times; rep from * to last st, sl1. Turn.

Bart & Francis

Row 7 LS LC: k1, sl1yo, [brk1, sl1yo] 3 times, *brRsl dec, sl1yo, [brk1, sl1yo] twice, brkyobrk, sl1yo, [brk1, sl1yo] 3 times; rep from * to last st, k1. Do *not* turn, slide.
Row 7 LS DC: sl1, brp1, [sl1yo, brp1] 3 times, *[sl1yo, brp1] 3 times, sl1yo, p1, [sl1yo, brp1] 4 times; rep from * to last st, sl1. Turn.

Row 9 LS LC: k1, sl1yo, [brk1, sl1yo] 3 times, *brRsl dec, sl1yo, brk1, sl1yo, brkyobrk, sl1yo, [brk1, sl1yo] 4 times; rep from * to last st, k1. Do *not* turn, slide.
Row 9 LS DC: sl1, brp1, [sl1yo, brp1] 3 times, *[sl1yo, brp1] twice, sl1yo, p1, [sl1yo, brp1] 5 times; rep from * to last st, sl1. Turn.

Row 11 LS LC: k1, sl1yo, [brk1, sl1yo] 3 times, *brRsl dec, sl1yo, brkyobrk, sl1yo, [brk1, sl1yo] 5 times; rep from * to last st, k1. Do *not* turn, slide.
Row 11 LS DC: sl1, brp1, [sl1yo, brp1] 3 times, *sl1yo, brp1, sl1yo, p1, [sl1yo, brp1] 6 times; rep from * to last st, sl1. Turn.

Row 13 LS LC: k1, sl1yo, *brkyobrk, sl1yo, [brk1, sl1yo] 5 times, brLsl dec, sl1yo; rep from * to last 7 sts, [brk1, sl1yo] 3 times, k1. Do *not* turn, slide.
Row 13 LS DC: sl1, brp1, *sl1yo, p1, [sl1yo, brp1] 7 times; rep from * to last 7 sts, [sl1yo, brp1] 3 times, sl1. Turn.

Row 15 LS LC: k1, sl1yo, *brk1, sl1yo, brkyobrk, sl1yo, [brk1, sl1yo] 4 times, brLsl dec, sl1yo; rep from * to last 7 sts, [brk1, sl1yo] 3 times, k1. Do *not* turn, slide.
Row 15 LS DC: sl1, brp1, *sl1yo, brp1, sl1yo, p1, [sl1yo, brp1] 6 times; rep from * to last 7 sts, [sl1yo, brp1] 3 times, sl1. Turn.

Row 17 LS LC: k1, sl1yo, *[brk1, sl1yo] twice, brkyobrk, sl1yo, [brk1, sl1yo] 3 times, brLsl dec, sl1yo; rep from * to last 7 sts, [brk1, sl1yo] 3 times, k1. Do *not* turn, slide.
Row 17 LS DC: sl1, brp1, *[sl1yo, brp1] twice, sl1yo, p1, [sl1yo, brp1] 5 times; rep from * to last 7 sts, [sl1yo, brp1] 3 times, sl1. Turn.

Row 19 LS LC: k1, sl1yo, *[brk1, sl1yo] 3 times, brkyobrk, sl1yo, [brk1, sl1yo] twice, brLsl dec, sl1yo; rep from * to last 7 sts, [brk1, sl1yo] 3 times, k1. Do *not* turn, slide.
Row 19 LS DC: sl1, brp1, *[sl1yo, brp1] 3 times, sl1yo, p1, [sl1yo, brp1] 4 times; rep from * to last 7 sts, [sl1yo, brp1] 3 times, sl1. Turn.

Row 21 LS LC: k1, sl1yo, *[brk1, sl1yo] 4 times, brkyobrk, sl1yo, brk1, sl1yo, brLsl dec, sl1yo; rep from * to last 7 sts, [brk1, sl1yo] 3 times, k1. Do *not* turn, slide.
Row 21 LS DC: sl1, brp1, *[sl1yo, brp1] 4 times, sl1yo, p1, [sl1yo, brp1] 3 times; rep from * to last 7 sts, [sl1yo, brp1] 3 times, sl1. Turn.

Row 23 LS LC: k1, sl1yo, *[brk1, sl1yo] 5 times, brkyobrk, sl1yo, brLsl dec, sl1yo; rep from * to last 7 sts, [brk1, sl1yo] 3 times, k1. Do *not* turn, slide.
Row 23 LS DC: sl1, brp1, *[sl1yo, brp1] 5 times, sl1yo, p1, [sl1yo, brp1] twice; rep from * to last 7 sts, [sl1yo, brp1] 3 times, sl1. Turn.

After working last set of DS rows, rep from Row 1 LS LC.

When desired length has been worked, ending with a Row 12 DS DC or Row 24 DS DC, bind off loosely, preferably with Italian Bind-Off. Work in ends and block as desired. I steam blocked the scarf shown. ∎

Row 24 DS DC →	
Row 24 DS LC →	
	← Row 23 LS DC
	← Row 23 LS LC
Row 22 DS DC →	
Row 22 DS LC →	
	← Row 21 LS DC
	← Row 21 LS LC
Row 20 DS DC →	
Row 20 DS LC →	
	← Row 19 LS DC
	← Row 19 LS LC
Row 18 DS DC →	
Row 18 DS LC →	
	← Row 17 LS DC
	← Row 17 LS LC
Row 16 DS DC →	
Row 16 DS LC →	
	← Row 15 LS DC
	← Row 15 LS LC
Row 14 DS DC →	
Row 14 DS LC →	
	← Row 13 LS DC
	← Row 13 LS LC
Row 12 DS DC →	
Row 12 DS LC →	
	← Row 11 LS DC
	← Row 11 LS LC
Row 10 DS DC →	
Row 10 DS LC →	
	← Row 9 LS DC
	← Row 9 LS LC
Row 8 DS DC →	
Row 8 DS LC →	
	← Row 7 LS DC
	← Row 7 LS LC
Row 6 DS DC →	
Row 6 DS LC →	
	← Row 5 LS DC
	← Row 5 LS LC
Row 4 DS DC →	
Row 4 DS LC →	
	← Row 3 LS DC
	← Row 3 LS LC
Row 2 DS DC →	
Row 2 DS LC →	
	← Row 1 LS DC
	← Row 1 LS LC
Set-Up Row DS DC →	
Set-Up Row DS LC →	

16 15 14 13 12 11 10 9 8 7 6 5 4 3 2 1

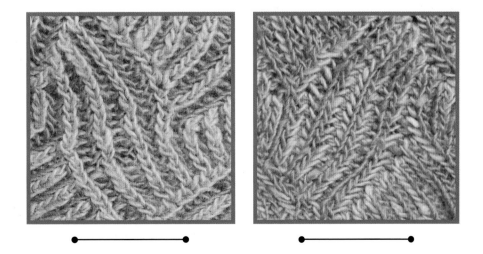

Useful Information

Two-Color Brioche in the Round

You might want to design a hat or a cowl using two-color brioche in the round. In this style of knitting two rounds are worked for every round that appears on the face of the fabric. Each round is worked once with the LC, and then once with the DC.

To make it easier to count the rounds, count the stitches in the dominant LC knit columns as viewed from the public side. When a pattern says 16 rounds, you will actually have worked 32 rounds total, 16 with each color.

Don't cross yarns when changing colors at the beginning of a round. At the end of a LC round, work the sl1yo, drop the LC to the front, pick up the DC and work the next round.

The last stitch at the end of a DC round will be a burp stitch. Since the LC is hanging to the front, you should be able to maintain the LC yarn over to work this last burp. Drop the DC to the front, pick up the LC, and take it to the back to work the next round.

Two-Color Brioche in the Round

Using Two-Color Italian Cast-On, cast on an even number of sts, beginning with LC knit st and ending with DC purl st. Join for working in the round, being careful not to twist sts.

Set-Up Round LC: *k1, sl1yo; rep from *. Place marker (pm) onto needle or hang marker on first st.

Set-Up Round DC: *sl1yo, brp1; rep from *.

Round 1 LC: *brk1, sl1yo; rep from *.

Round 1 DC: *sl1yo, brp1; rep from *.

Rep Rounds 1 LC and DC. ∎

Handling Yarns at the End of a Round

Leave the yarn hanging to the front at the end of every round.

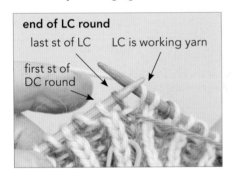

Approaching last st of LC round.

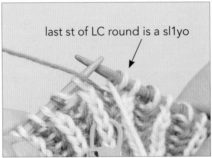

After making last sl1yo in LC round, keep LC to front (this will help maintain yarn over) and drop it. Then pick up DC hanging under it (do not cross yarns) and work first st of DC round, which is also a sl1yo.

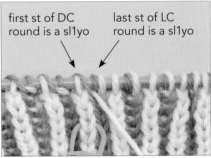

After working farther down DC round, this is what beginning/end sts should look like.

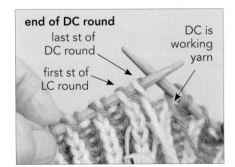

Approaching last st of DC round.

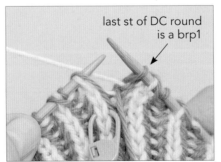

After making last brp in DC round, drop DC in front. Then pick up LC hanging above it, take it to back, and work first st of LC round, which is a brk1.

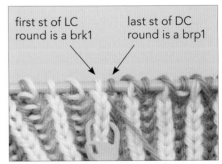

After working farther down LC round, this is what beginning/end sts should look like. ∎

How to Convert a Two-Color Brioche Flat Chart to Work in the Round

When working two colors in the round, you will work LC and DC *rounds*. You will not work LS or DS back-and-forth rows. Eliminate the selvedge stitches and work only those stitches between the blue and red repeat boundary boxes. Cast on a multiple of the number of stitches within the blue boundary box (always an even number of stitches).

These general instructions work only for stitch patterns that begin with a 2-stitch and end with a 1-stitch selvedge, such as Leafy Lacy I (page 76). The red boundary box is then a rectangle. If a stitch pattern has shifting selvedge stitches and the red boundary box also shifts, such as with Mr. Flood's (page 109), then the pattern must be redesigned to be knit in the round.

All rounds start from the right side of the chart, so each chart round must be read from right to left.

To make things easier, make a photocopy of the original chart. Cut around the blue and red boundary boxes, eliminating the selvedge stitches and the "Row" labels. Tape your cut-out chart to a piece of paper. Write "Round 1 LC," "Round 1 DC," then "Round 2 LC," "Round 2 DC" up the right edge of the chart. Your LC rounds will be in bark rounds, and your DC rounds will be in burps.

If you use the Two-Color Italian Cast-On, the first little knotted stitch on the needle doesn't count as a stitch and should be dropped before working the first Set-Up Round. The first stitch you create with the Italian Cast-On will be a LC knit stitch, and your last stitch will be a purl in the DC.

Two-Color Brioche Chart: Working Flat

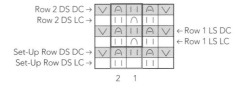

Two-Color Brioche Chart: Working in the Round

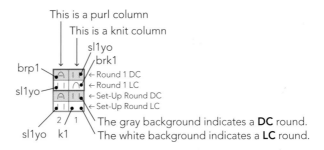

Reading a Chart for Two-Color Brioche in the Round

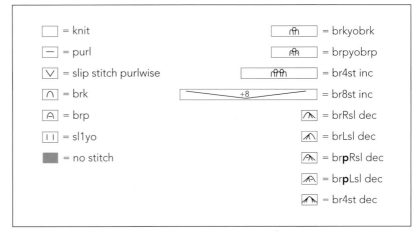

The red boundary line represents repeats.
The blue boundary line represents repeats in Set-Up Rounds.

Legend for Two-Color Brioche in the Round Symbols

☐	= knit	⋔	= brkyobrk
⊟	= purl	⋔	= brpyobrp
⋁	= slip stitch purlwise	⋔⋔⋔	= br4st inc
⋀	= brk	+8	= br8st inc
⋀	= brp	⟋⋀	= brRsl dec
⊟⊟	= sl1yo	⋀⟍	= brLsl dec
▓	= no stitch	⟋⋀	= brpRsl dec
		⋀⟍	= brpLsl dec
		⟋⋀⟍	= br4st dec

The chart symbols take on different meanings when the pattern is worked in the round.

Leafy Lacy I Translated into a Two-Color in-the-Round Chart

Original Leafy Lacy I Chart

Here you see the original Leafy Lacy I chart (see page 77).

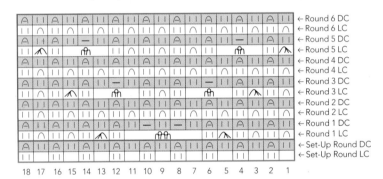

Leafy Lacy I Chart: Working in the Round

First, copy the chart and cut away the selvedge stitches so that only the blue and red boundary boxes remain. Then write your rounds as shown here.

Cast on a multiple of the number of stitches in the blue boundary box, in this case 18 stitches.

Using the legend for two-color brioche in the round symbols on page 229, work the stitch pattern. For the sample shown, I cast on 72 stitches.

Don't forget to work the plain even-numbered rounds (Rounds 2, 4 and 6 LC and DC)—they are easy to forget, because you are not turning your work.

This would make a beautiful cuff, hat, headband or cowl.

Converting a Two-Color Brioche Flat Chart to One Color

I am a two-color brioche enthusiast, but I realize that not all knitters want to work in two colors. If you want to work in only one color, here's how to translate the charts into that style.

In one-color brioche knitting, there is no sliding to the other end of the needle at the end of a LS row. You must turn the work after every worked row.

All LC rows will turn into RS rows and all DC rows will turn into WS rows. You still work each row twice, only you work it as a Row 1 RS, turn the work, then work a Row 1 WS, and turn the work. Every row is barked; there are no burp stitches.

You also need to treat the selvedge edges differently for one-color brioche knitting. For a nice selvedge edge, on the RS rows, knit the first stitch and, at the end of the row, knit 1 through the back of the loop (k1tbl). On the WS rows, slip the first stitch purlwise, take the yarn to the back, then work the following bark stitch. Work in pattern to the end, where you will bark the next-to-last stitch, then bring the yarn forward to the front and slip the last stitch purlwise.

Again, you may want to make a photocopy of the chart that you want to work in one color. Cut away the "Row" labels. Tape the chart to a piece of paper and write "Row 1 RS" at the right edge, where Row 1 LS LC was originally. Then write "Row 1 WS" at the left, by the grayed row that was Row 1 LS DC. Row 2 RS will begin at the same end as Row 1 RS. All RS rows will begin at the right side of the chart and are shown with a white background, and all WS rows will read from the left and are shown with a gray background.

You will use the legend for flat one-color brioche symbols on page 232 to follow the chart when working back and forth with one color.

If you use the One-Color Italian Cast-On, be aware that the very first loop of the cast-on counts as a stitch. The next stitch, which is the first stitch that you make, should be a knit, and you will end with a purl, since you are casting on an odd number of stitches. When you turn the work to begin your Set-Up Row, your first stitch will be a k1, as shown on the chart.

One-Color Brioche Chart: Working Flat

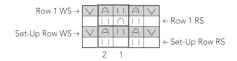

Row 1 WS →   ← Row 1 RS
Set-Up Row WS →   ← Set-Up Row RS
2   1

Flat One-Color Brioche Stitch

Cast on a multiple of 2 sts + 3.

Set-Up Row RS: *k1, sl1yo; rep from * to last st, k1tbl.
Set-Up Row WS: sl1, yb, *brk1, sl1yo; rep from * to last 2 sts, brk1, yf, sl1.

Row 1 RS: k1, sl1yo, *brk1, sl1yo; rep from * to last st, k1tbl.
Row 1 WS: sl1, yb, *brk1, sl1yo; rep from * to last 2 sts, brk1, yf, sl1.

Rep Row 1 RS and WS. ■

Reading a Chart as a Flat One-Color Brioche Chart

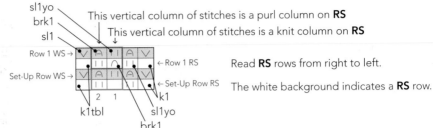

Read **WS** rows from left to right.

The gray background indicates a **WS** row.

Read **RS** rows from right to left.

The white background indicates a **RS** row.

The red boundary line represents repeats.
The blue boundary line represents repeats in Set-Up Rows.

Legend for Flat One-Color Brioche Symbols

☐ = knit on right edge, ktbl on left edge		⋔ = brkyobrk
— = knit		⋔ = brkyobrk
☑ = on right edge slip stitch purlwise, yb, on left edge, yf, slip stitch purlwise		⋔⋔ = br4st inc
		+8 = br8st inc
∩ = brk		⋏ = brRsl dec
A = brk		⋏ = brLsl dec
‖ = sl1yo		⋏ = brRsl dec
▓ = no stitch		⋏ = brLsl dec
		⋏ = br4st dec

The chart symbols take on different meanings when the pattern is worked in one color.

232

Leafy Lacy I Translated into a Flat One-Color Chart

Here you see the original Leafy Lacy I chart.

Original Leafy Lacy I Chart

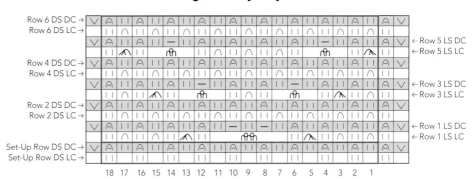

Photocopy the chart and cut away the "Row" labels. Tape it to a piece of paper and write your rows as shown. All RS rows will begin at the right edge of the chart and are shown with a white background, and all WS rows will read from the left edge and are shown with a gray background.

Leafy Lacy I Chart: Working Flat in One Color

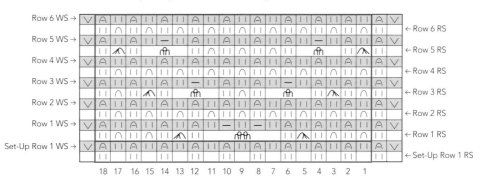

I cast on 39 stitches using the One-Color Italian Cast-On.

Note that Set-Up Row 1 begins at the right edge of the chart.

Remember that every other RS row needs to be worked, most often, in plain brioche knitting, no increases or decreases. In two-color brioche, these rows would be your DS rows.

APPENDIX III:

Converting a Two-Color Brioche Flat Chart to One-Color Brioche in the Round

When working one color in the round, you will work bark and burp *rounds*. Eliminate the selvedge stitches and work only those stitches between the blue and red repeat boundary boxes. Cast on a multiple of the number of stitches in the blue box.

These general instructions work only for those stitch patterns that begin with a 2-stitch and end with a 1-stitch selvedge, such as Leafy Lacy 1. The red boundary box is then a rectangle. If a stitch pattern has shifting selvedge stitches and the red boundary box also shifts, such as with Mr. Flood's (page TK), then the pattern needs to be redesigned to be knitted in the round.

All rounds start from the right side of the chart, so each chart round must be read from right to left.

To make things easier, make a photocopy of the original chart. Cut around the blue and red boundary boxes, eliminating the selvedge stitches and the "Row" labels. Tape your cut-out chart to a piece of paper. Write "Round 1 bark," "Round 1 burp," then "Round 2 bark," "Round 2 burp" up the right side of the chart. Your LC rounds will be in bark rounds, and your DC rounds will be in burps.

You will always be working with an even number of stitches. You will end a bark round with a sl1yo and also begin the following burp round with a sl1yo, so you will need to work 2 sl1yo's next to each other. You will end a burp round with a burp and begin the following bark round with a bark.

Working with One Color in the Round

When you work the brioche stitch in one color in the round, you must shift at the beginning of a round from a bark round to a burp round or from a burp round to a bark round.

Just as with two-color brioche in the round, the bark round ends with a sl1yo and the following burp round begins with a sl1yo.

One-Color Brioche Chart: Working in the Round

← Round 1 burp
← Round 1 bark
← Set-Up Round burp
← Set-Up Round bark

One-Color Brioche Stitch in the Round

Cast on an even number of sts. Place marker to indicate beginning of round and join, being careful not to twist the cast-on sts.

Set-Up Round bark: k1, sl1yo.
Set-Up Round burp: sl1yo, brp1.

Round 1 bark: brk1, sl1yo.
Round 1 burp: sl1yo, brp1.
Repeat Rounds 1 bark and burp. ■

Reading a Chart for One-Color Brioche in the Round

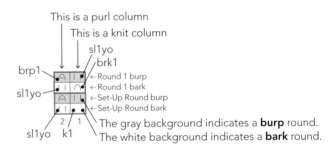

This is a purl column
This is a knit column
sl1yo
brk1
brp1
sl1yo
← Round 1 burp
← Round 1 bark
← Set-Up Round burp
← Set-Up Round bark
sl1yo   k1
The gray background indicates a **burp** round.
The white background indicates a **bark** round.

The red boundary line represents repeats.
The blue boundary line represents repeats in Set-Up Rows.

Legend for One-Color Brioche in-the-Round Symbols

☐ = knit		⋔ = brkyobrk
— = purl		⋔ = brpyobrp
⋁ = slip stitch purlwise		⋔⋔ = br4st inc
∩ = brk		+8 = br8st inc
⌴ = brp		⋏ = brRsl dec
‖ = sl1yo		⋏ = brLsl dec
■ = no stitch		⋏ = br**p**Rsl dec
		⋏ = br**p**Lsl dec
		⋏ = br4st dec

The chart symbols take on different meanings when the pattern is worked in one color and in the round.

Leafy Lacy I Translated into a One-Color in-the-Round Chart

Original Leafy Lacy I Chart

Here you see the original Leafy Lacy I chart.

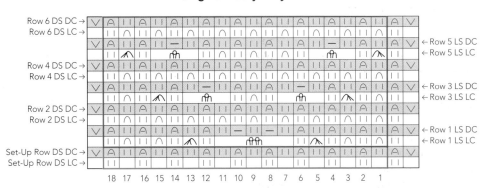

Photocopy the chart and cut away the "Row" labels. Tape it to a piece of paper. Write "Round 1 bark," "Round 1 burp," then "Round 2 bark," "Round 2 burp" up the right edge of the chart as shown. Your LC rounds will be in bark rounds, and your DC rounds will be in burps.

Leafy Lacy I Chart: Working One Color in the Round

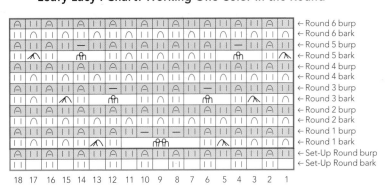

Designing Your Own Brioche Stitch Patterns

There are many ways to expand on this stitch dictionary. Here's some food for thought.

- Add more plain worked rows between the manipulation rows or between repeats.

- Add plain columns between repeats or between stitches within one repeat.

- Work one pattern, then a different second pattern, etc.

- Mirror a repeat (if possible) horizontally and vertically.

- Use two different thicknesses of yarn. Work on two different size needles, one for LC and one for DC.

- Use color-changing yarns.

- Introduce a garter stitch block or column, or some other common knitting stitch, in combination with the brioche stitch. You could work a lace pattern in between Mr. Flood's repeats. Or add cables running up the side of a repeat.

- Combine several different brioche patterns, such as in the Aran design

shown below (which I created in Photoshop).

- Syncopate columns and rows and repeats.

- Shift increases or decreases to other rows or from LS to DS.

- Change a 2-stitch increase to a 4-stitch increase.

- Change a 2-stitch decrease to a 4-stitch decrease.

- Shift a decrease from a Rsl to a Lsl and vice versa. This causes the "line" of decreases to be either straight up and down or scalloped.

- Shift colors (use the DC as LC and vice versa).

- Work a repeat with LC, then with DC. Shift registration or use other patterning techniques; for example, start the repeat 4 stitches in.

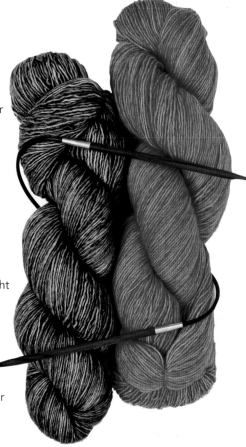

- Add garter stitches between the brioche patterns shown in the photo, instead of the brioche ribs, and create horizontal and/or vertical striping.

Yarn Resources

All of the stitch pattern samples were knit with Malabrigo *Lace* (100% baby wool; 470yd/430m per 1¾oz/50g hank). I used Knitter's Pride size 1 (2.5mm) double-pointed needles, 8" long.

BART & FRANCIS
www.bart-francis.be
Shantung Yaspee used in Nan's Other Cowl, page 210.
Silk's & Wool's used in Bart & Francis, page 222.

CRYSTAL PALACE
CrystalPalaceYarns.com
Mini Mochi used in Cathedral, page 200.

FREIA HANDPAINT YARNS
www.freiafibers.com
Ombré Worsted used in Reptilian Cowl, page 176.

HAND MAIDEN FINE YARN
Handmaiden.ca
Maiden Hair used in Ring of Fire, page 166.

KNITWITCHES YARNS
www.knitwitchesyarns.co.uk
Seriously Gorgeous Kid Silk used in Miss B, page 204.

MADELINETOSH
Madelinetosh.com
Tosh Merino Light used in Veda's Peacock, page 190;
and Icicle, page 180.

MANOS DEL URUGUAY
Distributed in the U.S. by Fairmount Fibers
FairmountFibers.com
Silk Blend used in Stegosaurus, page 184.

PIGEONROOF STUDIOS
www.pigeonroofstudios.com
Siren Two Sock Yarn used in Sister Janie, page 196.
Note: This yarn has been discontinued, but Pigeonroof produces several other sock-weight yarns.

ROWAN
www.knitrowan.com
Kidsilk Haze used in Willow, page 170.

SOLITUDE WOOL
www.solitudewool.com
Corriedale used in Gretchen's Zigzag, page 216.

Index

■ I dedicate this book, again, to my mother and to my children. Thanks, Mom, for teaching me how to knit, and thanks, Mathilde and Rosalie, for encouraging me to continue.

Acknowledgments

Thanks to Alexandra Feo, the fabulous photographer who made the look of the book possible.

I would like to thank my dear knitting friend Alexandra Richards, who tech read all of the stitch patterns and project patterns. Also, Anne Cohen, who proofread a lot of the text.

Thanks to the staff at Soho Publishing/Sixth&Spring Books, especially Lisa Silverman and Diane Lamphron (who really kept their patience with me!), for accepting my proposal (thanks, Trisha!) and helping me to make it a reality.

A special thanks to Jared Flood, who loves the graphic elements of charting, and to JC Briar, who loves the visual communication of charting. They helped me immensely when I designed the symbols and created the charts for this book.

Finally, thanks to all of my knitting and non-knitting friends who made this book possible. Edo Camstra, for the use of his scanner. My wonderful V&D colleagues for keeping me "in stitches." Veda Harloff, for listening to my complaints. Nancy Bush, for making great suggestions. Cat Bordhi, for encouragement. My Amsterdam knitting groups, Stitch 'n Bitch de Jaren and Penelope Craft, for all of the enjoyable conversations.